The Australian way of COOKING Pictorial

Gaslight
PUBLISHING
PTY. LTD.
INCORPORATED in N.S.W.

Published by:

Gaslight Publishing Pty Limited (Incorporated in N.S.W.)
173 Commonwealth Street, Surry Hills, N.S.W., 2010, Australia
Phone: (02) 212 2522, Fax: (02) 212 6428
Telex No.: 121822 User Sy. 3909

National Library of Australia
Cataloguing-in-Publication Data
The Australian Way of COOKING Pictorial
Includes Index
ISBN 0-9588122-0-9
1. Cookery, Australian
2. Cookery, Australian – Pictorial Works
Copyright ©

SYDNEY HARBOUR BRIDGE VIEW CELEBRATING AUSTRALIA'S BIRTHDAY

Design, Art and Photographic Direction By:	**YON TARPSTRA**
Artwork:	**HELEN REYNOLDS**
Home Economist and Food Editor:	**ELLEN ARGYRIOU**
Location Photography:	**HUGH SCARLETT**
Chapter Introductions:	**JOE WOLFF**
Finished Art and Typesetting:	**GAS GRAPHICS TGC PTY LIMITED AND A.P.T. PTY LIMITED,** Sydney, Australia.
Production:	**ANN ALBERTS** **KAY BARNES** **DAPHNE MOLONY** **MARK SWADLING** **GLOBE PRESS PTY. LTD.**

The Australian way of COOKING Pictorial

Gaslight
PUBLISHING
PTY. LTD.
INCORPORATED in N.S.W.

MORTON NATIONAL PARK NEAR TAPITALLIE, NOWRA, NEW SOUTH WALES

AUSTRALIA DAY (JANUARY 26 1788) REMEMBERED IN THE ROCKS AREA, SYDNEY, NEW SOUTH WALES

Foreword

Dear Reader:

There's an Australian bush tale that underscores the importance of the cook. The old bush doctor, whenever called to a sick person's home, boarding house or wherever, went first of all directly to the kitchen and thanked the cook for giving him a new patient.

From this story, it's easy to see that whoever is running the kitchen has a tremendous influence over the people they're feeding. The food they choose and the way they cook it has a direct bearing on good nutrition, health and happiness.

The cook's job is to present food in such a way that essential nutrients can be best absorbed by the body. This means fresh, unrefined ingredients in proportions that are easy to digest. If smell, flavour and colour are at their best, this usually means the cook is on the right track.

The common sense rules for healthy eating are simple and straightforward:
1. Try to eat a variety of foods.
2. Find your desireable weight and maintain it.

3. Try to eat foods without a high content of fat, saturated fat and cholesterol.
4. Look for foods with adequate starch and fibre.
5. Avoid large amounts of sugar.
6. Avoid large amounts of sodium.
7. If you drink alcohol, do it in moderation.

Healthy eating starts with good recipes. And this is what you'll find in THE AUSTRALIAN WAY OF COOKING – healthful recipes using ingredients from the basic food groups and, for the most part, unrefined, nutritious foods.

Nutrition is more than a study of how to produce health. It's about how life is lived. Francis Bacon once wrote, "A healthy body is a bounteous host to the soul, a sick body, it's prison."

I believe this cookbook will give you the opportunity to have fun cooking delicious foods with health building ingredients. I wish you joy and success in the kitchen; may your fish never be dry, may your meat never be tough, and may your salads, vegetables, and desserts be delicious and healthful.

Ellen Argyriou
HOME ECONOMIST

VIEW OF PERTH, WESTERN AUSTRALIA

CONTENTS

FISH IN ABUNDANCE NEAR DOCTORS CREEK, DARWIN, NORTHERN TERRITORY

KOALAS, ONE OF THE NATIVE MARSUPIALS FOR WHICH AUSTRALIA IS WORLD RENOWNED

Introduction

Australia is a country slightly larger than the United States in size with a population smaller than that of California. Needless to say, we have plenty of room. And because we're "the lucky country", there's plenty of everything else, too: long white beaches, glittering air, sparkling sea, and food. The Australian food industry is one of the most self-sufficient in the world. There is an abundance of grains, fruit and vegetables, dairy foods, meat and seafood. We also have a world class wine industry (the beer isn't a bad "drop" either).

This beautifully photographed cookbook — you can almost reach out and touch the food — caters for every occasion from spontaneous get togethers to the more formal dinner party.

Australians love to get together with friends, and one of the most popular ways to do this is the barbecue. With our excellent meat, shrimp isn't the only thing we throw on the "barbie". There's tender and juicy beef, veal, lamb, pork and poultry. This book offers you a number of tasty meat recipes for barbecue dishes, the traditional Sunday roast and more.

As an island continent, we have access to a tremendous amount of seafood. The seafood

section, full of fish and shellfish recipes, will inspire you to make use of our exotic fish and succulent crayfish, oysters, prawns and crab.

Since 45% of Australia is in the tropics, we have a section devoted to what you'd eat in a tropical paradise. The recipes here use pineapple, mangoes, paw paws, rockmelon, avocadoes, passionfruit, and our excellent seafood.

This book also features many recipes that focus on natural cooking. Some are old-fashioned recipes in the style of our early settlers. Others use our bounty of fresh fruits and vegetables to put flavour, nutrition and fibre into your diet.

To help when you're in a hurry, there is a section full of tempting recipes using the microwave. You'll be able to prepare either a simple meal or a banquet with the minimum of fuss.

The influence of Australia's migrants on our diet is tremendous. We've gone from a meat and potatoes country to one where you find all types of cooking. The international section has some of our favourite multi-national dishes.

As you can see, THE AUSTRALIAN WAY OF COOKING has a lot to offer. It's both a comprehensive collection of useful recipes and a reflection of who Australians are today. We hope this book gives you an opportunity to enjoy yourself in the kitchen.

Mike Alberts
MANAGING DIRECTOR

Gaslight PUBLISHING
PTY. LTD.
INCORPORATED in N.S.W.

MT AUGUSTUS (LARGEST MONOCLINE IN AUSTRALIA 2.5 TIMES LARGER THAN AYERS ROCK) LOCATION WESTERN AUSTRALIA

PART OF AUSTRALIA'S SEAFARING HISTORY AND THE OPERA HOUSE DEPICTED DURING THE BICENTENARY IN SYDNEY, AUSTRALIA

The Australian way of

PICNICS, BARBECUES BRUNCHES & BUFFETS

Hospitality Down Under

Australians are an unpretentious and friendly lot. You're likely to be greeted just about anywhere with "Lets 'ave a beer" or "I'll put on the kettle." We know how to enjoy our friends, and our free time. Australians get four weeks holiday a year (which usually turns "The Yanks" green with envy).

Because "the weather's usually right" and there is plenty of beef, lamb and seafood, the barbecue has become one of our favourite ways of getting together with people. Barbecues in Australia vary from large affairs with huge quantities of meat and beer to small informal backyard gatherings around the pool.

Brunch is another way Australians entertain. While you still might not invite "the mates" around for brunch, it's becoming a popular and relaxed way of spending time with friends.

Whatever kind of party or gathering you have, the idea is to entertain with the minimum of fuss. The following recipes will allow you to do just that, and have fun at your own party.

WITCHETTY GRUBS, A TRADITIONAL ABORIGINAL MEAL FOUND IN THE OUTBACK. (FULL OF PROTEIN)

Bacon and Veal Pate

6 large rashers bacon
500g (1lb) minced veal
1 onion, chopped
2 hard-boiled eggs

1 egg
¼ teaspoon nutmeg
2 bay leaves
seasoning to taste

Line a 22cm (8½") x 12cm (5") loaf tin or terrine dish with three of the bacon rashers. Cut the remaining bacon and place in a food processor with the veal, onion, eggs, nutmeg and seasoning. Press into the prepared dish, decorate with bay leaves and cover with foil. Stand in a water bath and bake at 180°C (350°F) for 1-1½ hours or until cooked. Allow to cool, refrigerate overnight. Unmould and serve with salad.
Serves 10-12.

PHOTOGRAPH   PAGES 30-31

Barbecue Dip

250g (8oz) packet cream cheese, cubed
½ small red capsicum, seeded, cubed
¼ cup parsley
1 large gherkin, halved

3 stuffed olives
1 shallot, chopped
1 tablespoon barbecue sauce
seasoning to taste

Combine all the ingredients in a food processor and blend until well combined. Refrigerate, then serve with savoury biscuits.
Makes approximately 1½ cups.

"TREPHINA GORGE" NEAR ALICE SPRINGS, NORTHERN TERRITORY

Avocado Dip

1 large avocado, peeled
½ small onion
3 teaspoons lime or lemon juice

¼ teaspoon chilli powder
seasoning to taste

Combine all the ingredients in a food processor and blend until smooth. Serve with corn chips or carrot straws.
Makes approximately 1½ cups.

Smoked Salmon Dip

1 x 100g (3oz) can* smoked salmon spread
125g (4oz) cream cheese, cubed

¼ cup chopped chives
2 teaspoons lemon juice
seasoning to taste

Combine all ingredients in a food processor and blend until smooth. Refrigerate until ready to serve.
*nearest equivalent can size.
Makes approximately 1 cup.

Mousse of Trout

2 trout
60g (2oz) butter or margarine
½ cup milk
½ cup white wine
pinch of cayenne pepper

1½ teaspoons of port
1 cup of cream, whipped
30g (1oz) ground almonds
cucumber and lettuce for garnish
seasoning to taste

Simmer trout gently in half the butter, milk, white wine and seasonings until tender. Remove from liquid and cool. Skin and bone the trout and pound the flesh in a bowl, or place in a food processor with the remaining softened butter and the port. Fold in the cream and almonds. Season, then spoon into individual moulds and chill. Garnish with rings of cucumber and lettuce leaves.
Serves 2.

Salami Slice

1 x 375g (12oz) packet frozen puff pastry
125g (4oz) salami, chopped
2 onions, chopped
1 x 310g (10oz) can* 4 bean mix,

drained, liquid reserved
125g (4oz) Mozzarella cheese, coarsely grated
seasoning to taste

Roll pastry out thinly on a floured board. Trim to a 35cm (14") square reserving pastry scraps. In a small frying pan sauté salami and onion together over moderate heat until tender. Drain on absorbent paper and cool. Combine salami and onion with beans, cheese and seasonings. Scatter evenly over pastry leaving a 2cm (¾") border along one side. Brush this border with reserved bean liquid. Carefully roll up pastry towards border, seal edges. Keeping join underneath, place onto a lightly greased baking sheet and glaze with reserved bean liquid. Using pastry scraps decorate top with a lattice design of 1cm (½") wide pastry strips. Glaze and bake at 200°C (400°F) for 20-25 minutes or till pastry is crisp and golden.
*nearest equivalent can size.
Serves 6.

Nutty Cheese Balls

125g (4oz) Cheddar cheese, grated
1 cooking apple, grated
½ cup chopped cashews
2 tablespoons chopped parsley
500g (1lb) green beans, sliced

1 head broccoli, cut into small florets
1 large red capsicum seeded, thinly sliced
3-4 shallots, finely chopped
French dressing

Combine cheese, apple and cashews in a bowl. Mould into 20 walnut sized balls. Roll in parsley and refrigerate. Cook the beans and broccoli in boiling salted water until tender but crisp. Drain and transfer to a serving bowl. Add the capsicum and shallots. Toss in French dressing and serve with the nutty cheese balls.
Makes approximately 20 balls.

"BUGS, BEEF AND BANGERS" WITH ALL THE GOODIES. A TYPICAL AUSSIE BARBECUE

Cheese Filled Prunes

125g (4oz) blue vein cheese
90g (3oz) cream cheese
2 tablespoons chopped parsley
2 tablespoons French mustard
½ cup finely chopped toasted almonds
2 doz dessert prunes, de-seeded

Combine all the ingredients in a bowl with the exception of the prunes. Place the mixture into a piping bag and pipe along the centre of each prune. Chill until required and serve.   Makes 2 doz.

Curacao Fruit Cheese

¾ cup chopped dried apricots
½ cup sultanas
½ cup orange liqueur
250g (8oz) cream cheese, softened
2 tablespoons milk
chopped unblanched almonds
walnuts or poppy seeds

Combine the apricots in a bowl with the sultanas, orange liqueur and soak for at least 3 hours. Beat the cream cheese and milk together until smooth then fold in the fruit and refrigerate until firm. Mould into a ball or flat round, pressing nuts or poppy seeds into the surface, then chill until required.   Serves 10-12.

Cheesy Spinach Quiches

3 sheets ready rolled puff pastry
125g (4oz) tasty cheese, coarsely grated
2 spinach leaves, shredded
½ small onion, finely chopped
1 egg
3 tablespoons cream
1 tablespoon finely chopped parsley
1 tablespoon French mustard
seasoning to taste

Cut pastry into 6cm (2½") rounds with a pastry cutter and press into shallow patty tins. Combine all the remaining ingredients and divide equally between the pastry cases. Bake at 200°C (400°F) for approximately 20 minutes or until cooked.   Serve immediately. Makes approximately 1 doz.

PHOTOGRAPH   PAGES 30-31

Cheese and Cucumber Passrounds

3 large green cucumbers, halved lengthwise, peeled, seeded
salt
155g (5oz) cream cheese, softened
¼ cup cream
2 teaspoons chopped dill
2 tablespoons pernod
1 teaspoon green peppercorns, crushed

Sprinkle the cut side of the cucumber with salt and turn upside down to drain on kitchen towelling. Beat the cream cheese and cream together, add the dill, pernod and peppercorns. Combine well. Pipe the cheese along the hollowed-out centre of each cucumber half. Refrigerate, cut into 2½cm (1") pieces and serve.   Makes approximately 24.

Apricot Passrounds

A very colourful passround. The filling can be made well ahead of time and chilled until required.

12-15 fresh apricots
250g (8oz) cottage cheese
¼ cup chopped shallots
2 tablespoons apricot brandy
1 hard-boiled egg
1 teaspoon salt
1 teaspoon Tabasco sauce
1 teaspoon chopped chives

Halve and stone the apricots and place on a flat tray. Combine all the other ingredients and spoon some of the cheese mixture into each apricot half. Refrigerate until ready to serve.   Makes 2-3 doz.

Prawn and Avocado Passrounds

A creamy tasty mixture which is very simple to make.

125g (4oz) cooked prawns, shelled, deveined, finely chopped
1 large avocado, peeled, stoned, finely chopped
¼ cup chopped shallots
½ teaspoon vinegar
½ teaspoon Worcestershire sauce
½ cup Baileys Irish Cream
½ cup sour cream
½ cup freshly grated coconut
1 teaspoon salt

Combine all the ingredients together in a bowl. Refrigerate and serve spooned onto water biscuits.   Makes approximately 15-20.

STUFFED ZUCCHINI (RECIPE PAGE 37)

Savoury Eggs

6 hard-boiled eggs
1 small onion
2 tablespoons chutney
30g (1oz) butter or margarine
2 tablespoons mayonnaise
1 teaspoon chilli sauce
seasoning to taste

Remove the yolks from eggs and place into a food processor with the remaining ingredients; mix until well combined. Spoon or pipe the mixture into the egg halves and garnish with chopped parsley.   Makes 1 doz.

Curried Cashews

2 tablespoons oil
2 teaspoons curry powder
2 teaspoons Worcestershire sauce
pinch chilli powder
2 cups cashew nuts

Heat the oil in a frying pan and add the curry powder, Worcestershire sauce, chilli powder and cashew nuts. Stir well to coat the nuts. Spread on to a foil lined baking sheet and bake at 150°C (300°F) for 20-25 minutes, or until crisp.

TRADITIONAL HORSE AND CART RIDE, BOURKE STREET MALL, MELBOURNE, VICTORIA

MOUNT WARNING NEAR MURWILLUMBAH, NEW SOUTH WALES

Sausage Rolls

6 slices bread
½ cup hot water
2kg (4lb) sausage meat
1 onion, finely chopped
½ teaspoon mixed herbs

750g (24oz) packet ready rolled
puff pastry, thawed
1 egg beaten
seasoning to taste

Remove crusts from bread and soak in a bowl of hot water for 5 minutes; squeeze to remove excess moisture. Combine the bread in a bowl with the sausage meat, onion, herbs and seasoning. Place into a piping bag. Cut sheets of pastry in half and pipe the filling along the edges of the pastry, turning the edge of the pastry over the filling. Turn again so that the filling is completely encased in the pastry. Repeat process with remaining pastry and filling. Score the pastry at 5cm (2") intervals and brush with beaten egg. Bake at 230°C (450°F) for 20 minutes, then reduce temperature to 180°C (350°F) and bake a further 10-15 minutes.

Makes approximately 4 doz.

Traditional Meat Pie

1 onion, chopped
750g (1½lb) minced steak
1½ cups beef stock
½ cup tomato sauce
pinch nutmeg
2 tablespoons flour blended with

a little water
375g (12oz) packet shortcrust pastry,
thawed
1 sheet ready rolled puff pastry,
thawed
seasoning to taste

Sauté the onion and meat in a frying pan until browned, draining off any excess fat. Add the beef stock, tomato sauce and seasoning; cover and bring to the boil then simmer for 15 minutes. Stir in the blended flour, allow the mixture to thicken, then cool. Lightly grease a 23cm (9") deep pie dish and line with the shortcrust pastry. Spoon in the cold filling, moisten the edges with water and top with the puff pastry, pressing down gently to seal. Trim and score the edges, brush the top with lightly beaten egg and make a slight cut in the centre of the pastry. Bake at 230°C (350°F) for 10 minutes then reduce heat to 180°C (350°F) and bake a further 30 minutes.

Serves 4-6.

ONE OF THE MANY BEAUTIFUL BEACHES AROUND SYDNEY, NEW SOUTH WALES

SUNSET OVER THE TWELVE APOSTLES, PORT CAMPBELL NATIONAL PARK, VICTORIA

LENNA HOUSE (NOW LENNA HOTEL), RUNNYMEDE STREET, BATTERY POINT, HOBART, TASMANIA

Pork Spare Ribs in Black Bean Sauce

1.5kg (3lb) pork spare ribs	2 tablespoons soy sauce
3 cloves garlic	1 tablespoon honey
1 apple, sliced	1 tablespoon sherry
1 onion, sliced	½ cup water
¼ cup black beans	seasoning to taste

Place the pork ribs into a baking dish and bake at 200°C (400°F) for approximately 30 minutes, draining off any excess fat. Reduce the heat to 180°C (350°F). Combine all the remaining ingredients in a food processor and pour over the meat, cooking for a further 45 minutes, basting occasionally until the meat is cooked.

Serves 4-6.

Pork and Veal Terrine

250g (8oz) minced pork	1 egg
250g (8oz) minced veal	¼ teaspoon thyme
4 rashers bacon, chopped	3 tablespoons brandy
125g (4oz) lambs fry, chopped	1 bay leaf
1 small onion, chopped	seasoning to taste
1 clove garlic	

Combine all the ingredients with the exception of the bay leaf in a food processor; blend until well mixed. Press into a terrine dish or a 22cm (8½") x 12cm (5") loaf tin, smooth top and decorate with a bay leaf. Cover with foil and place into a water bath. Bake at 180°C (350°F) for 1½ hours. Refrigerate and serve with fresh crusty bread.

Serves 6-8.

Barbecue Pork Parcels

2 tablespoons soy sauce	1 teaspoon five spices
2 tablespoons dry red wine	4 pork fillets
2 tablespoons honey	2 sheets ready rolled puff pastry,
1 clove crushed garlic	thawed

Combine the soy sauce, wine, honey, garlic and spices in a bowl and add the pork, marinating for at least 1 hour or cover and refrigerate overnight. Drain the pork fillets, reserving the marinade. In a small saucepan reduce the marinade to half the quantity by boiling gently, then cool. Cut each pastry sheet in half and place each fillet onto the pastry, brushing with the marinade. Moisten the edges of the pastry with milk and seal. Place onto a lightly greased baking sheet, seam-side down, glaze with milk and bake at 250°C (450°F) for 15-20 minutes or until pastry is golden brown. Serves 4.

Baked Cutlets

2 onions, sliced	6 lamb cutlets
rind 1 lemon	seasoned flour
¼ cup parsley	1 egg beaten
¼ cup mint	2 tablespoons milk
2 cups fresh breadcrumbs	3 rashers bacon, halved

Combine the onions, lemon rind, parsley, mint and breadcrumbs together in a food processor. Dip the cutlets in the seasoned flour, egg and milk. Coat with the breadcrumb mixture and wrap in bacon. Place onto individual pieces of foil; wrap into parcels. Place on a baking sheet and bake at 200°C (400°F) for 1 hour, opening foil 10 minutes prior to end of the cooking to allow bacon to crispen.

Serves 4-6.

PHOTOGRAPH PAGES 30-31

Baked Lamb with Crusty topping

2 kg (4lb) leg of lamb
1 egg yolk
3 tablespoons butter or margarine, melted
1½ cups fresh breadcrumbs
1 tablespoon sesame seeds
¼ teaspoon salt
½ teaspoon mixed herbs
1 small onion, sliced

Remove excess fat from lamb and brush with a little egg yolk. Combine butter, breadcrumbs, sesame seeds and seasonings with half of the remaining yolk. Press mixture firmly over lamb. Press the onion rings firmly into the crumb surface with the palm of the hand to form a decorative pattern. Brush with the remaining yolk. Bake in a roasting dish at 180°C (350°F) for approximately 2 hours. When crust is golden and crisp, cover with foil for remainder of cooking period.   Serves 6.

Marinated Lamb Skewers

2 x 200g (7oz) cartons natural yoghurt
¼ cup French mustard
pinch ground allspice
750g (1½lb) lean boneless lamb
seasoning to taste

Combine 1 carton of yoghurt with the mustard and seasonings in a large bowl. Add meat and stir well until thoroughly coated. Cover and refrigerate overnight. Thread meat onto six metal skewers and grill for 15-20 minutes. Blend the remaining carton of yoghurt with left over marinade in a saucepan and heat gently. Do not boil. Serve kebabs on a bed of boiled rice and spoon over the yoghurt sauce.   Serves 6.

Chicken Drumsticks with Kiwi Fruit Sauce

2 cups fresh breadcrumbs
¼ cup finely chopped shallots
¼ teaspoon Tabasco sauce
2 eggs
60g (2oz) butter or margarine, melted
a little milk
18 large chicken legs
Sauce
3 kiwi fruit
1 teaspoon curry powder
1 teaspoon salt

Combine the breadcrumbs, shallots, Tabasco sauce, eggs and butter with a little milk in a bowl. Lift the skin away from the flesh, right to the end of the leg. Spoon the seasoning evenly under the skin of each leg, pressing the seasoning so that it is evenly distributed around the flesh. Bake at 180°C (350°F) until brown; basting regularly. Serve hot or cold.

Sauce
Purée the kiwi fruit, curry powder and salt, and serve with the chicken.   Serves 6.

PHOTOGRAPH   PAGE 35

Guinea Fowl and Herb Stuffing

2 guinea fowl
¼ chopped parsley
1 teaspoon chopped rosemary
1 teaspoon chopped marjoram
1 teaspoon caraway seeds
¼ cup chopped mushrooms
1 tablespoon grated Cheddar cheese
seasoning to taste

Split the fowls in half down the backbone and breast. Combine the herbs, caraway seeds, cheese, mushrooms and seasoning together in a bowl. Lift the skin from the flesh of the fowls and spread the herb mixture evenly under the skin. Place in a roasting dish and bake at 190°C (370°F) until cooked and browned and the juices are clear. Serve with the pan juices or as it is.

Variation
1 cup chicken stock
½ cup grapefruit juice
1 tablespoon chopped chives

Bring the stock and grapefruit juice to the boil in a saucepan. Boil until reduced by half then stir in the chives. Boil for one more minute; pour over the guinea fowl and serve.   Serves 4.

PHOTOGRAPH   PAGE 35

Kebabs, Sweet'n'Sour

¼ cup soy sauce
2 tablespoons oil
2 cloves garlic, crushed
2 tablespoons brown sugar
1 onion, finely chopped
1 tablespoon lemon juice
2 teaspoons grated root ginger
1 x 450g (14oz) can* pineapple pieces, drained, juice reserved
dash Tabasco sauce
4 chicken breasts cut into strips

Combine soy sauce with the oil, garlic, sugar, onion, lemon juice, ginger, pineapple juice and Tabasco sauce. Add the chicken and marinate for 2 hours. Thread chicken onto skewers alternately with pineapple. Grill until cooked, basting with the marinade and serve on a bed of parsley rice.   Serves 4.
*nearest equivalent can size.

A TYPICAL BULLDUST TRACK IN NORTH QUEENSLAND

Bacon and Scallop Kebabs

8 rashers bacon
500g (1lb) scallops
¼ cup melted butter or margarine
seasoning to taste
little extra butter
½ cup chopped shallots
¼ cup finely chopped parsley

Cut each rasher of bacon into three pieces and roll. Thread the bacon and scallops alternately onto metal or pre-soaked bamboo skewers; brush with melted butter and season. Grill on the barbecue for approximately 4-5 minutes, turning regularly. Melt a little extra butter in a pan, sauté the shallots and parsley and serve poured over the barbecued scallops.   Serves 4.

PORK AND VEAL TERRINE (RECIPE PAGE 28); BACON AND VEAL PATE (RECIPE PAGE 20)

CHEESY SPINACH QUICHES (RECIPE PAGE 22); INDIVIDUAL HAM QUICHES (NO RECIPE)

Seafoods Skewers

250g (8oz) scallops
250g (8oz) green king prawns,
shelled, deveined
grated rind, juice 1 lemon
juice ½ orange
3 tablespoons orange liqueur

Combine all ingredients in a bowl and marinate overnight. Thread scallops and prawns alternately onto four skewers. Grill, basting frequently with the marinade until just cooked. Serve on a bed of thinly sliced oranges and cucumbers.   Serves 4.

Bordeaux Prawns

125g (4oz) butter or margarine
1 carrot, diced
1 onion, sliced
1 shallot, sliced
3 sprigs parsley
1 bay leaf
¼ teaspoon thyme
3 doz king prawns, shelled,
deveined
¾ cup brandy
3 teaspoons tomato purée
1½ cups white wine
2 egg yolks
1 tablespoon water
1 teaspoon butter
seasoning to taste

Melt half the butter in a saucepan and cook the vegetables with the bay leaf and thyme until tender. In another saucepan melt the remaining butter and sauté the prawns until just cooked; pour in brandy and ignite. When flames have subsided add tomato purée, cooked vegetables, seasoning and white wine. Cover, bring to the boil and simmer for 15 minutes. Remove prawns to a serving dish and keep warm. Reduce sauce slightly then beat in the egg yolks, water and butter. Pour over prawns and serve.   Serves 6.

Prawn Satay

The Satay Sauce
¾ cup coconut milk
1 small nob root ginger, chopped
2 cloves garlic, crushed
seasoning to taste
2 tablespoons soy sauce
1 teaspoon brown sugar
1 teaspoon chilli powder
1 tablespoon lime juice
For Serving
500g (1lb) green king prawns,
shelled, deveined

Combine all the ingredients for the sauce in a bowl. Place the prawns in the base of a shallow dish, pour over the sauce and allow to marinate for at least 30 minutes. Thread onto metal or pre-soaked bamboo skewers and grill on the barbecue for 2 minutes on each side, basting frequently with the marinade. DO NOT overcook.   Serves 4.

Fish Mornay

1 cup grated cheese
3 cups cooked, flaked fish
grated cheese, for topping
lemon slices, for garnish
Cheese Sauce
6 tablespoons butter or margarine
6 tablespoons flour
3¾ cups milk
seasoning to taste

Make the sauce in the usual way with butter, flour, seasonings and milk. Add the cheese and heat through. Place the fish in a greased ovenproof casserole, cover with sauce and top with cheese. Bake at 200°C (400°F) until golden brown and serve garnished with lemon slices and parsley.

SUNSET OVER SYDNEY HARBOUR

CASINO IN BEAUTIFUL HOBART, TASMANIA

Malay Prawns Satay

500g (1lb) green king prawns, shelled, deveined
1 small clove garlic, bruised
½ teaspoon sugar
1 teaspoon cornflour
¼ teaspoon curry powder
¼ teaspoon salt

2 tablespoons satay sauce
1 teaspoon soy sauce
1 tablespoon dry sherry
1 tablespoon peanut oil
2 teaspoons sesame oil
1 large onion, sliced

Marinate prawns in the combined garlic, sugar, cornflour, curry powder, salt, satay sauce, soy sauce and sherry; drain, reserve marinade. Heat oils in a frying pan and sauté the onion for 1 minute. Add prawns and stir fry for 2 minutes. Pour over the marinade, reheat and serve on braised lettuce leaves.   Serves 4.

Prawn and Salmon Salad

1 x 220g (7oz) can* pink salmon, drained, flaked
1 x 410g (13oz) can* grapefruit segments, drained
½ cup chopped celery

1 x 185g (6oz) can* prawns, drained
½ cup chopped parsley
seasoning to taste
½ cup coleslaw dressing
shredded lettuce

Gently toss together all the ingredients with the exception of the dressing and the lettuce. Chill until ready to serve. Serve on a plate with the dressing spooned over the salad surrounded by shredded lettuce.   Serves 4-6.
*nearest equivalent can size.

Rice and Chicken Salad

¾ cup long grain rice
1 clove garlic, crushed
3 tablespoons oil
1 tablespoon tarragon vinegar
pinch mustard
1 tablespoon sultanas

1 large tomato, peeled, chopped
2 tablespoons chopped walnuts
250g (8oz) cooked chicken, chopped
125g (4oz) ham, chopped
1 green capsicum, chopped
seasoning to taste

Cook rice in boiling salted water until tender, drain thoroughly. Whisk garlic, oil, vinegar, seasoning and mustard together. Pour over hot rice, stir in the remaining ingredients, cover and refrigerate until required.   Serves 2-4.

Vegetable and Rice Salad

2 cups rice
3 tablespoons of French dressing
250g (8oz) frozen peas, thawed
¼ cup green capsicum, chopped
¼ cup celery, chopped
1 tablespoon black olives, stoned, chopped

3 tomatoes, chopped
¼ cup onion, finely chopped
2 radishes, thinly sliced
¼ cup mayonnaise
½ teaspoon salt
lettuce cups.

Cook rice in boiling salted water until just tender, drain and toss in the French dressing, allow to cool then stir in all the remaining ingredients with the exception of the lettuce. Refrigerate until required then serve in lettuce cups.   Serves 6-8.

Patio Salad

4 x 300g (10oz) cans* kidney
beans, drained
8 hard-boiled eggs, chopped
1 cup finely chopped onion

2 cups chopped celery
1/3 cup relish, pickles or chutney
2 cups grated Cheddar cheese
2 cups sour cream

Combine all ingredients in a bowl and serve.   Serves 4-6.
*nearest equivalent can size.

Stuffed Potatoes

6 large pontiac potatoes, cooked
60g (2oz) melted butter or margarine
250g (8oz) cooked prawns, deveined,
chopped
60g (2oz) shallots, chopped

1 teaspoon grated lemon rind
1/2 teaspoon chopped parsley
1 tablespoon chopped dill
seasoning to taste

Cut the potatoes in half, scoop out flesh and mash with the
butter. Combine with all the other ingredients and spoon back
into the potato shell. Bake at 200°C (400°F) until heated through.
Serves 6.

SALAMANDA MARKET, HOBART, TASMANIA

Tasty Brown Rice Salad

To serve as a hot salad, simply heat all the ingredients together in
a saucepan with a little chicken stock until warmed through.

3 cups cooked brown rice
1/2 cup corn kernels
1/2 cup cooked peas
1 cup sliced celery
3 shallots, chopped
1 red capsicum, de-seeded, chopped

1 carrot, chopped
6 rashers bacon, chopped, cooked
1/4 cup chopped walnuts
1/4 cup mayonnaise
1/2 red chilli, de-seeded, chopped

Place all the ingredients in a large bowl and combine thoroughly.
Chill until required.   Serves 8.

Moulded Potato Salad

3 cups potatoes, diced
1 cup cooked peas
1 cup cooked carrots, chopped
2 gherkins, chopped
1 tablespoon chopped mint

1 teaspoon ground black pepper
1 tablespoon gelatine
2 tablespoons creme de menthe
1/4 cup warm water
1 cup mayonnaise

Combine the potatoes with the peas, carrots, gherkins, mint and
pepper in a bowl and refrigerate. Dissolve the gelatine in the
creme de menthe and the water. Cool and stir into the
mayonnaise. Combine with the potatoes and spoon into a wetted
5-6 cup mould and refrigerate until set. Turn out and serve
decorated with sprigs of fresh mint or watercress.   Serves 6-8.

GUINEA FOWL AND HERB STUFFING (RECIPE PAGE 29); CHICKEN DRUMSTICKS WITH KIWI FRUIT SAUCE (RECIPE PAGE 29)

KARANDA TOURIST TRAIN IN SCENIC ATHERTON TABLELAND, QUEENSLAND

Cider Flavoured Potatoes

1kg (2lb) potatoes, peeled, thinly sliced	1 cup cider
1 cup grated Cheddar cheese	1 tablespoon chopped parsley
60g (2oz) butter or margarine	seasoning to taste

Place half the potatoes over the base of a greased ovenproof dish. Sprinkle with half the cheese and season, cover with the remaining potatoes and cheese. Dot with butter and pour over the cider. Bake uncovered at 190°C (375°F) for 1½ hours. Serve sprinkled with freshly chopped parsley. Serves 4.

Stuffed Zucchini

6 medium zucchinis	2 tomatoes, roughly chopped
30g (1oz) butter or margarine	1 stick celery, sliced
250g (8oz) minced steak	seasoning to taste
1 onion, roughly chopped	

Slice the zucchinis in half lengthways and scoop out the seeds and flesh. Melt the butter in a saucepan and sauté the meat until lightly browned. Add the remaining ingredients and simmer for 5 minutes. Spoon the mixture into the zucchinis and place onto a greased baking sheet. Bake at 200°C (400°F) for 45 minutes or until tender. Serves 6.

PHOTOGRAPH   PAGE 22

Gratin Cauliflower

½ medium cauliflower	1 cup milk
90g (3oz) butter or margarine	seasoning to taste
8 slices wholemeal bread, crumbed	90g (3oz) tasty cheese, grated
2 tablespoons flour	4 shallots, chopped

Divide cauliflower into florets, cook in boiling salted water until tender; drain. Melt half the butter in a saucepan and saute the breadcrumbs until browned. Make a white sauce in the usual way with the remaining butter, flour and milk. Season and stir in the cheese and shallots. Arrange cauliflower in an ovenproof dish, spoon over the sauce and sprinkle with the breadcrumbs. Bake uncovered at 180°C (350°F) for 20 minutes or until browned. Serves 4-6.

PHOTOGRAPH   THIS PAGE

Mixed Vegetable Casserole

3 capsicums cut into strips	2 cloves crushed garlic
3 eggplants, sliced	3 onions, thinly sliced
6 zucchini, sliced	1 cup chicken stock
3 tomatoes, skinned, chopped	seasoning to taste
⅔ cup olive oil	

Toss vegetables in oil and transfer to a casserole. Cover and bake at 180°C (350°F) for 1 hour. Serve as an entree or as a vegetable accompaniment. Serves 4-6.

Pumpkin Cream Soup

2kg (4lb) pumpkin, peeled	2 cups water
2 onions, peeled	2½ cups milk
2 apples, cored	freshly ground pepper to taste
2 cups chicken stock	½ cup light sour cream
1 teaspoon nutmeg	chopped chives
1 teaspoon salt	

Roughly chop pumpkin, onions and apples. Place in a heavy based saucepan. Add stock, nutmeg and salt. Bring to the boil. Cover and simmer 35-40 minutes until pumpkin is tender. Purée in a food processor or rub through a sieve. Return to pan and stir in the milk. Adjust seasonings, serve garnished with sour cream and chopped chives. Serves 6.

Stuffed Capsicums

6 large capsicums	1 tablespoon chopped dill
2 tablespoons oil	¾ cup rice
250g (8oz) minced steak	1 tablespoon chopped parsley
250g (8oz) minced veal	**Sauce**
1 onion, chopped	1 cup tomato soup
1 tablespoon tomato paste	½ teaspoon garlic salt
1 cup water	1 tablespoon sherry

Cut top from the capsicum and remove the seeds. Reserve tops. Heat the oil in a large frying pan and add the meat. Lightly brown then stir in the onion, tomato paste and water. Cook for a further 5 minutes. Add the dill, rice and parsley and simmer until all the moisture is absorbed. Spoon into the capsicums, replace the top and place in a baking dish. Combine all the ingredients for the sauce and pour over the capsicums. Cover with foil and bake at 180°C (350°F) for approximately 30-40 minutes or until cooked. Serves 6.

GRATIN CAULIFLOWER (RECIPE THIS PAGE)

STRAWBERRY & BANANA ROLL (RECIPE PAGE 40); PAW PAW SOUFFLE (RECIPE PAGE 40)

Fruit and White Burgundy Punch

juice and rind 2 oranges	*¼ cup sugar*
juice and rind 2 lemons	*2 bottles white burgundy*
1¼ cups water	*1 cup brandy*
1 tablespoon honey	*crushed ice*

Place the orange and lemon rind in a saucepan together with the water, honey and sugar. Simmer for 5 minutes, then strain into a punch bowl. Add the juice from the fruit, wine, brandy and crushed ice. Garnish with slices of orange and lemon; chill until required. Serves 15-20.

Strawberry Pavlova

1 punnet strawberries, hulled	**Filling**
little caster sugar	*4 egg whites*
½ cup fresh orange juice	*250g (8oz) sugar*
½ cup port	*½ teaspoon vanilla essence*
Reserve a few strawberries for	*1 teaspoon vinegar*
decoration	*2 teaspoons cornflour*

Combine the strawberries, reserve a few for decoration in a bowl, with the caster sugar, orange juice and port; chill for approximately 2 hours. Whisk the egg whites in a bowl with the sugar, vanilla and vinegar until stiff, then fold in the cornflour. Place onto a lightly greased baking sheet, and bake at 120°C (250°F) for 1½ hours without opening the oven. Leave to cool in the oven. Fill the pavlova with the strawberry filling and decorate with the extra strawberries. Serves 8.

Rum Trifle

2 egg yolks	*2 bananas, sliced*
2 tablespoons sugar	*⅓ cup coarsely chopped cashew nuts*
1 cup scalded milk	*1 cup thickened cream*
½ cup rum	*cherries*
1 sponge sandwich cake	*angelica for decoration*
raspberry jam	

Make a soft custard by placing the egg yolks, sugar and milk in a double saucepan. Heat, stirring constantly until thickened. Allow to cool, then blend in 1 teaspoon of the rum and chill. Arrange one of the sponge cake layers in a serving dish and spread liberally with raspberry jam, slices of banana and sprinkle liberally with cashews. Pour over some of the rum and top with the chilled custard. Repeat with remaining sponge, jam and rum. Top with whipped cream and decorate with cherries and angelica. Chill thoroughly before serving. Serves 6-8.

Meringues with Ginger Cream

3 egg whites	*1 cup thickened cream, whipped*
¾ cup caster sugar	*3 tablespoons, finely chopped ginger*

Whisk the egg whites and half the sugar until stiff then fold in the remaining sugar. Lightly grease a baking sheet and spoon the meringue mix into six heaps, slightly hollowing out the centres. Bake at 110°C-120°C (225°F-250°F) for 2½-3 hours; cool. Combine the whipped cream with half the ginger and pile into the meringue shells. Top with the remaining ginger. Makes 6.

MAGNIFICENT FITZROY FALLS, NEW SOUTH WALES

Pawpaw Souffle

500g (1lb) peeled, seeded pawpaw
¼ cup Kirsch liqueur
4 egg whites
60g (2oz) caster sugar

1⅓ cups cream
For Decoration
kiwi fruit and mandarin segments

Purée the pawpaw in a blender or a food processor with the liqueur; chill. Whip the egg whites until stiff, gradually adding the caster sugar. Chill, then whip the cream until a thick consistency is obtained. Combine all the ingredients and serve in a glass bowl and decorate with the fruit.   Serves 6.

PHOTOGRAPH   PAGE 38

Strawberry and Banana Roll

1 punnet strawberries, hulled, sliced
3 bananas, sliced
2 tablespoons caster sugar
3 tablespoons Cointreau
3 cups milk

vanilla essence
90g (3oz) butter or margarine
¾ cup flour
4 eggs, separated

Place the strawberries and bananas in a glass bowl, sprinkle with sugar, cover and soak with the liqueur. Heat the milk and vanilla in a saucepan. In another saucepan, melt the butter, add the flour and stir to a paste. Remove from the heat and stir in the heated milk slowly mixing to a smooth paste. Return to the heat and cook 4-5 minutes; cool. Grease and line a swiss roll tin and sprinkle with caster sugar. Whisk the egg whites until stiff and beat the egg yolks separately. Add the egg yolks to the sauce mixture, then fold in the stiffly beaten egg whites. Pour into the prepared tin and bake at 180°C (350°F) until lightly browned. Turn onto a piece of greaseproof paper lightly coated with sugar. Strain the fruits and place them onto sponge. Carefully roll into the Swiss roll. Serve with whipped cream and extra strawberries and bananas if wished.   Serves 6-8.

PHOTOGRAPH   PAGE 38

Coffee Cream Profiteroles

1 cup water
1 tablespoon caster sugar
pinch salt
30g (1oz) butter or margarine
125g (4oz) flour, sifted

3 eggs
whipped cream
2 tablespoons coffee Marsala
125g (4oz) cooking chocolate, melted

Combine the water, sugar, salt and butter in a saucepan and bring to the boil. Remove from the heat and stir in the flour. Return to the heat and beat until a smooth paste forms and the mixture leaves the side of the pan; remove from the heat and cool slightly. Add the eggs one at a time, beating well after each addition; refrigerate until cold. Place spoonfuls of mixture onto greased baking sheets spacing well. Bake at 200°C (400°F) for 10 minutes, reduce heat to 180°C (350°F), baking a further 30 minutes. Cool. To the whipped cream add the coffee Marsala, spoon into the meringues then coat with the melted chocolate.   Makes 20.

Double Layer Truffles

1½ cups ground walnuts
1½ cups sifted icing sugar
2 tablespoons rum

200g (6oz) light cooking chocolate
60g (2oz) butter or margarine
¾ cup condensed milk

Combine the walnuts, icing sugar and rum in a bowl and press over the base of a greased and foil lined 20cm (8") square tin. Combine the chocolate and butter in a double saucepan. Add the milk and cook for 5 minutes. Pour over nut mixture and refrigerate overnight. Cut into desired squares.   Makes 25

POPULAR HOT AIR BALLOONING OVER CANBERRA, AUSTRALIAN CAPITAL TERRITORY

SAILING ON SYDNEY'S BEAUTIFUL HARBOUR, NEW SOUTH WALES

ENJOYING FISH

Seafood From the Island Continent

Australia is an island continent. That means it is surrounded by a tremendous amount of water — and fish. There are over 2,500 species of fish off our shores. This is enough to have a different fish dinner once a week for the next fifty years. With this variety of fish, there is something for everyone's taste.

Fish shops were once limited to flake (shark) and flathead which were used to make the old stand by "fish and chips". Now you can find a wide and exciting range of fish: gemfish, jewfish, redfish, flounder, sole and John Dory. You'll also find Australians using a variety of recipes that put the ol' fish batter to shame.

It's important to buy fresh fish on the day you plan to use it. A fresh fish is unmistakeable. It has full bright eyes, gills that are flat and red underneath, skin that's slippery to the touch and a "sea smell."

There is also an astonishing variety of shellfish in Australian waters. Rock lobster from Western Australia, crayfish from Tasmania, oysters from Sydney, Northern Territory barramundi, giant Queensland mud crabs and Morton Bay Bugs are all fabulous eating.

The following recipes, using seafood found off our island continent, will make a fish lover out of anyone.

LAKE ST. CLAIR, TASMANIA

Mussels in Lemon Sauce

1kg (2lbs) mussels
1 small onion, chopped
1 shallot, chopped
1 clove garlic, crushed
½ cup finely chopped parsley
freshly ground black pepper
75g (2½oz) butter or margarine
1¼ cups white wine
1½ tablespoons lemon juice

Scrub the mussels thoroughly and place in a saucepan with the onion, shallot, garlic, parsley, pepper, half the butter and the wine. Cover and cook the mussels for a few minutes over a high heat. Shake in the pan several times to ensure even cooking. When all the mussels have opened, transfer to a heated serving dish and keep warm. Strain the liquid into a small saucepan and reduce over a high heat until one-third remains. Remove from the heat and whisk in the remaining butter. When thick and foamy whisk in the lemon juice and pour over the mussels. Serve very hot with chunks of fresh crusty french bread.　　　　Serves 4.

PHOTOGRAPH　　PAGE 48

PEACHES & SQUID (RECIPE PAGE 49)

Mussels in Garlic Butter

Mussels are always available in your local fish shop. Try this very quick and simple recipe.

125g (4oz) butter or magarine, cubed
2 cloves garlic, crushed
¼ cup chopped parsley
2 dozen mussels, washed, beards removed
¼ cup chopped shallots
2 sprigs thyme
1 bay leaf
¼ teaspoon salt
1 cup dry white wine

Cream the butter with the garlic and parsley in a bowl, set aside. Place the mussels in a saucepan with the remaining ingredients. Bring to the boil and simmer for 3 minutes or until the mussels open. Detach the lid from the base of the mussels and place the mussels still sitting in the shell on a baking sheet. Dot generously with the garlic butter and grill until the butter has melted.

Serves 2-3.

PHOTOGRAPH　　PAGE 57

Creamed Crab

A special dish for entertaining when crabs are not too expensive.

4 small crabs
1 tablespoon chopped shallots
½ cup chopped mushrooms
1 tablespoon butter or margarine
2 tablespoons Cognac
seasoning to taste.

Gratin Sauce
2 tablespoons butter or margarine
2 tablespoons flour
1½ cups fish stock
½ cup cream
1 teaspoon French mustard
1 teaspoon cayenne pepper
½ cup grated cheese

Prepare crabmeat in the usual way and set to one side, being careful to keep the shells intact. Sauté the shallots and mushrooms in the butter, season and pour over the warmed Cognac ignited. Remove from the heat. Make the sauce by melting the butter in a saucepan and stirring in the flour over a low heat for 1-2 minutes. Gradually add the fish stock and stir until the sauce thickens then stir in the cream, mustard and seasoning. Allow to simmer for 2-3 minutes then remove from heat and stir in the crabmeat and mushrooms. Spoon the mixture into the crab shells, sprinkle with cheese and bake at 150°C (300°F) for 5 minutes.　　　　Serves 4.

PHOTOGRAPH　　PAGE 67

Calamari Rings

This makes an excellent appetizer to serve with cocktails.

½ cup flour
½ cup self-raising flour
1 teaspoon salt
1 egg
½ cup water
1 tablespoon oil
1kg (2lb) squid
oil for frying
For serving: tartare sauce, lemon wedges

Make a batter by beating the flours and salt together in a bowl with the combined egg, water and oil. Prepare the squid by gently pulling the tentacles from the body. Rinse under running cold water until the ink is removed. Slide out the piece of cuttle which forms the backbone and peel the skin from the squid and cut the body into rings. Cut away and discard the hard sections from the tentacles. Cut tentacles and flat fins into strips. Dry thoroughly on kitchen paper. Heat the oil, dip the squid in the batter and deep fry until golden brown. Drain and serve with tartare sauce and lemon wedges.　　　　Serves 4-6.

PHOTOGRAPH　　PAGE 57

Seafood Bowl

For individual serves, the pastry could be cut into six and used to line individual quiche tins.

8 shallots, chopped
1 clove garlic, crushed
30g (1oz) butter or margarine
375g (12oz) green prawns, shelled, deveined
375g (12oz) scallops
¾ cup dry white wine
½ teaspoon salt
pinch cayenne pepper
2 tablespoons cornflour
½ cup cream
8 sheets filo pastry
60g (2oz) butter or margarine, melted
½ cup grated Gruyere or Swiss cheese

Sauté the shallots and garlic in the butter. Add the prawns, scallops, wine and seasonings. Bring to the boil and simmer uncovered for 1 minute. Gradually blend the cornflour and cream to a smooth paste and stir into the prawns and scallops. Bring to the boil and boil gently for 1 minute, stirring constantly. Brush each sheet of pastry with melted butter and layer. Line a lightly greased 18cm (7") x 20cm (8") quiche tin, folding the edges over or under to neaten. Spoon the prawn mixture into the pastry case and sprinkle with the cheese. Bake at 190°C (370°F) for 10 minutes or until cooked and brown.　　　　Serves 6.

SYDNEY OPERA HOUSE AND CITY FROM THE AIR, NEW SOUTH WALES

MUSSELS IN LEMON SAUCE (RECIPE PAGE 46)

Oyster Savouries

An elegant passround to serve with drinks.

½ cup cream
¼ cup sour cream
1 small onion, finely chopped
¼ teaspoon salt

⅛ teaspoon cayenne pepper
24 frozen vol-au-vent cases, cooked
24 oysters
small jar black or red caviar

Combine the creams and whip until thick. Fold in the onion and seasonings. Spoon into cold pre-baked vol-au-vent cases and garnish with oysters and caviar.

Baked Avocado with Crab

2 avocadoes
1 cup crabmeat
½ cup white sauce

¼ cup brown breadcrumbs
¼ cup grated cheese

Halve the avocadoes removing the seed. Mould a little crab into the cavity, spoon over some white sauce and top with the combined breadcrumbs and cheese. Bake at 220°C (440°F) until the cheese has melted. Serve at once as an entree.   Serves 4.

PRAWN AND WHITING ROLLS (RECIPE PAGE 59)

Oysters au Fromage

Parmesan or Gruyere cheese could be used to add extra flavour to the oysters.

2 rashers bacon, chopped
¼ cup chopped shallots
90g (3oz) grated tasty cheese
1 tablespoon Worcestershire sauce

12 oysters in their shell
3 lettuce leaves
seasoning to taste

Sauté the bacon and shallots in a frying pan for 2 minutes, drain. Combine the cheese, bacon mixture, Worcestershire sauce and seasoning in a bowl. Place the oysters on a baking sheet and top with a spoonful of cheese mixture. Grill until cheese has melted and browned. Serve on the lettuce, garnished with sprigs of parsley.   Serves 2.

Peaches and Squid

Squid is available cleaned and cut ready to use.

60g (2oz) butter or margarine
½ cup chopped onion
750g (1½lb) squid tubes, rings or slices

1 cup sliced peaches
¼ cup orange liqueur
chopped chives
seasoning to taste

Melt the butter in a frying pan and add the onion. Sauté until tender then stir in the squid and gently cook until it changes in colour. Stir in the peaches, liqueur and seasoning. Cook for a further 3 minutes and serve with cooked pasta garnished with chopped chives.   Serves 6.

PHOTOGRAPH   PAGE 46

Seafood Cases

1 packet frozen vol-au-vent cases
12 scallops
16 prawns, shelled, deveined
¼ cup water
28g (1oz) packet* white wine sauce mix
½ cup milk
1 tablespoon butter or margarine
1 jar oysters, well drained

Cook vol-au-vents as instructed on the packet and keep warm. Poach scallops and prawns in the water for 1 minute. Blend the sauce mix with the milk, add the seafood together with the butter and bring to the boil. Reduce heat and simmer for 3 minutes, stirring constantly. Fold in the oysters, adjust seasoning if necessary and spoon into the vol-au-vent cases. Serve garnished with a sprig of dill or fennel. Serves 4.
*nearest equivalent packet size.

Prawn Cocktail

Any of the mayonnaise recipes from this section would make an ideal accompaniment to this recipe, in particular the tomato mayonnaise from "Prawns in Tomato Cases".

4 lettuce leaves, shredded
2 shallots, chopped
1kg (2lb) prawns, shelled
1 cup mayonnaise
lemon wedges

Combine lettuce and shallots and divide between six cocktail dishes. Toss the prawns with mayonnaise and spoon into dishes. Garnish with lemon wedges, serve. Serves 6.

Tomato Prawns

This is suitable to serve as an entree.

30g (1oz) butter or margarine
1 onion, finely chopped
1 clove garlic, crushed
500g (1lb) ripe tomatoes, puréed
¼ teaspoon dried basil
½ cup dry white wine
1 tablespoon tomato paste
500g (1lb) prawns
1 tablespoon parsley, finely chopped
1 shallot, sliced
seasoning to taste

Melt the butter in frying pan, add the onions and garlic and sauté until onion is tender. Add tomatoes, seasoning, basil, wine and tomato paste. Bring to the boil and simmer uncovered for 20 minutes until the sauce has reduced and thickened. Stir the prawns into the tomato sauce and simmer gently until heated through. Sprinkle with chopped parsley and shallots and serve with hot fluffy rice. Serves 4.

Artichokes with Prawn Filling

6 large artichokes
water
The Dressing
1½ cups mayonnaise
2 tablespoons white vinegar
½ tablespoon lemon juice
½ tablespoon anchovy sauce
1 small clove garlic, crushed
pinch of cayenne pepper
1 teaspoon chopped tarragon
2 tablespoons chopped parsley
3 tablespoons sherry
For Serving
500g (1lb) prawns shelled, chopped
¼ cup chopped shallots

Trim the artichokes so that they sit upright in a suitably sized saucepan. Cover with water and boil until tender. The artichokes are cooked when one of the leaves close to the top comes out easily when pulled with a pair of tongs. Remove from the heat and drain upside down until cool. Pull out the centre, leaving enough "wall" to support the shape of the artichoke. Make the dressing by combining all the ingredients together in a blender or food processor. Pour over the combined prawns and shallots. Spoon into the artichokes and serve garnished with a sprig of herbs. Serves 6.

Prawns in Tomato Cases

Tomatoes filled with prawns can make an ideal main dish, or an accompaniment to salads.

6 tomatoes
½ cup chopped onion
2 teaspoons parsley
1 tablespoon tomato paste
chicken stock
1 cup mayonnaise
500g (1lb) king prawns, shelled, deveined, chopped
¼ cup chopped celery
¼ cup chopped shallots

Cut a slice from the top of each tomato and scoop the pulp into a saucepan. Place tomatoes upside down on kitchen paper to drain and refrigerate. Make a tomato sauce by stirring the onion, parsley and tomato paste into the reserved pulp. Add sufficient stock to cover and boil rapidly until reduced and slightly thickened, strain into a bowl, cool and refrigerate. Stir sufficient tomato sauce into the mayonnaise to obtain a coating consistency. Toss the prawns, celery and shallots together in a bowl and add the tomato mayonnaise. Stir carefully to combine. Spoon into the tomato cases replacing lids and serve on a bed of watercress. Serves 6.

REDFISH SANDWICHES WITH SOUR CREAM SAUCE (RECIPE PAGE 63)

Sauted Prawns in Liqueur

Prawns cooked in this way could be chopped and used as a filling for vol-au-vents.

30g (1oz) butter or margarine
30 large green prawns, shelled, deveined
2 tablespoons brandy
¼ cup coffee cream liqueur
¼ cup cream
½ teaspoon salt
1 tablespoon desiccated coconut

Melt the butter in a frying pan and stir fry the prawns until just cooked. Pour in the brandy and flambe, add the coffee cream liqueur, cream and salt and stir over a low heat until the sauce thickens. Serve the prawns with cooked pasta and sprinkle with desiccated coconut. Serves 6.

FISHING AT SUNSET ON A ROCKY BEACH

SYDNEY WATERWAYS FROM THE AIR, NEW SOUTH WALES

Chilli Prawns

Prawns are a favourite dish in Australia. The addition of fresh chilli gives them a delicious spicy flavour.

¼ cup tomato sauce	2 cloves garlic, crushed
1 tablespoon sherry	1 teaspoon finely chopped root ginger
1 tablespoon sugar	6 shallots, chopped
2 tablespoons oil	750g (1½lb) green prawns, shelled,
1 red chilli, seeded, finely chopped	deveined

Combine the tomato sauce with the sherry and sugar. Heat the oil in a wok over a medium heat, add the chilli, garlic and ginger. Stir in the shallots and tomato mixture. Simmer for 2-3 minutes, stirring occasionally. Add the prawns and simmer until just cooked. Serve on a bed of spaghetti, garnished with chopped parsley.   Serves 4.

Trevally and Prawn Casserole

If trevally is unavailable any white fish fillets may be used.

1kg (2lb) trevally fillets	deveined
juice 1 lemon	2 firm tomatoes, sliced
water	1 green capsicum, seeded, sliced,
2 cups white sauce	blanched
1 cup dry sherry	seasoning to taste
250g (8oz) cooked prawns, shelled,	

Place fillets in a shallow dish, add the lemon juice and sufficient water to cover. Cover with foil and bake at 180°C (350°F) for 10 minutes. Remove fish and cool. Reheat the white sauce and stir in the sherry and seasoning. Cut fish into pieces and stir into the sauce, together with the prawns, tomato and capsicum. Simmer until re-heated and serve hot, with a green salad.   Serves 4.

PHOTOGRAPH   THIS PAGE

TREVALLY & PRAWN CASSEROLE (RECIPE THIS PAGE)

Creamed Scallops with Mushrooms

Do not overcook the scallops as they will toughen. These are delicious served on a bed of saffron rice accompanied with a fresh herb and cucumber salad.

1½ tablespoons butter or margarine	½ teaspoon curry powder
2 cups mushrooms, roughly chopped	2 teaspoons lemon juice
¼ cup shallots, chopped	cornflour to thicken
750g (1½lb) scallops	seasoning to taste
1 cup sour cream	

Melt the butter in a saucepan and add the mushrooms and shallots and sauté 2-3 minutes. Season and add the scallops, sour cream, curry powder and lemon juice. Cook for a further 2 minutes and thicken with cornflour if wished.   Serves 4.

Coquilles St. Jacques

¾ cup white wine	1 cup cream
4 shallots, finely chopped	½ cup grated Parmesan cheese
500g (1lb) scallops	½ cup fresh breadcrumbs
2 tablespoons butter	2 tablespoons melted butter
1 tablespoon flour	seasoning to taste

Heat the wine, shallots and seasoning in a saucepan until boiling. Add the scallops, remove from the heat, cover and stand for 5 minutes. Remove scallops with a slotted spoon and divide between four scallop shells. Continue to cook the wine mixture over a high heat until reduced to ¼ cup. Make a sauce in the usual way with the butter, flour and cream. Stir in the wine and pour over the scallops. Combine the Parmesan cheese with the melted butter and divide equally between the shells. Grill until lightly browned and serve at once.   Serves 4.

Scallop Brouchettes

1 tablespoon lemon juice	½ teaspoon crushed green
1 clove crushed garlic	peppercorns
1 teaspoon finely chopped fennel	500g (1lb) scallops
3 tablespoons peanut oil	250g (8oz) bacon rashers, rind
2 teaspoons soy sauce	removed

Combine the first seven ingredients in a bowl to make a marinade. Wash and clean the scallops, stir into the marinade and leave for 1½ hours. Drain and wrap each scallop in a piece of bacon. Thread onto skewers and grill for 5-7 minutes. The bacon should be crisp so turn the scallops once or twice during the cooking being careful not to overcook.   Serves 4-6.

Crayfish Scallop Supreme

A delightful combination of these two popular Australian shellfish.

2 cups rice	750g (1½lb) scallops
1kg (2lb) crayfish	6 shallots, chopped
3 tablespoons butter or margarine	1 tablespoon chopped parsley
2 tablespoons lemon juice	

Cook rice in boiling salted water for 12-15 minutes. Drain and keep warm. Halve the crayfish lengthwise and remove the digestive tract. Chop flesh into bite-size pieces. Melt 1 tablespoon of the butter in a frying pan with the lemon juice and sauté scallops and shallots until just tender. Add the crayfish and allow to heat through. Toss parsley and remaining butter through rice and spoon onto a heated serving plate. Spoon the seafood mixture into the shells and serve with the rice.   Serves 4.

TOURISTS ON THE GREAT BARRIER REEF, QUEENSLAND

TROUT WITH ALMONDS AND CRABMEAT STUFFING (RECIPE PAGE 64)

Honey Mayonnaise Scallops

The flavour of the honey and dill mayonnaise is quite unusual.

1kg (2lb) scallops	1½ cups vegetable oil
fish stock	2 tablespoons honey
The Mayonnaise	2 tablespoons chopped dill
3 egg yolks	seasoning to taste
1 teaspoon vinegar	

Poach the scallops in the stock until just cooked. Drain, cool and refrigerate. Make a mayonnaise in the food processor by combining the egg yolks with the vinegar and slowly dribbling in the oil. Transfer to a bowl and add honey, dill and seasoning. Stir the scallops into the mayonnaise and serve in a scallop shell on a bed of watercress. Serves 6.

Scallops and Broccoli

3 tablespoons oil	drained
1 onion, roughly chopped	2 tablespoons soy sauce
2 cloves garlic, crushed	1 teaspoon satay sauce
1 knob root ginger, finely chopped	¾ cup beef stock
6 shallots, chopped	1 tablespoon cornflour
125g (4oz) mushrooms, sliced	water to mix
250g (8oz) broccoli, in florets	500g (1lb) scallops
230g (7oz) can* sliced bamboo shoots,	

Heat oil in a frying pan and sauté onions, garlic and ginger for approximately 2 minutes. Add the shallots, mushrooms, broccoli, bamboo shoots and cook a further 3 minutes then stir in the soy sauce, satay sauce and stock and allow to boil. Blend the cornflour with a little water, add to vegetables and stir until the sauce boils and thickens. Add scallops and simmer until just cooked. Serve with boiled rice. Serves 4.
*nearest equivalent can size.

Scallop Nuggets on Peach and Carrot Purée

1 x 425g (14oz) can* peaches may replace fresh peaches when not in season. These should be well drained then puréed with the cooked carrots.

1 cup breadcrumbs	**The Purée**
½ teaspoon salt	2 carrots
½ cup apricot brandy	2 peaches, peeled, sliced
36 scallops	⅓ cup cream
220g (7oz) butter or margarine, melted	2 tablespoons apricot brandy

Combine the breadcrumbs with the salt into a mixing bowl and stir in approximately ¼ cup apricot brandy. Dip the scallops into the butter, coat with the breadcrumbs and refrigerate for 1 hour. Steam the carrots and peaches until soft then purée in a blender or food processor with the cream and the apricot brandy. Keep warm. Pan fry the crumbed scallops until just browned, being careful not to overcook them. Serve on a base of the purée, garnished with fresh herbs. Serves 6.
*nearest equivalent can size.

Grilled Crayfish

155g (5oz) butter	1 teaspoon dill seeds or fennel
juice 1 lemon	3 large green crayfish tails
2 tablespoons Pernod	

Melt the butter in a saucepan and add the lemon juice, Pernod and dill. Stir well over medium heat and set to one side. Cut the crayfish tails in half removing the meat and cut into chunks and then return to the shell. Sit the tails on a grilling rack, brush liberally with the butter and place under the griller. Grill, brushing regularly with the butter until cooked. Serve with a tossed mixed lettuce and watercress salad. Serves 6.

Crayfish in Pernod Sauce

A delicious recipe.

1½ cups mayonnaise
1 tablespoon Pernod
4 large sorrel leaves, finely shredded
¼ cup finely chopped celery

¼ teaspoon chilli sauce
500g (1lb) cooked crayfish
alfalfa sprouts

Combine the mayonnaise, Pernod, sorrel, celery and chilli sauce. Chop the crayfish into bite-size pieces and gently fold into the sauce. Serve the crayfish on a bed of sprouts with thin slices of buttered wholemeal bread.   Serves 4-6.

The Crayfish is found in great quantities on the South Eastern and Western coasts of Tasmania. Southern Crayfish is also known as "Southern Rock Lobster". The annual catch is in the region of 1,500 tonnes. Southern Rock Lobsters are recognised as a gourmet's delight and are exported both live and frozen to all parts of the world. The most popular size for the gourmet market is for lobster under 750g (1½lb).

Tahitian Fish Salad

220g (7oz) white fish
1 medium onion, peeled, sliced
juice 2 lemons
½ cup coconut milk
½ cup cream

1 tablespoon whisky
dash of Tabasco sauce
½ teaspoon chopped fresh parsley
3 cups cooked macaroni

Cut the fish fillets into very thin slices across the grain and place in a glass dish with the onion, lemon juice, coconut milk, cream, whisky, Tabasco and parsley. Marinate for at least 24 hours in the refrigerator. Combine the macaroni with the fish and spoon into lettuce cups just prior to serving.   Serves 6.

Crayfish in Mustard Sauce

Always make sure the crayfish is very fresh when purchased and cleaned thoroughly when halved.

3 medium, cooked crayfish
45g (1½oz) butter or margarine
1 small onion, chopped
4 tablespoons flour
1 cup milk
3 tablespoons cherry liqueur

2 tablespoons grated mild Cheddar cheese
2 teaspoons French mustard
½ teaspoon English mustard
breadcrumbs
butter

Halve the crayfish lengthwise and remove meat; cut into chunks. Melt the butter and sauté the onions until tender. Add the flour and stir over a low heat for 2 minutes. Gradually add the milk and allow the sauce to thicken. Add the liqueur and simmer for 2 minutes then stir in the cheese and mustards. Spoon a little of the sauce into the crayfish shells, add the crayfish and coat with the remaining sauce. Sprinkle with breadcrumbs and dot with butter. Grill until brown and bubbling. Serve immediately.   Serves 6.

Fruity Fillet Rolls

3 slices wholemeal bread, crumbed
½ cup sultanas
¼ cup walnuts
1 tablespoon lemon juice
little orange juice to bind

500g (1lb) fish fillets, redfish, bream
1 egg white, lightly beaten
wheatgerm for coating
oil for deep fat frying

Purée the wholemeal crumbs, sultanas and walnuts in a blender or food processor. Add the juices and continue processing until a soft mixture is achieved. Spread a layer of the filling onto each fillet, then roll up and secure. Dip each fillet in the egg white, coat with wheatgerm and deep fry in oil until golden. Serve with sautéed silverbeet and a carrot and apple salad.   Serves 4.

CALAMARI RINGS (RECIPE PAGE 46) TOP; MUSSELS IN GARLIC BUTTER (RECIPE PAGE 46) BOTTOM

SMOKED COD CASSEROLE (RECIPE PAGE 67)

Red Salmon Mousse

This is an excellent dish for a buffet.

Aspic Glaze
2 tablespoons lemon juice
2 teaspoons gelatine
2 radishes, thinly sliced
2 gherkins, sliced into thin strips
1 olive
5-cup salmon mould
seasoning to taste
The Mousse
1 x 250g (8oz) packet cream cheese, cubed

¾ cup yoghurt
½ cup mayonnaise
¼ cup gherkin juice
¼ cup lemon juice
5 teaspoons gelatine
2 x 220g (7oz) cans* red salmon, drained, flaked
4 gherkins, sliced
10 stuffed olives, sliced
parsley and lemon wedges for garnish

Heat the lemon juice with the seasoning in a saucepan, sprinkle over the gelatine, and stir until dissolved. Pour ¾ of mixture into the wetted salmon mould, and refrigerate until almost set, then arrange the radishes and gherkins in a decorative pattern using the olive for the eye, pour over the remaining aspic, refrigerate. Meanwhile combine the cheese, yoghurt and mayonnaise in a blender or food processor. Heat the juices in a small saucepan, sprinkle over the gelatine, and stir until dissolved. Add to the blended mixture with the salmon, gherkins and olives, blend until well combined. Pour the mixture onto the chilled aspic and refrigerate until firm. Unmould onto a serving platter and garnish with parsley and lemon wedges. Serves 10-12.
*nearest equivalent can size.

PHOTOGRAPH   THIS PAGE

Microwave Fish Medly

Fish just tastes so good when cooked in the Microwave.

1.5kg (3lb) whole snapper
90g (3oz) butter or margarine
2 cloves garlic, crushed
freshly ground black pepper
pinch salt
250g (8oz) prawns, shelled, deveined,

chopped
125g (4oz) scallops
1 cup breadcrumbs
¼ cup chopped shallots
grated rind, lemon
juice 1 orange

Place snapper in a shallow dish and dot with butter, cover with plastic wrap and Microwave on MEDIUM for 10 minutes and allow to stand. Melt the remaining butter on HIGH for approximately 1 minute, add garlic, black pepper and salt then stir in the prawns, scallops, shallots, breadcrumbs, lemon rind and orange juice. Microwave on MEDIUM for 3 minutes, stirring once and serve poured over the fish. Serves 4.

PHOTOGRAPH   PAGE 64

Seafood in Whisky Sauce

Whisky particularly enhances seafood and adds a finishing touch to the sauce.

1 onion, roughly chopped
1 tablespoon butter or margarine
500g (1lb) large green prawns, shelled, deveined
½ cup whisky
500g (1lb) white fish fillets

1-1½ cups dry white wine
1½-1¾ cups fish stock
2 tablespoons butter or margarine
2 tablespoons flour
¼-½ cup cream
salt and cayenne pepper to taste

Sauté the onion in the butter using a large frying pan with a lid. Add the prawns. Warm the whisky, ignite and add to the pan. When the flames have subsided add the fish fillets and pour over the wine. Cover and simmer 3 -5 minutes. Transfer the fish and prawns to a serving platter, cover and keep warm. Make the whisky sauce by adding the stock to the frying pan and whilst heating cream the butter and flour together. Gradually stir the creamed mixture into the stock and stir until smooth and slightly thickened. Add the cream and gently simmer for approximately 10 minutes. Season and pour over the fish just prior to serving. Serves 4-6.

PHOTOGRAPH   PAGE 67

Tropical Baked Fish

Snapper is the ideal fish for this recipe.

2½kg (5lb) fish
The Stuffing
1 cup cooked rice
1 tablespoon desiccated coconut
1 tablespoon chopped shallots

1 egg
1 teaspoon salt
1 teaspoon lemon pepper
2 tablespoons white wine

Fill the cavity of the fish with the combined stuffing ingredients. Secure opening and place the fish on a large piece of buttered foil. Wrap up into a secure parcel and bake at 180°C (350°F) for approximately 40-50 minutes or until cooked.

RED SALMON MOUSSE (RECIPE THIS PAGE)

Prawn and Whiting Rolls

The delicate flavouring of the whiting enhances the flavour of the prawns.

250g (8oz) green prawns, shelled
¼ cup chopped shallots
220g (7oz) butter or margarine
1.5kg (3lb) whiting fillets

1 onion, chopped
water and milk
seasoning to taste
cornflour for thickening

Blend the prawns, shallots, butter, seasoning in a food processor until smooth. Spread a little of the prawn paste onto each fillet, roll up and secure with a toothpick. Place with the onion in a baking dish with sufficient water and milk to cover. Bake, covered, at 180°C (350°F) until the fish flakes when tested. Remove and keep warm. Combine the cornflour with the stock, bring to the boil and stir until the mixture thickens. Serve the sauce poured over the fish rolls garnished with lemon and sprigs of dill. Serves 6.

PHOTOGRAPH   PAGE 49

ROWING ON THE YARRA RIVER AND SKYLINE OF MELBOURNE, VICTORIA

Stuffed Baked Snapper

The Stuffing
1 tablespoon butter or margarine
1 onion, chopped
2 cups fresh breadcrumbs
grated rind and juice ½ lemon
1 tablespoon chopped parsley

½ cup chopped shallots
For Cooking
4 x 500g (1lb) Snapper
melted butter
lemon juice

Melt butter in a saucepan and sauté the onion until tender and stir into the combined remaining stuffing ingredients. Spoon into the cavity of the fish and secure the openings. Place in a shallow greased baking dish and pour over sufficient butter and lemon juice to coat the fish. Cover with foil and bake at 190°C (370°F) for 30-35 minutes or until cooked. Serve hot with the juices spooned over the fish. Serves 4.

PHOTOGRAPH   THIS PAGE

Gemfish Parcels

2 tablespoons chopped dill
2 tablespoons chopped pine nuts
1 teaspoon grated lemon rind
½ teaspoon lemon pepper

90g (3oz) butter, melted
12 sheets filo pastry
6 gemfish fillets

Combine the dill, pine nuts, lemon rind, pepper and 2 tablespoons melted butter. Brush six sheets of filo pastry with the melted butter and stack. Repeat with remaining pastry and divide each stack into three even strips lengthwise.
Place a gemfish fillet on each strip of pastry and spread with some of the dill and nut butter. Fold each one into a neat parcel sealing the edges. Place on a baking sheet and brush with melted butter. Bake at 180°C (350°F) for 20-30 minutes. Serves 6.

Fish Provencale

1kg (2lb) sea bream fillets, skinned
nutmeg
1 tablespoon olive oil
1 large onion, sliced
1 red capsicum, seeded, sliced
56g (1-2oz) can* anchovy fillets, drained

1 tomato, sliced
1 tablespoon stuffed olives
½ cup sliced mushrooms
½ cup white wine
15g (½oz) butter or margarine
seasoning to taste

Sprinkle fish fillets with seasoning and nutmeg, pour the olive oil into an ovenproof dish with the onion and capsicum and arrange the fish on top. Scatter with the remaining ingredients and dot with butter. Cover and bake at 180°C (350°F) for 40 minutes or until cooked. Serves 4.
*nearest equivalent can size.

Gemfish Casserole

4 tablespoons butter or margarine
1 cup mushrooms, sliced
750g (1½lb) smoked gemfish
⅓ cup dry white wine
2 bay leaves

⅓ cup cream
½ cup grated cheese
½ cup fresh breadcrumbs
sliced tomato for garnishing
seasoning to taste

Melt the butter in a frying pan, add the mushrooms and sauté for 1 minute. Remove from the pan and scatter over the base of a greased casserole dish. Place the fish on top, pour over the wine and add the bay leaves. Cover and cook at 180°C (350°F) for 10 minutes. Remove the bay leaves and add the cream and season. Sprinkle with the cheese and breadcrumbs. Return to the oven for 10 minutes. Serve garnished with tomato slices. Serves 4.

STUFFED BAKED SNAPPER (RECIPE THIS PAGE)

CRAYFISH CATCH

WINDSURFING AT MANLY BEACH, SYDNEY, NEW SOUTH WALES

Redfish Sandwiches with Sour Cream Sauce

1 lettuce
1 bunch silverbeet
4 shallots chopped
6 slices Gouda cheese
6 slices smoked salmon

12 redfish fillets
1 tablespoon capers chopped
½ teaspoon salt
1 cup sour cream

Finely shred the lettuce and silverbeet and lightly steam, then cool. Purée in a food processor together with the shallots and reheat. Sandwich the slices of cheese and smoked salmon between two fillets of fish, secure with toothpicks and grill until cooked and cheese has melted. Combine the capers, salt and sour cream. Serve the sandwiches of fish with the vegetable purée and the sour cream sauce.   Serves 6.

PHOTOGRAPH   PAGE 50

Tasty Fish Loaf

1 tablespoon butter or margarine
1 tablespoon flour
1 cup milk
500g (1lb) redfish fillets, poached, flaked
2 cups fresh breadcrumbs
1 onion, finely chopped

1 capsicum, finely chopped
½ cup chopped bacon
½ cup grated Cheddar cheese
extra breadcrumbs for topping
1 tablespoon butter or margarine
seasoning to taste

Make a sauce in the usual way with the butter, flour and milk. Season to taste then combine with the redfish, breadcrumbs, onion and capsicum. Grease and line a loaf tin and alternate the fish mixture with the bacon and cheese ending with a layer of fish. Sprinkle with extra breadcrumbs and dot with butter. Bake at 190°C (370°F) for approximately 1 hour.   Serves 6-8.

Redfish Fillets in Zucchini Cream

1½ teaspoons butter or margarine
500g (1lb) redfish fillets
½ cup sliced zucchini

⅓ cup buttermilk
1½ tablespoons sour cream
seasoning to taste

Melt the butter in a frying pan and gently fry the fish until lightly golden, approximately 4 minutes. Remove from the pan and keep warm. Sauté the zucchini in the same pan until cooked but still crisp, then stir in the buttermilk, sour cream and seasoning. To serve, pour the zucchini cream over the red fish fillets and serve on a bed of lightly steamed leeks and carrot straws.

Serves 4.

Whiting with Cottage Cheese Accompaniment

6 whole whiting
1 small onion, finely sliced
finely grated rind 1 lemon
¼ cup lemon juice
¾ cups water
1 bay leaf
seasoning to taste

Accompaniment
1 tomato, sliced
1 lemon, sliced
1 x 200g (6-7oz) carton cottage cheese
finely grated rind 1 lemon
1 tablespoon lemon juice
salt, cayenne pepper, to taste
1 tablespoon chopped parsley

Arrange fish in the base of an electric frying pan with the remaining ingredients. Cover and simmer for 5 minutes or until the fish are just cooked. Using a slotted spoon, carefully remove fish onto a serving platter. When cool, cover and refrigerate. Prepare the accompaniment by arranging the slices of tomato and lemon around the fish. Combine the remaining ingredients together and serve with the fish.

Trout with Cognac Cream Sauce

90g (3oz) butter
4 small trout
½ cup cream
2 tablespoons orange liqueur

2 tablespoons Cognac
½ cup almond flakes, toasted
seasoning to taste

Melt the butter in a frying pan and pan fry the trout until cooked. Warm the cream in a small saucepan but do not allow to boil. Stir in the liqueur, Cognac, and seasoning. Transfer trout to a serving platter. Pour over the sauce, garnish with almonds and serve.

Serves 4.

Smoked Trout and Fettucine

2 tablespoons garlic butter
410g (13oz) cooked fettucine
½ cup cream
2 smoked trout filletted, boned, flaked

¼ cup cherry liqueur
½ cup slivered almonds, toasted
seasoning to taste

Melt the butter in a frying pan and add the fettucine, cream, fish and liqueur. Stir all the ingredients together over a low heat until the sauce thickens, season and serve liberally sprinkled with the toasted almonds.

Serves 6.

FISH MEDLEY (RECIPE PAGE 59)

Trout with Almonds and Crabmeat Stuffing

The delicate fine texture of the trout with the combination of crabmeat makes for a delicious meal.

6 trout
⅓ cup rice
30g (1oz) butter or margarine
4 shallots, chopped
90g (3oz) mushrooms, chopped

1 x 220g (7oz) can* crab, drained
1 teaspoon lemon juice
seasoning to taste
flour to coat
60g (2oz) almonds, browned in butter

Wash and clean trout. Cook rice in pan of boiling salt water for 10 minutes or until tender, drain well. Melt the butter in a frying pan and sauté the shallots and mushrooms for 1 minute. Stir in the rice, crab, lemon juice and seasoning. Coat the fish with flour and fill the cavity with the crabmeat stuffing. Secure opening to prevent filling from spilling out while frying. Pan fry the trout until cooked and golden. Sprinkle with the almonds and serve.
*nearest equivalent can size. Serves 6.

PHOTOGRAPH PAGE 56

Mullet in Vegetable Cases

The Mullet Filling

410g (13oz) mullet fillets, skinned, minced
1 onion finely chopped, sautéed
2 cloves garlic crushed, sautéed
¼ teaspoon dried thyme leaves
½ teaspoon dried basil leaves
finely chopped parsley

1 tomato, skinned, finely chopped
2 tablespoons tomato paste
10 black olives, seeded
seasoning to taste
choose either:-
2 eggplant
2 capsicums

Combine the ingredients for the filling in a bowl and mix well. Set aside whilst preparing your choice of vegetables.
Eggplant – cut eggplant in half lenthwise, remove flesh leaving a layer of 1cm (½") next to the skin. Finally chop the flesh and add to the mullet filling, mixing well. Pack the fish mixture back into each half. Capsicum – cut capsicums in half lengthwise, removing seeds, par boil for approximately 5 minutes. Remove from the water and pack the fish mixture back into each half. Place each vegetable into a shallow ovenproof dish and bake at 180°C (350°F) for 20-25 minutes.

TRAWLER AT SEA, SORTING PRAWNS

THE FAMOUS SYDNEY TO HOBART YACHT RACE

Smoked Cod Casserole

1kg (2lb) smoked cod
1 onion, sliced
1 cup dry white wine
peppercorns
1 small clove garlic, crushed

little chopped fennel or dill
4 tomatoes, quartered
few black olives
6 shallots sliced

Cut fish into serving pieces and place in a casserole with the onion, wine, peppercorns, garlic and herbs. Cover and bake at 180°C (350°F) for 30-40 minutes adding the tomatoes and olives during the last ½ hour of cooking. Serve the fish with its juice, garnish with shallots.   Serves 6-8

PHOTOGRAPH   PAGE 58

Stuffed Baked Trout

Fish prepared in this may be cooked on the barbecue.

2 large trout
The Stuffing
60g (2oz) fresh bread, crumbed
¼ cup chopped onion

1 rasher bacon, chopped
grated rind ½ orange
¼ cup chopped fresh herbs
seasoning to taste

Fill the cavity of the fish with the combined stuffing ingredients, secure opening and wrap each fish in a large square of buttered foil. Bake at 180°C (350°F) for approximately 20 minutes or until cooked. Serve garnished with slices of lemon and parsley.
                                                                          Serves 2.

SEAFOOD IN WHISKY SAUCE (RECIPE PAGE 59)

CREAMED CRAB (RECIPE PAGE 46)

Fruity Ling Fillets

500g (1lb) ling fillets
1 onion, finely sliced
1 orange, peeled, finely sliced
2 bananas, peeled, finely sliced

2 tablespoons lemon juice
lemon pepper
salt to taste

Place the ling fillets on a sheet of lightly buttered foil, layer with the onion, orange and bananas. Pour over the lemon juice. Season with the lemon pepper and salt. Fold the foil over to form a neat parcel and seal well. Cook on the barbecue for approximately 10-12 minutes. The fish is cooked when it flakes easily with a fork. Serve with a spinach and cashew nut salad.
                                                                          Serves 4.

Flathead Parcels

grated rind ½ lemon
6 sprigs dill
90g (3oz) butter, softened

12 sheets filo pastry
90g (3oz) butter, melted
6 large flathead fillets

Cream the lemon rind, dill and butter together. Brush a sheet of filo pastry with the melted butter, place another sheet on top and brush with butter. Repeat until 6 sheets are used. Make a second stack of 6 sheets. Spread half the lemon dill butter over each rectangle of pastry and divide each piece into three even strips lengthwise. Place a fillet of fish down the centre of each strip and fold into a neat parcel, sealing the edges. Place on a baking sheet, brush with melted butter and bake at 180°C (350°F) for 20-30 minutes, until cooked and golden.   Serves 6

SURF BOAT IN FULL FLIGHT

BEEF, LAMB, VEAL & PORK HABITS

Meat, Part of our Pioneer Heritage

In Australia, meat is almost as important as beer. Meat has been an essential part of our diet since the pioneer days. Traditionally, Australians ate meat two or three times a day — steak for breakfast meant you were in "fat city". This is understandable with the vast numbers of sheep and cattle and the abundance of great tasting beef, veal, lamb and pork.

Although we've cut our meat consumption for health reasons, it's still an essential and nutritious part of the Australian diet. We enjoy grills, barbecues, casseroles and the traditional roast. (It's interesting to note that lamb and beef are less expensive in Australia than in North America.)

The traditional Sunday roast dinner is something we inherited from our "Pommy" ancestors, and it's still popular with many Australians.

European migrants have contributed their flair for using aromatic herbs and interesting sauces to get the best out of inexpensive cuts of meat.

This section gives you recipes for the traditional roast as well as a variety of other tasty meat dishes.

MUSTERING SHEEP

Veal and Chicken Liver Pate

250g (8oz) chicken livers
2 tablespoons butter or margarine
1 onion, finely chopped
500g (1lb) minced veal
grated rind ½ lemon

1 tablespoon brandy
1 tablespoon dry white wine
½ teaspoon thyme
4 rashers bacon, rinds removed

Sauté the chicken livers in the butter with the onion. Pureé in a food processor and add the remaining ingredients with the exception of the bacon. Line a small terrine with the bacon and spoon in the meat mixture. Press down firmly and cover. Cook in water bath at 180°C (350°F) for approximately ¾-1 hour and cool. Refrigerate until required, unmould and serve with hot buttered toast. Serves 6-8.

PHOTOGRAPH PAGES 76-77

Supreme Pate

2 tablespoons butter or margarine
3 chicken livers, chopped
1 onion, finely chopped
250g (8oz) minced veal
250g (8oz) minced pork
1 egg, lightly beaten
1 teaspoon fresh mixed herbs, chopped

½ teaspoon freshly grated lemon rind
1 tablespoon chopped parsley
seasoning to taste
2 tablespoons dry sherry
½ cup soft wholemeal breadcrumbs
250g (8oz) chicken breasts, finely chopped

Melt the butter in a frying pan and sauté chicken livers with the onion until tender. Pureé in food processor adding all the remaining ingredients with the exception of the chicken. Process until smooth. Spoon ⅓ of the mixture into base of a greased terrine. Cover with a layer of chicken. Repeat layers ending with the chicken, and smooth over the surface. Cover and cook in a water bath at 180°C (350°F) for approximately 1-1½ hours. Remove from the oven, drain off excess fat and when cool, refrigerate. Unmould and serve with melba toast. Serves 6.

PHOTOGRAPH PAGES 76-77

Potted Meat Paste

Delicious served on hot buttered muffins or as a sandwich spread.

500g (1lb) gravy beef
½ teaspoon thyme
½ teaspoon Angostura bitters
seasoning to taste

2 onions, chopped
½ cup red wine
½ cup beef stock

Remove fat and sinew from meat and roughly chop. Combine with the other ingredients in a saucepan. Cover and simmer for 2-3 hours or until the meat is tender. Allow to cool then pureé in a food processor. Transfer to a serving bowl and refrigerate. Serves 4.

PHOTOGRAPH PAGES 76-77

Brawn

500g (1lb) gravy beef, roughly chopped
1 veal knuckle, cut into 3
250g (8oz) pickled pork, roughly chopped
6 peppercorns
3 cloves

½ teaspoon nutmeg
pinch herbs
1 large onion, chopped
1 carrot, chopped
1 tablespoon vinegar
2 teaspoons salt

Place meat in a large saucepan, and barely cover with water. Add remaining ingredients, cover saucepan and bring to the boil. Simmer gently for 2½-3 hours until meat is cooked and will flake easily with a fork. Drain, reserve stock and remove bones and tissue. Strain stock and return four cups to the saucepan. Bring to the boil and simmer for approximately 20 minutes or until stock has reduced by half. Stir into the prepared meat and vegetables. Place into a 15cm (6") x 23cm(9") wetted loaf tin or a suitable mould. Cool, then chill in refrigerator until set.

MINT JELLIED LAMB (RECIPE PAGE 82)

Picnic Sausage Loaf

Ideal for a buffet luncheon or picnic.

500g (1lb) sausage mince
6 shallots, chopped
2 teaspoons Angostura bitters
1 teaspoon dried mixed herbs

½ clove garlic, crushed
seasoning to taste
1 egg, beaten
1 tomato, chopped

Combine all ingredients together mixing well. Lightly grease a meatloaf tin and spoon in the mixture, pressing down well. Cover and bake at 180°C (350°F) for 1-1½ hours. Drain off excess fat and refrigerate. When cold serve thinly sliced. Serves 6.

PHOTOGRAPH PAGES 76-77

Farmstyle Sausages

Home made sausages are always a treat; they are also simple to make.

500g (1lb) minced veal
250g (8oz) minced pork
¼ teaspoon nutmeg
½ teaspoon marjoram
½ teaspoon caraway seeds

seasoning to taste
¼ cup brandy
¼ cup water
sausage casing, from your local butcher

Place all the ingredients, with the exception of the sausage casings, into a bowl and combine well. To fill sausage cases, knot one end of the casing. Use a piping bag to fill them. Pull the open end over the nozzle and squeeze the mixture into casing. Tie into sausage lengths that suit you. Refrigerate for 1 hour before cooking. Serves 3-4.

CITY OF BRISBANE SKYLINE, QUEENSLAND

CATTLE IN NORTHERN TABLELANDS, NEW SOUTH WALES

Potato Scallops

Delicious served with fish or as an accompaniment to a barbecue.

2 cups self-raising flour
salt, pepper
1¾ cups beef stock

750g (1½lb) small potatoes, thinly sliced
oil for deep frying

Make a batter in the usual way with the flour, seasoning and stock. Dip the potato slices in the batter and deep fry until golden brown and cooked through. Drain and serve. Serves 6-8.

Corned Silverside with White Onion Sauce

1-2kg (2-4lb) piece corned silverside
2 bay leaves
6 peppercorns
6 whole allspice
1 tablespoon lemon juice
2 carrots
3 onions
3 potatoes

White Onion Sauce
1½ cups milk
1 cup reserved stock
3 onions, sliced
5 tablespoons cornflour
seasoning to taste

Soak piece of silverside for 30 minutes in cold water. Place in a large saucepan with bay leaves, peppercorns, allspice and lemon juice. Cover with water, bring to the boil and simmer for 1 hour per 500g (1lb). Add vegetables to the pan 40 minutes before cooking time has elapsed. When cooked, remove meat and vegetables to a large platter; keep warm. Strain liquid through sieve and reserve one cup. Make the white sauce by pouring the milk and stock into saucepan. Add onions. Bring to the boil, simmer gently for 15-20 minutes or until onions are tender. Blend cornflour and a little milk and add to the sauce, stirring constantly until thickened. Season and serve with the meat. Serves 8-10.

Seasoned Steak Roll

The Marinade
½ cup olive oil
⅓ cup red wine
1 cup chopped onions
1 clove garlic, crushed
1 teaspoon oregano
½ teaspoon cayenne pepper
1 teaspoon salt
1 teaspoon black pepper

For Cooking
1kg (2lb) piece skirt steak "butterflied"
¼ bunch silverbeet, shredded
2 carrots cut into strips
2 onions, sliced
2 hard-boiled eggs sliced
chopped parsley
seasoning to taste

Combine the ingredients for the marinade. Open out the meat and top with shredded silverbeet, the carrots, the onion rings and eggs. Sprinkle with chopped parsley and seasoning. Roll and tie the meat tightly and place in the marinade. Refrigerate for six hours. Cook in the marinade until tender. Serve sliced with the cooking juices served seperately. Serves 6.

Kummel Flambe Steaks

Kummel is extracted from caraway seeds, and with the two combined, they add an unusual flavour to the veal.

125g (4oz) butter or margarine
1 onion, finely chopped
1 clove garlic, crushed
1 teaspoon caraway seeds
seasoning to taste

8 veal escalopes, flattened
½ cup Kummel liqueur
½ cup thickened cream
2 cooking apples peeled, cored, quartered

Melt half the butter in a large frying pan and add onion, garlic and caraway seeds; sauté until onion is tender. Season meat, add to pan and brown well on both sides. Pour in liqueur, ignite, then stir in cream. Reduce heat and stir until sauce thickens. Serve garnished with apple quarters which have been sautéed in the remaining butter. Serves 4.

STOCKMEN DISCUSSING THE NEXT DROVE

Rib Roast Piquant

1.5kg (3lb) Rib Roast
seasoning to taste
1 teaspoon paprika

2 cloves garlic, crushed
1¼ cups red wine
1¼ cups wine vinegar

Rub the seasoning and garlic into the meat. Marinate in the combined wine and vinegar for 4-6 hours. Roast on a rack at 180°C (350°F) allowing about 40 minutes per kg for medium to rare and serve with jacket potatoes, sour cream and horseradish sauce. Serves 4.

PHOTOGRAPH PAGE 88

Beef with Green Peppercorn Sauce

A simple dish to make, but looks very impressive served with the peppercorn sauce.

1 clove garlic
4 thick beef tenderloin steaks
butter
½ cup orange liqueur

1 x 55g (2oz) can* green peppercorns, drained
½ cup cream

Cut garlic in half and rub all over the surface of the steaks. Melt butter in a heavy-based frying pan. Sear the steaks on both sides then cook as desired. Pour over the liqueur, ignite and allow the flames to die down. Remove steaks to a platter and keep warm. Stir in the peppercorns and a little extra liqueur to de-glaze the pan. Stir in the cream, adjust the seasonings if necessary, reduce heat and stir for 2-3 minutes until pan juices are blended. Spoon over steaks and serve with vegetables. Serves 4.
*nearest equivalent can size.

PICNIC SAUSAGE LOAF (RECIPE PAGE 72) BOTTOM LEFT; TERRINE (NO RECIPE) MIDDLE LEFT; POTTED MEAT PASTE (RECIPE PAGE 72)

TOP CENTRE; SUPREME PATE (RECIPE PAGE 72) RIGHT; MIDDLE VEAL AND CHICKEN LIVER PATE (RECIPE PAGE 72)

Beef Burgundy

This traditional French dish has a delicious flavour which is greatly enhanced with a good red wine.

1kg (2lb) blade steak, cubed	½ cup red wine
3 rashers bacon, chopped	seasoning to taste
6 small white onions	1 bay leaf
1 tablespoon brandy	1 tablespoon chopped parsley
250g (8oz) mushrooms	½ teaspoon thyme
1 clove garlic, crushed	1 carrot sliced
1½ cups beef stock	

Sauté meat, bacon and onion in a frying pan until browned. Warm brandy, ignite and pour into the pan. Add mushrooms and garlic then stir in stock, wine, seasoning, herbs and carrot. Cover and simmer 1½-2 hours. Serve garnished with chopped parsley.

Serves 6-8.

PREPARING FOR A BARBECUE

Beef Stroganoff

A beautifully flavoured dish suitable for easy entertaining.

750g (1½lb) round steak, cut into strips	2 onions, sliced
seasoned flour	250g (8oz) mushrooms, sliced
½ teaspoon nutmeg	2 tablespoons tomato paste
60g (2oz) butter or margarine	¼ cup beef stock
1-2 cloves garlic, crushed	½ cup white wine
	½ cup sour cream

Toss meat in seasoned flour and nutmeg. Melt butter in a saucepan and sauté the garlic with the onions. Add the meat and brown well, then stir in the mushrooms. Combine tomato paste, stock and wine and stir into the meat. Cover and simmer approximately 20-30 minutes until meat is tender. Add sour cream, DO NOT BOIL. Serve with buttered noodles. Serves 4.

Ratatouille Beef

Beautifully tender beef cooked in a rather attractive way with delicious fresh vegetables. Would make an ideal meal for a special occasion.

2kg (4lb) piece Scotch fillet	2 zucchinis, sliced
90g (3oz) butter or margarine	2 cloves garlic, crushed
2 onions, sliced	¼ cup chopped parsley
1 red capsicum, sliced	½ teaspoon dried basil
1 green capsicum, sliced	seasoning to taste

Trim excess fat from fillet and slice meat at 8cm (3") intervals being careful not to slice meat right through. Melt butter in a frying pan, add prepared vegetables, herbs and seasoning, sauté gently for 3 minutes. Pack cooked vegetables into pockets of the fillet, place meat into a large roasting dish and pour over pan juices. Bake at 180°C (350°F) for 1¼ hours for rare beef, 1½ hours medium rare, 1¾ hours for well done. Serves 6-8.

PHOTOGRAPH   PAGE 83

Boeuf a la Mode

A tasty dish that needs little else but a crusty bread, a green salad and a glass of wine.

1.5-2kg (3-4lb) topside beef	2 pig's trotters, chopped
1-2 cloves garlic, slivered	1 cup beef stock
2 tablespoons oil	3 carrots, roughly chopped
1 onion, sliced	2 bay leaves
3 tablespoons brandy	seasoning to taste
½ cup red wine	3 extra carrots, diagonally sliced

Make small incisions all over the beef and insert slivers of garlic. Heat the oil in a large saucepan and sauté the onions until tender, add the meat, turning occasionally and brown on all sides. In a smaller saucepan heat the brandy, ignite and pour over the meat, add the wine then simmer for 5 minutes. Transfer to a large casserole dish with the trotters and the remaining ingredients, cover and cook at 180°C (350°F) for approximately 1-1½ hours or until tender. Allow the meat to cool in the stock, when cold remove from the stock and set aside. Skim off fat from the stock, then strain into a clean saucepan and re-boil until stock has slightly reduced; remove from heat and allow to cool. Slice the cold meat and arrange decoratively on a large platter with the extra carrots. Carefully spoon over the cold stock and garnish with fresh herbs if desired. Allow to set completely before serving.

PHOTOGRAPH   PAGE 85

Serves 6-8.

Beef with Sour Cream and Mushroom Sauce

4 rashers bacon, rind removed	½ cup beef stock
1kg (2lb) fillet beef	¾ cup red wine
2 tablespoons butter or margarine	**The Sauce**
2 onions, chopped	pan juices
¼ cup carrot, chopped	1 tablespoon butter or margarine
¼ cup celery, chopped	2 tablespoons flour
seasoning to taste	125g (4oz) button mushrooms, sliced
1 teaspoon thyme	½ cup sour cream
1 bay leaf	

Wrap the bacon around the beef and secure. Melt the butter in a roasting pan and sauté the onion with the vegetables until tender. Add the beef, brown all over then add the seasonings, stock and wine. Bake at 180°C (350°F) for 1-1½ hours or until cooked. Remove from heat, keep warm. Make the sauce by bringing the pan juices to the boil. Add the combined butter and flour and cook until thickened. Add the mushrooms, gently cook for 2-3 minutes then stir in the sour cream. Reheat and serve the sauce spooned over the meat. Serves 4.

SHEARING SHEEP

RURAL COTTAGE IN SUNSET

Peach Stuffed Beef Roll

1 tablespoon butter or margarine
1 onion, finely chopped
2 cups breadcrumbs
lightly beaten egg

seasoning to taste
1 teaspoon rosemary
3 peach halves, roughly chopped
2.5kg (5lb) boned loin of beef

Melt butter and sauté the onion until soft. Place in a bowl and combine with the remaining ingredients except beef. Place beef skin side down onto a board and spread with the stuffing. Roll up and tie securely with string. Bake at 180°C (350°F) for approximately 1 hour depending on the rareness of beef required. Carve and serve with green beans garnished with sautéed, flaked almonds.   Serves 8-10.

Pocket Steak

1kg (2lb) piece fillet steak
¼ bunch silverbeet
1 egg
grated rind 1 orange

2 tablespoons orange liqueur
1 tablespoon finely chopped almonds
1 teaspoon salt
a good dash chilli sauce

Cut a pocket through the centre of the beef. Shred the silverbeet finely and combine with the remaining ingredients. Pack the filling into the pocket of the beef and set aside for 30 minutes, close pocket with small skewers. Place on a roasting rack and roast the fillet at 180°C (350°F) allowing 10-15 minutes per 500g (1lb) and 10-15 minutes over, depending on how rare you like the beef. Allow to stand for 5-10 minutes before slicing.   Serves 4-6.

Lamb Creole

2 tablespoons oil
6-8 lamb chops
4 zucchinis, sliced
4 tomatoes
2 cloves garlic, crushed
1 capsicum, de-seeded, sliced
3 onions, sliced
½ teaspoon oregano
¼ teaspoon cumin

¼ teaspoon chilli powder
seasoning to taste
¼ cup red wine
2 teaspoons brown sugar
2 beef stock cubes
2 tablespoons tomato sauce
2 tablespoons flour
3 tablespoons water

Heat oil in pan, add chops and sauté both sides until browned, remove from pan. Add all prepared vegetables, oregano, cumin, chilli powder, seasoning, red wine, brown sugar, stock cubes and tomato sauce. Return meat to pan, bring to boil and reduce heat, simmer covered for 30 minutes or until meat is tender. Remove meat from pan; keep warm. Mix flour and water until smooth, add to vegetable mixture stirring until sauce boils and thickens. Place chops onto serving plate. Spoon vegetable mixture over and serve with noodles or rice.   Serves 6.

Roast Lamb with Fig Sauce

An unusual but very delicious dish.

1 large leg of lamb, 2 kg (4 lbs)
1 cup water
2 cloves garlic, slivered
1 medium onion, chopped

4 large or 6 small figs
1 cup chicken stock
½ teaspoon ground ginger
seasoning to taste

Stud the leg of lamb with the garlic. Scatter the onion over the base of a roasting dish and place the lamb on top and add water. Roast at 200°C (400°F) for about 1½ hours. Half an hour before the lamb is cooked, add the figs; remove meat from dish and keep warm. Skim fat from pan, add the stock, ginger and seasoning, simmer for 5 minutes. Mash the figs into the sauce which will have a lumpy appearance. Slice the lamb and serve with the accompanying sauce.

PHOTOGRAPH   PAGE 92   Serves 4-6.

Brain Vol-au-vent

4 sets lamb's brains
2 rashers bacon, finely chopped
90g (3oz) butter or margarine
1 tablespoon lemon juice

1 tablespoon finely chopped parsley
½ teaspoon lemon pepper
8 vol-au-vent cases, pre-baked
1 hard boiled egg, finely chopped

Cover brains with cold water and allow to stand for 1 hour, drain, remove skin and membranes. Poach brains in boiling salted water uncovered for 15 minutes. Drain and cut into thick slices. Sauté bacon and brains in butter for 1 minute. Remove from heat, add lemon juice, parsley and lemon pepper, toss lightly. Spoon into warm pre-baked vol-au-vent cases. Garnish with crisp bacon and finely chopped egg.   Serves 4.

Mint Jellied Lamb

Delicious served with a potato salad and a jellied beetroot.

6 teaspoons gelatine
1½ cups hot water
2 tablespoons sugar
⅓ cup vinegar
½ cup finely chopped mint leaves
seasoning to taste

2 carrots, cooked, sliced
3-4 stuffed olives
1-2 gherkins, sliced
½ cup cooked peas
500g (1lb) cooked lamb

Dissolve the gelatine in the hot water and stir in the sugar, vinegar, mint and seasoning, allow to cool. Pour a little of the gelatine mixture into the base of a chilled wetted mould and refrigerate until the consistency of unbeaten egg white. Arrange the carrot, olives and gherkin in a decorative pattern over the jelly and refrigerate until partially set, then layer the peas alternately with the meat, seasoning well between each layer. Carefully pour in the remaining gelatine mixture and refrigerate until set. Unmould and serve with a salad.   Serves 4-6.

PHOTOGRAPH   PAGE 72

Crown Roast of Lamb

Your butcher will prepare this joint for you with reasonable notice. The roast will usually consist of twelve cutlets, sufficient for 6 people.

1 crown roast
stuffing of choice (see recipes below)

Fill the cavity with chosen stuffing and place roast in baking dish. Bake at 180°C (350°F) for 1 hour.

Sweet Potato Stuffing

500g (1lb) sweet potato, cooked, mashed
2 tablespoons sherry
seasoning to taste

1 egg, lightly beaten
1 cup soft breadcrumbs
1 onion, finely chopped
1 tablespoon chopped parsley

Combine all ingredients together and use to stuff the meat.

Herbed Stuffing

60g (2oz) butter or margarine
4 rashers bacon, chopped
1 onion, finely chopped
3 cups soft breadcrumbs
4 tablespoons chopped parsley

1 teaspoon marjoram
1 teaspoon thyme
½ teaspoon sage
1 egg, lightly beaten
seasoning to taste

Heat butter and sauté bacon and onion together until onion is tender. Add breadcrumbs and herbs and when cool beat in the egg to bind ingredients together. Season to taste.

RATATOUILLE BEEF (RECIPE PAGE 78)

Rack of Lamb with Cranberry Mousse

3 tablespoons cranberry jelly
1 tablespoon sweet fruit chutney
2 tablespoons gelatine, dissolved
in water

4 egg whites
⅓ cup whipped cream
seasoning to taste
6 racks of lamb, 4 cutlets per rack

Purée the cranberry jelly, chutney and gelatine in a food
processor. Pour into a glass bowl and refrigerate. Beat the egg
whites stiffly, refrigerate. When the cranberry is starting to set, fold
in egg whites and cream; refrigerate until set. Season lamb and
bake at 200°C (400°F). Slice the lamb into single cutlets or leave
in pairs and serve with the mousse.   Serves 6.

Lamb Parcels

250g (8oz) mushrooms
1 cooking apple, peeled, cored
4 sprigs mint
seasoning to taste

1.5kg (3lb) loin lamb chops, boned
butter for frying
1 packet frozen puff pastry
egg for glazing

Purée the mushrooms, apple, mint and seasoning in a food
processor. Tie the chops into neat rounds and pan fry in butter
for 1 minute on each side; allow to cool. Roll out pastry and cut
into large squares allowing one square per chop, remove string
and top each chop with some of the mushroom purée. Wrap the
chops in the pastry and refrigerate for 1 hour. Glaze with beaten
egg and bake at 180°C (350°F) for 20-25 minutes or until cooked.
                                                             Serves 6.

PHOTOGRAPH   PAGE 93

Rack of Lamb with Parsley and Sesame Seeds

6 racks of lamb, 4 cutlets per rack.

Stuffing
½ cup breadcrumbs
2 tablespoons finely chopped parsley
1 tablespoon sesame seeds

1 clove garlic, crushed
1 egg
seasoning to taste

Trim the racks and cut a pocket in each rack. Combine all the
ingredients for the stuffing and fill pocket with some of the
stuffing. Roast at 180°C (350°F) until cooked.   Serves 6.

PHOTOGRAPH   PAGE 92

Lamb in Apple Marinade

1 small onion, finely chopped
1 small knob root ginger, finely
chopped
½ cup brown sugar, lightly packed
1 cup apple juice
⅓ cup lemon juice

¼ cup oil
1 teaspoon curry powder
seasoning to taste
1.5kg (3lb) lamb chops
1 tablespoon cornflour

Combine onion, ginger, sugar, fruit juices, oil, curry powder and
seasoning. Place chops into a shallow dish and pour over the
marinade and leave for at least 4 hours, turning occasionally.
Remove chops from marinade and grill or pan fry until cooked.
Blend marinade and cornflour; heat until sauce boils and thickens,
then simmer 3 minutes and serve with the chops.   Serves 4-6.

"HOME ON THE SHEEPS BACK". RED KELPIE MUSTERING SHEEP, WAGGA WAGGA, NEW SOUTH WALES

Noisettes of Lamb with Strawberry Hollandaise

2 punnets strawberries
4 sprigs tarragon
2 teaspoons green peppercorns
4 egg yolks

250g (8oz) clarified butter, melted
3 tablespoons dry sherry
12-18 noisettes of lamb

Hull and wash strawberries then purée with the tarragon and peppercorns. Make the Hollandaise sauce by beating the egg yolks in the top of a double saucepan over simmering water; when very thick, remove from the heat and pour in the butter, drip by drip to start with and then faster as it combines more easily into the egg. Beat in half of the strawberry purée and refrigerate. Stir the sherry into the remaining purée and refrigerate. Grill or pan fry the lamb to your liking. Spoon 2-3 tablespoons of the strawberry and sherry purée onto the base of warm plates and spread over evenly. Place two or three noisettes (with skewers or string removed) in the centre of the purée so they overlap and spoon over some of the strawberry Hollandaise sauce. Serve garnished with small sprigs of fennel or dill.

Serves 4-6.

Veal and Peach Grill

6 large thinly sliced veal steaks
flour
60g (2oz) butter or margarine
3 peaches, peeled, sliced

1 cup ground macadamia nuts
seasoning to taste
6 slices Swiss cheese

Lightly toss the meat in the flour and melt the butter in a frying pan. Pan fry steaks on each side until cooked. Remove from the pan and keep warm. Carefully sauté the peaches and spoon onto the veal steaks, sprinkle with macadamia nuts and season. Cover with a slice of cheese and grill until cheese melts.   Serves 6.

Blue Vein Schnitzels

4 veal steaks
125g (4oz) butter or margarine
60g (2oz) blue vein cheese
seasoned flour
1 egg, beaten

¼ cup milk
dried breadcrumbs
¼ cup oil
60g (2oz) butter or margarine
lemon wedges

Pound veal steaks until thin. Cream butter and blue vein cheese together until smooth. Spread a little of the blue vein butter onto one side of each steak and dust with seasoned flour. Dip in combined egg and milk. Press breadcrumbs on firmly, then refrigerate for 1 hour. Melt oil and butter and sauté steaks until golden brown, turning once. Serve garnished with lemon wedges.

Serves 4.

Veal and Prune Terrine

12 prunes, pitted
4 tablespoons Creme de Cacao liqueur
1 tablespoon Cognac
500g (1lb) veal mince

2 shallots, chopped
2 eggs
1 teaspoon salt
1 teaspoon pink peppercorns
4 rashers rindless bacon

Soak the prunes in the Creme de Cacao and Cognac for 24 hours before use. Combine the veal, shallots, eggs, salt and peppercorns in a bowl. Stir well. Line a 4-5 cup terrine dish with 3 rashers of bacon. Place half the veal mixture into the dish. Strain the prunes and place them down the middle of meat; cover with remaining veal. Spoon over 2 tablespoons of the Creme de Cacao mixture and top with the remaining rasher of bacon. Cook at 190°C (370°F) for 1-1½ hours, until cooked. Remove the terrine from the oven and place a weight on the top. Allow to cool then remove from the dish and refrigerate. Serve sliced, with hot toast.

Serves 6.

Glazed Lamb Rosemary

30g (1oz) butter or margarine
1kg (2lb) lamb chops
2 large onions, sliced
4 tomatoes, sliced
¼ cup chopped parsley
2 cloves garlic, crushed

1 tablespoon dried rosemary or
2 teaspoons fresh rosemary sprigs
2 cups beef stock
2 teaspoons brown sugar
seasoning to taste

Melt butter in a large pan and sauté the chops until browned on both sides. Add onions, cook a further 2 minutes. Add tomatoes, parsley, garlic, rosemary, stock, sugar and seasoning. Simmer uncovered for 45 minutes or until meat is tender, stirring occasionally.

Serves 4-6.

BOEUF A LA MODE (RECIPE PAGE 78)

Veal Pudding

500g (1lb) minced veal
60g (2oz) butter or margarine
30g (1oz) Parmesan cheese
125g (4oz) tomatoes, skinned, seeded, chopped
4 eggs
seasoning, nutmeg to taste
3 leaves silver beet, shredded
1 slice wholemeal bread, soaked in milk
3 tablespoons breadcrumbs

The Sauce
125g (4oz) tuna
4 anchovy fillets
2 teaspoons capers
2 teaspoons lime juice
seasoning to taste
1 egg yolk
¾ cup oil, approximately

Sauté the veal in the butter until just browned, mashing well with a fork to break up lumps, transfer to a bowl and stir in the remaining ingredients with the exception of the breadcrumbs. Pour into a well greased 4-cup mould, sprinkle with breadcrumbs and bake at 180°C (350°F) for 1 hour or until cooked. Meanwhile make the sauce by combining all the ingredients for the sauce in a blender or food processor, add sufficient oil to make a thin pouring sauce and heat gently. To serve, turn the pudding onto a serving plate and serve with the warm sauce.

Serves 3-4.

CATTLE IN SCRUB COUNTRY

Veal Rolls with Banana

6 veal escalopes, flattened	2 eggs beaten
seasoning to taste	breadcrumbs for coating
½ cup chopped marjoram	1 cup sliced mushrooms
½ cup parsley butter	½ packet pre-cooked pasta
4 bananas	½ cup sour cream
3 tablespoons banana liqueur	2 tablespoons mustard

Lay the veal flat onto the work surface, season and sprinkle with the herbs. Roll up and secure, then sauté in the butter for 10 minutes until golden and cooked on both sides. Remove from the pan and keep warm. Dip the bananas in the liqueur, egg and breadcrumbs, then sauté until golden; remove from the pan and keep warm. Add a little more butter to the pan, sauté the mushrooms then add the pasta, sour cream and mustard, stir until heated through and the pasta is well coated. Arrange the veal and bananas on a serving plate and serve the pasta sauce as an accompaniment.   Serves 4.

Roast Pork with Prune and Apple Stuffing

60g (2oz) butter or margarine	¼ teaspoon mixed herbs
1 green apple, finely chopped	seasoning to taste
125g (4oz) prunes, pitted	2kg (4lb) loin of pork, boned
1 onion, finely chopped	2 teaspoons salt
1 knob root ginger, finely chopped	¼ cup oil
6 slices stale bread, crumbed	

Melt butter in a frying pan and sauté the apple with the prunes, onion and ginger for 3 minutes. Remove from heat and stir in breadcrumbs, herbs, seasoning. Unroll loin, skin side down, and place prepared stuffing down centre of meat. Roll up firmly and secure with string. Rub rind with salt and oil. Bake at 220°C (440°F) for 1½-2 hours or until cooked.   Serves 4-6.

Roast Veal with Paprika Sauce

Paprika Sauce

½ cup finely chopped carrot	seasoning to taste
½ cup finely chopped celery	dash Worcestershire sauce
¼ cup finely chopped onion	2 cups chicken stock
1 tablespoon paprika	1 cup tomato purée
1 bay leaf	**For Cooking**
1 clove crushed garlic	2kg (4lb) boned, rolled loin of veal
pinch thyme	1 clove crushed garlic
	seasoning to taste

Make the sauce by combining all the ingredients in a saucepan. Bring to the boil, reduce the heat and simmer for 25 minutes. Allow to cool slightly, then puree in a food processor. Place the veal on a rack in a roasting dish, rub with garlic and season. Roast at 180°C (350°F) for approximately 1¾ hours or until cooked to suit your taste. Carve and serve with reheated sauce.   Serves 6-8.

Loin of Pork with Avocado and Apple Sauce

1.5kg (3lb) pork of loin, boned	¼ teaspoon Tabasco sauce
seasoning to taste	½ tablespoon lemon juice
½ teaspoon tarragon	½ cup cream
The Sauce	**For Garnish**
1 large ripe avocado, peeled, seed removed	1 small avocado, sliced
2 small granny smith apples, peeled, cored	

Dust the inside of the pork with the seasoning and tarragon. Roll up and secure. Bake at 200°C (400°F) until cooked about 1 hour. Make the sauce by puréeing the avocado with 1 apple, a dash of Tabasco and the lemon juice. When smooth add the cream and refrigerate. Reheat carefully. Just prior to serving add the remaining finely chopped apple and serve with the carved meat, garnished with slices of avocado.   Serves 6.

RIB ROAST PIQUANT (RECIPE PAGE 75)

CHARMING LONDON COURT IN PERTH, WESTERN AUSTRALIA

SERENE RURAL SCENE

ROAST LAMB WITH FIG SAUCE (RECIPE PAGE 82) TOP; RACK OF LAMB WITH PARSLEY AND SESAME SEEDS (RECIPE PAGE 83) BOTTOM LEFT

LAMB PARCELS (RECIPE PAGE 83)

YARRA RIVER AND SKYLINE OF MELBOURNE, VICTORIA

The Australian way of
COOKING COUNTRY STYLE

The Unhurried Approach of Country Cooking

Australia has marvellous produce (rivalling anything coming from the great central valley in California). You can't miss this fact when you travel through the countryside and visit the Australian country towns. You'll also notice that time doesn't pass quickly here.

Part of the country tradition is to take the time to make what you need from local produce. Summer fruits like raspberries and strawberries are made into jam and marmalade and then ladled on homemade bread.

Farmers often open their "tucker boxes" to a lunch of tasty cheese or meat seasoned with homemade chutneys — far superior to what you find in the shops.

We've taken afternoon tea, part of our English heritage, and improved it with a number of homemade goodies: wholemeal fruit scones, nutty gingerbread, apple pies and shortbread. In this section, you'll find country inspired recipes for these delights and many others.

"DAYS END" AUSTRALIAN STOCKMAN

Pork and Veal Pie

You require: Loaf Tin 13cm x 22cm x 7.5cm (5¼in x 8½in x 3in).

Filling
450g (1lb) Pork pieces
450g (1lb) Veal Steak, cubed
1 teaspoon mixed herbs
1 teaspoon salt
½ teaspoon pepper
2 small onions, finely chopped

3 teaspoons gelatine
3 hard-boiled eggs
Pastry
400g (3½ cups) plain flour
½ teaspoon salt
115g (4oz) lard
250ml (1 cup) milk

Place pork, veal, herbs, salt, pepper and onion into a saucepan, cover with water and simmer until meat is tender about 40 minutes. Remove from heat, set aside and allow to cool. Strain off stock from the meat and reserve stock.

Pastry
Sift flour and salt into a bowl. Place lard and milk into a saucepan and bring to the boil. Make a well in the flour and pour in boiling milk mixture. Mix thoroughly until pastry mixture leaves the sides of the bowl, form into a ball, cover and refrigerate for 1 hour.

How to do the Pie

Take ⅔ of the pastry and roll out (on floured bench) to 1.2cm (½in) thickness. Grease and flour the base and sides of the tin and press in pastry so that it slightly overlaps the edge. Spread ½ the cooled meat mixture into the pie shell. Place the hard boiled eggs on top and cover with remaining meat mixture. Roll out the remaining pastry and place it over the pie, trimming off the edges. Carefully pinch the sides so as to seal pie and make a small hole in the centre of pie top. Lightly brush top with milk and bake at 190°C (375°F) for 30 to 40 minutes or until golden brown. Remove from oven and allow to cool for 15 minutes. Heat 1 cup of reserved meat stock and dissolve gelatine in this. Using a funnel, very carefully pour the meat stock into the pie. Refrigerate for 5-6 hours. Serve cut into slices with fresh garden salads. Serves 6-8.

PHOTOGRAPH   PAGE 110

Brunch Pie

A hearty country breakfast, incorporating the natural taste of cream and cheese.

2-3 tablespoons oil
2 cups uncooked potatoes, cubed
1 onion, finely chopped
220g (7oz) chopped ham
2 sticks celery, finely sliced

6 eggs, beaten
pinch thyme
¼ cup cream
½ cup grated cheese
freshly chopped parsley

Heat oil in a large frying pan and sauté the potatoes and onion for approximately 15-20 minutes. Stir frequently until they are cooked. Reduce heat and stir in the ham and celery. Combine the eggs, thyme and cream together and pour over the potatoes. Cover and cook until the eggs are almost set, approximately 8-10 minutes. Sprinkle with cheese, stand covered for 5 minutes for eggs to set and cheese to melt. Serve. Serves 4-6.

Braised Pheasant in Brandy and Port

The fruity flavour of the port and brandy really penetrates through the pheasant making a very tasty dish.

1kg (2lb) pheasant
flour
30g (1oz) butter or margarine
2 tablespoons oil
2 rashers bacon, chopped
1 large onion, chopped

60g (2oz) button mushrooms
4 tablespoons brandy
4 tablespoons port
1 cup water
seasoning to taste
1 teaspoon fresh thyme

Lightly toss pheasant in flour. Heat butter and oil in a frying pan, and brown the pheasant all over. Transfer to a casserole. Sauté the bacon, onion and mushrooms in the frying pan for 3 minutes, then add ½ the brandy and port. Simmer for 2-3 minutes. Add the water, seasoning and thyme and stir to lift pan juices. Pour over pheasant, cover tightly and bake at 180°C (350°F) for 1½-2 hours; add the remaining port and brandy ½ hour before serving. Serves 4.

PHOTOGRAPH   PAGES 108-109

"PINEAPPLE ROW" MOUNT COONOWRIN, QUEENSLAND

"HOLD ON THERE!", AUSTRALIAN RODEO

THE BICENTENNIAL SYDNEY BALLOON FLY-OVER EVENT AT PARRAMATTA PARK. PHOTOGRAPH BY DAVID CUMMING. ORGANISED BY PETER VIZZARD & JUDY LYNNE. FEATURING THE AUSTRALIAN FLAG BALLOON (OWNER MR. VIC. ALBERTS). THIS BALLOON IS THE SYMBOL OF "CAMP QUALITY" WHO GIVE CHILDREN WITH CANCER THIS UNIQUE OPPORTUNITY OF FLYING WITH A BALLOON DURING THEIR SHORT LIVES. MRS. VERA ENTWISTLE IS THE MAIN INSTIGATOR OF SUCH MEMORABLE EVENTS.

Chicken with Sour Cherry Sauce

A rather delicious meal, and very colorful with the addition of the cherry sauce.

8 chicken breast fillets
dark soy sauce

8 thin slices lemon
freshly ground black pepper

Brush the chicken with soy sauce. Place a slice of lemon on each breast and season with pepper. Line a grill pan with foil and grill chicken until tender. Remove lemon slices. Serve with the sour cherry sauce.

Sour Cherry Sauce

2 tablespoons cider vinegar
4 tablespoons soft brown sugar
2 tablespoons cornflour
1 x 425g (14oz) can* black cherries,
pitted, drained, juice reserved

1 cup chicken stock
1 tablespoon grated orange rind
1 tablespoon grated lemon rind
½ cup orange juice
2 tablespoons lemon juice

Place vinegar and sugar in a saucepan, bring to the boil and cook, stirring constantly until mixture caramelizes. Blend cornflour with 2 tablespoons of cherry liquid, stir the remainder into the sugar mixture with the stock, rinds, juices and cherries, cook for a further 3 minutes. Add cornflour paste, stirring thoroughly until combined. Stir until sauce thickens.   Serves 8.
*nearest equivalent can size.

PHOTOGRAPH   PAGES 102-103

Quick Damper

2 cups self-raising flour
½ teaspoon salt

1¼ cups milk, approximately

Sift the flour and salt into a bowl, add sufficient milk to make a manageable dough. Turn out onto a floured board and knead lightly. Form into a round. Place onto a greased baking sheet, brush top with milk. Place into a hot oven·220°C (440°F) for 25-30 minutes. Serve warm with butter.

Spicy Mustard

Marvellous to serve with cold meats, and so easy to make.

150g (5oz) dry mustard seeds
1 medium onion, chopped
2 cloves garlic, crushed
1 teaspoon salt
2 teaspoons ground black pepper
1 bay leaf

2 teaspoons Tabasco sauce
2 tablespoons golden syrup
1 tablespoon curry powder
1 cup white wine
1 chicken stock cube

Combine all the ingredients in a saucepan and cover with water. Leave to soak for 1 hour, drain and add fresh water to cover. Leave for 2 hours then simmer for the next hour, stirring frequently to prevent the mixture catching, adding more water or wine as required. Remove from the heat and cool. Place in a processor or blender and roughly chop but do not purée. Pour into sterilised bottles or jars and store in a cool place for 1 week.

Spicy Tomato Sauce

2kg (4lb) ripe tomatoes, halved
2 onions, quartered
1 clove garlic, crushed
1 cup white vinegar
¾ cup firmly packed brown sugar
½ teaspoon chilli powder
1 teaspoon cloves

1 teaspoon peppercorns
1 teaspoon curry powder
1 tablespoon salt
½ teaspoon allspice
1 teaspoon paprika
¼ teaspoon black pepper
pinch cayenne pepper

Finely chop the tomatoes and place into a large pan. Chop onions, add to tomatoes with garlic and vinegar. Bring to boil, reduce heat and simmer 45 minutes. Pass tomato mixture through a strainer, pressing mixture with the back of a spoon to extract all juices. Discard pulp and return liquid to saucepan. Add remaining ingredients to pan. Bring to boil, reduce heat and simmer until sauce has thickened, approximately 30 minutes. Pour into hot, sterilised jars, seal and store.

PHOTOGRAPH   PAGE 106

Paw-Paw and Apple Chutney

Excellent served with cold meats, and makes an excellent gift for friends.

1kg (2lb) paw-paw peeled, seeded, chopped
1 large green apple, peeled, cored, chopped
500g (1lb) onions, chopped
1¾ cups sugar
2 cups white vinegar
1 cup raisins
1 tablespoon caraway seeds
1 tablespoon ground cumin
1 teaspoon salt

Combine all ingredients in a preserving pan or heavy based saucepan. Bring to the boil, then allow to simmer for approximately 50 minutes until the mixture thickens, stirring occasionally to prevent the mixture catching. Pour into sterilised jars when cool, seal and store.

PHOTOGRAPH   PAGE 106

Pineapple and Tomato Chutney

A sweet and spicy chutney which will accompany almost anything to add an extra touch of flavour.

1kg (2lb) pineapple, peeled, finely chopped
1.5kg (3lb) tomatoes, peeled, seeded, chopped
1½ cups raisins
2½ cups raw sugar
2 cups vinegar
1 green apple, peeled, cored, chopped
1½ tablespoons salt
3 tablespoons curry powder
2 teaspoons ground ginger
1 tablespoon Tabasco sauce
1 teaspoon powdered cloves

Combine all the ingredients in a large preserving pan or saucepan. Boil uncovered for 1-1½ hours or until the mixture thickens, then remove from the heat. Cool, pour into sterilised jars and seal well. Store in a cool place for 1 month before using.

PHOTOGRAPH   PAGE 106

Spiced Pickled Beetroot

Delicious served with salads and cold meats.

4 beetroots
1½ cups white vinegar
¾ cup water
¾ cup sugar
½ teaspoon peppercorns
½ teaspoon cloves
1 bay leaf
½ teaspoon mustard seeds
½ cinnamon stick
¼ teaspoon salt

Wash beetroots well, cook in boiling salted water until tender. Cool, and remove skins, either peeling by hand for a smooth surface or with a knife. If beetroots are large, cut in half, then slice into julienne strips. Place vinegar, water, sugar, peppercorns, cloves, bay leaf, mustard seeds, cinnamon stick and salt into pan, bring to boil. Simmer 5 minutes and strain. Spoon beetroots into hot, sterilised jars and top up with the vinegar mixture to overflowing.

Seal. Store in a cool place.

Pepper Pickle

6 red capsicums or peppers
6 green capsicums or peppers
6 cups tarragon or white wine vinegar
1 teaspoon salt
1 tablespoon sugar
sprigs fresh tarragon
1 small onion
1 small tablespoon black peppercorns

Wash capsicums, slice in half lengthwise, removing seeds and cores, cut into thin strips. Arrange capsicums in layers of colour in hot sterilised jars. Bring vinegar, salt and sugar to boil, pour over capsicums and decorate pickle with sprigs of fresh tarragon, onion rings and peppercorns.

Seal and store.

CREME CARAMEL (RECIPE PAGE 104) RIGHT; PEACH AND APPLE FLAN (RECIPE PAGE 110) LEFT

CHICKEN WITH SOUR CHERRY SAUCE (RECIPE PAGE 100)

Bran Biscuits

Healthy wholemeal bran biscuits.

3 cups wholemeal self-raising flour, sifted
1 cup bran
2 tablespoons brown sugar
½ cup dates, chopped
1 teaspoon mixed spice
60g (2oz) butter or margarine
2 tablespoons honey
1-1½ cups milk

Place the flour, bran, brown sugar, dates and spice into a bowl. Melt the butter and honey in the milk and stir into the dry ingredients. Turn onto a floured board and knead lightly, cut out using 6cm (2½") cutter. Place on a greased baking sheet. Brush with milk and bake at 220°C (440°F) for 12-14 minutes or until golden.   Makes 18 biscuits.

Pecan Topped Muffins

125g (4oz) butter or margarine
¾ cup brown sugar
grated rind ½ orange
1 egg, beaten
1 cup cereal, crushed
½-¾ cup milk
1½ cups self-raising flour, sifted
¼ teaspoon salt
Topping
½ cup brown sugar
½ cup pecan nuts, chopped
½ teaspoon cinnamon

Cream the butter and sugar together with the grated orange rind. Add the egg gradually, then the cereal. Add the milk alternately with the flour and salt and divide the mixture equally between 16 greased muffin or deep patty tins. Combine the ingredients for the topping and sprinkle over the muffins. Bake at 190°C (370°F) for 15-20 minutes. Serve warm.   Makes 16 muffins.

**PRUNE AND APPLE DESSERT CAKE (RECIPE PAGE 106) TOP
SPICED APPLE CAKE (RECIPE PAGE 106) BOTTOM**

Blueberry Muffins

Delicious served hot, but are a treat buttered and served in a lunch box.

1½ cups flour
1½ teaspoons baking powder
pinch salt
90g (3oz) butter or margarine
½ cup caster sugar
1 egg, beaten
½ cup milk
1 x 425g (14oz) can* blueberries, drained

Sift the flour, baking powder and salt together in a bowl. Cream the butter and sugar together in another bowl until light and fluffy. Stir in the milk and flour alternately, mixing well after each addition. Fold in the blueberries and spoon into greased muffin tins. Bake at 180°C (350°F) for 30 minutes.   Makes 12.
*nearest equivalent can size.

Mixed Fruit Wholemeal Biscuits

The name tells the story, your taste buds do the rest.

1½ cups wholemeal self-raising flour
½ cup self-raising flour
¼ teaspoon salt
30g (1oz) butter or margarine
¾ cup mixed fruit
2 tablespoons brown sugar
¾-1 cup milk

Sift the flour and salt together. Rub the butter into the flour and stir in the mixed fruit and sugar. Mix to a soft dough with the milk. Turn onto a floured board and lightly knead until smooth and elastic. Roll or press out to 2cm (¾") thickness. Cut into shape; using a 6cm (2½") fluted cutter. Place on greased baking sheet and glaze with milk. Bake at 220°C (440°F) for 10-15 minutes or until cooked. Serve warm with butter or margarine.
                   Makes 10-12 biscuits.

Blueberry Spiced Cobbler

2 x 425g (14oz) cans* blueberries, drained
2 cups flour
2 teaspoons baking powder
1 teaspoon mixed spice
125g (4oz) butter or margarine
¼ cup caster sugar
1 egg, beaten
sufficient milk for mixing
For Topping
milk and sugar

Place the blueberries in an ovenproof dish and gently heat. Sift the flour, baking powder and spice together in a bowl then rub in the butter until mixture resembles fine breadcrumbs. Add the sugar, egg and sufficient milk to make a soft manageable dough. Turn onto a lightly floured board and knead gently. Roll out to 1¼cm (½") thickness and cut into rounds with a fluted cutter. Place on top of the blueberries, slightly overlapping. Brush with milk and sprinkle with a little sugar. Bake at 200°C (400°F) for approximately 30 minutes.   Serves 6.
*nearest equivalent can size.

Creme Caramel

90g (3oz) caster sugar
½ cup water
2¼ cups milk
30g (1oz) sugar
¼ teaspoon vanilla essence
2 eggs, beaten
2 egg yolks

Dissolve sugar in the water and bring to the boil without stirring until a rich brown colour is achieved. Pour immediately into 4 dry, hot individual moulds, allow to coat the base and sides, leave to cool. Heat the milk and sugar with the vanilla and pour onto the beaten eggs. Cool and strain. Pour into the prepared moulds, cover with greaseproof paper or foil and cook in a water bath at 180°C (350°F) for 25-30 minutes or until set when tested. Leave to cool, then turn out and serve with chocolate-coated strawberries.   Serves 4.
PHOTOGRAPH   PAGE 101

"SHE'LL BE RIGHT MATE!", KANGAROOS, MOTHER AND SON

PINEAPPLE AND TOMATO CHUTNEY (RECIPE PAGE 101) TOP LEFT; SPICY TOMATO SAUCE (RECIPE PAGE 100) TOP MIDDLE; PAW PAW AND APPLE CHUTNEY (RECIPE PAGE 101) TOP RIGHT; QUINCE JELLY (RECIPE PAGE 117) CENTRE RIGHT; CITRUS MARMALADE (RECIPE PAGE 116) FRONT LEFT

Spiced Apple Cake

Delicious served warm with fresh cream.

The Topping
2 tablespoons brown sugar
½ teaspoon cinnamon
½ teaspoon nutmeg
3 tablespoons flour
15g (¾oz) melted butter or margarine
The Cake
¾ cup milk
1 cup muesli

1 egg, beaten
⅓ cup brown sugar
60g (2oz) melted butter or margarine
1 cup peeled, grated apple
1¾ cups self-raising flour
1 teaspoon baking powder
½ teaspoon cinnamon
½ teaspoon nutmeg

Mix dry topping ingredients together and stir in the butter. Combine the milk and muesli and stand for 5 minutes, then add the egg. Add sugar, butter and apple, then fold in the sifted dry ingredients. Pour into a prepared 20cm (8") springform tin. Crumble the topping over the cake mixture. Bake at 180°C (350°F) for 30-35 minutes. Allow cake to stand 15-20 minutes before turning out. Eat within 2-3 days.   Serves 6.

Raisin Rum Cake

½ cup raisins
¼ cup rum
3 cups self-raising flour
¼ teaspoon salt
1 teaspoon bicarbonate of soda
185g (6oz) butter or margarine

1¼ cups caster sugar
3 eggs
1½ cups milk
100g (3½oz) cooking chocolate, melted, cooled

Soak the raisins in the rum for at least 2 hours. Grease and line 3 x 20cm (8") sandwich tins with greaseproof paper. Sift the flour, salt and bicarbonate of soda together. Cream the butter and sugar together, add the eggs one at a time, beating well after each addition. Add the milk, chocolate and strained rum alternately with the flour mixture and beat well. Pour the mixture into the tins and bake at 200°C (400°F) for 30-40 minutes. Allow to cool, then serve the cakes plain, with icing cream or with a chocolate frosting.

Prune and Apple Dessert Cake

The Topping
¼ cup walnuts, chopped
10 prunes
1 apple, peeled, cored, sliced
The Base
125g (4oz) butter or margarine
⅓ cup brown sugar
½ cup honey

2 eggs, beaten
1 cup cereal, finely crushed
2 cups self-raising flour or wholemeal self-raising flour
½ teaspoon salt
½ teaspoon mixed spice
½ teaspoon nutmeg
⅔-¾ cup water

Grease and flour a 20cm (8") springform tin. Arrange topping ingredients in a decorative pattern in base of tin. Make the base by creaming the butter, sugar and honey together until light and fluffy. Gradually add the beaten eggs, alternately with the cereal. Sift the flour, salt and spices together and add to the creamed mixture alternately with the water and spoon into the prepared tin. Bake at 180°C (350°F) for 45-50 minutes or until cooked. Stand 5 minutes. Invert onto a wire rack, gently release the spring and remove rim. Carefully remove tin base so as not to disturb topping.   Serves 6.

Apricot Brazil Ring Cake

½ cup chopped dates
¼ cup chopped dried apricots
1 cup muesli
1 cup boiling water
125g (4oz) butter or margarine
¾ cup caster sugar
2 eggs, beaten

2 cups self-raising flour
½ teaspoon mixed spice
⅓ cup brazil nuts, chopped
lemon icing
extra chopped or whole dried apricots
flaked brazil nuts

Soften dates, apricots and muesli in a bowl with the water for 15 minutes. Cream butter and sugar together until light and fluffy then gradually add the eggs. Stir in the fruits, muesli, flour, spice and brazil nuts. Spoon into a 20cm (8") ring tin and bake at 180°C (350°F) for 45-55 minutes, or until cooked. Allow to cool in the tin before turning out. Ice whilst warm, and decorate with apricots and brazil nuts.

Date Cake Delicious

¾ cup evaporated milk, scalded
1 cup chopped dates
125g (4oz) butter or margarine
½ cup caster sugar
1 egg lightly beaten

1 cup self-raising flour
½ cup chopped walnuts
1 tablespoon butter or margarine, melted, (optional)
3 teaspoons cinnamon sugar, (optional)

Pour the milk over the dates and leave to cool. Cream the butter and sugar in a bowl then add the egg and beat well to combine. Fold in the flour, mixing alternately with the milk and dates; finally add the walnuts. Place the mixture into a greased 20cm (8") ring tin and bake at 180°C (350°F) for 45 minutes approximately. Brush with a little butter and cinnamon sugar if desired.

Date and Walnut Roll

1½ cups chopped dates
60g (2oz) butter or margarine
1 cup brown sugar
1 cup water

½ teaspoon bicarbonate of soda
1 egg, lightly beaten
½ cup chopped walnuts
2 cups self-raising flour, sifted

Combine dates, butter, brown sugar and water in a saucepan and stir over low heat until the sugar has dissolved. Bring to the boil, remove from heat and allow to cool. Stir in the bicarbonate of soda, egg and walnuts, then add the flour. Spoon mixture into two greased nut roll tins and bake at 180°C (350°F) for 40-45 minutes.
Makes 2 rolls.

Apple Pie

A family favourite.

8 large green apples
¼ cup sugar
½ cup water
¼ teaspoon cinnamon
⅓ cup sultanas
185g (6oz) butter or margarine, cubed
½ cup sugar

1 egg separated
1½ cups flour
¾ cup self-raising flour
⅓ cup cornflour
½ cup milk approximately, for glazing
extra sugar
extra cinnamon

Peel, quarter, core and slice apples and place in a large saucepan with the sugar, water and cinnamon. Bring to the boil, reduce heat and simmer, covered for 8 minutes, or until apples are tender but still holding their shape. Drain apples if any liquid remains and stir in the sultanas. Cool. Cream the butter and sugar together, then beat in the egg yolk. Add the dry ingredients and knead into a dough. Roll out ⅔ of pastry and use to line base and sides of greased 20cm (8") springform tin and spread the apple mixture evenly over base. Roll out remaining pastry, to cover the pie. Seal edges together and trim. Brush top with the lightly beaten egg white, sprinkle with the extra sugar and cinnamon. Cut 2 slits in the top. Bake at 180°C (350°F) for 15 minutes, reduce heat to 150°C (300°F), cook a further 35 minutes, or until pie is golden brown and pastry is cooked. Serve hot or cold with cinnamon cream, or ice cream.
Serves 8-10.

PHOTOGRAPH PAGE 114

AUSTRALIAN COUNTRY KITCHEN, QUEENSLAND

BRAISED PHEASANT IN BRANDY AND PORT (RECIPE PAGE 98)

Chocolate Dipped Hazelnut Squares

125g (4oz) butter or margarine
½ cup sugar
¾ cup roasted hazelnuts, finely chopped
1 cup flour
pinch salt
125g (4oz) cooking chocolate, melted

Cream butter and sugar together and stir in hazelnuts, then add flour and salt and mix well. Press mixture into a greased 18cm (7") x 28cm (11") slab tin. Bake at 150°C (300°F) for 30-40 minutes until pale brown and firm, then cut into squares. Dip each square diagonally into the melted chocolate and leave to set.

Makes approximately 25

Peach and Apple Flan

1 quantity sweet shortcrust pastry
1 cup custard
2 apples, cored, thinly sliced
2 x 410g cans peach halves, drained
2 x 312g (10oz) cans* mandarin segments, drained
4 tablespoons apricot jam

Line a 30cm (12") flan tin with pastry and bake blind at 190°C (370°F) for 15-20 minutes. Remove blind bake and return to oven for 5 minutes. Allow to cool. Spoon the custard into the base of the flan. Arrange fruit over the top and sprinkle with lemon juice. Heat the jam in a small saucepan, and gently brush over the fruit. Allow to cool before slicing.

Serves 8-10.

*nearest equivalent can size

PHOTOGRAPH   PAGE 101

BRUNCH PIE (RECIPE PAGE 98)

Macadamia Nut Chiffon Pie

Macadamia nuts have a lovely sweet and buttery flavour, and although quite expensive to buy, are well worth the treat in this delicious pie.

The Pie Crust
250g (8oz) plain sweet biscuits
125g (4oz) butter or margarine, melted
1 teaspoon ground cinnamon
The Filling
½ cup macadamia nuts, crushed

2 cups milk
5 eggs
1¼ cups cream
¾ cup sugar
3 teaspoons gelatine, dissolved in a little hot water

Make the pie crust by crushing the biscuits and stirring in the melted butter and cinnamon. Press into a suitably sized pie dish or springform tin and refrigerate until firm. To make the filling, combine the nuts and milk in a saucepan, bring to the boil, allow to simmer for 3 minutes, remove from heat. Strain the milk from the nuts, reserve. Place 1 whole egg and 4 egg yolks in the top of a double saucepan, add strained milk with half the sugar, stir over a medium heat and while stirring, add the dissolved gelatine. Stir until the custard thickens. Remove from heat and allow to cool. Scatter the reserved nuts over the base of the pie crust. Whip the cream with half the remaining sugar and whip the egg whites stiffly with the remaining sugar. Fold half of the cream and egg whites into the custard and pour into the pie crust over the nuts. Refrigerate until set and decorate with remaining whipped cream, chopped nuts and chocolate leaves.

Serves 8-10.

Nougat Bars

1 cup caster sugar
1 cup self-raising flour
1 cup coconut
1 cup rolled oats
pinch salt
¼ cup chopped walnuts
1 egg, lightly beaten
125g (4oz) butter or margarine, melted
1 tablespoon golden syrup

Combine the first six ingredients in a bowl. Stir in the remaining ingredients and combine well. Pour the mixture into two greased slab tins and bake at 180°C (350°F) for 20 minutes. When cool, cut into 5cm (2") squares.

Jam Fingers

3 cups flour
1 teaspoon baking powder
250g (8oz) butter or margarine
1 cup caster sugar
1 egg, lightly beaten
2 teaspoons vanilla essence
1 cup raspberry jam, warmed

Sift the flour and baking powder into a bowl then rub in the butter and stir in the sugar. Add the egg and vanilla essence and mix to a stiff dough. Knead lightly. Press two-thirds of dough into a greased and paper lined slab tin, spread with the jam. Roll out the remaining dough and cut into 1 cm (½") strips. Decorate the top in the form of a lattice pattern and bake at 180°C (350°F) for 40 minutes approximately. Cool in the tin and cut into small squares to serve.

Makes approximately 25.

SCENIC BRISBANE, QUEENSLAND

"BACK TO THE PASTURES", SHEEP AFTER SHEARING, NEW SOUTH WALES

Rhubarb Tart

A very "country style" dessert, delicious served on a cold night with hot custard, or cream.

1 quantity shortcrust pastry
1 x 540g (16oz) can* rhubarb, drained, syrup reserved
2 tablespoons cornflour
1 cup rhubarb syrup
1 egg, separated

grated rind, 1 lemon
½ juice 1 lemon
1 teaspoon ground ginger
1 tablespoon chopped, preserved ginger
little extra milk and caster sugar

Line a pie plate with the pastry reserving pastry strips and set aside. Make the reserved syrup up to 1 cup with cold water. Mix the cornflour to a smooth paste with a little water. Bring the rhubarb syrup to the boil in a saucepan then stir in the cornflour mixture and cook, stirring constantly until the mixture thickens. Cool, stir in the egg yolk, rhubarb purée, lemon rind, juice, ground and preserved ginger. Allow to cool. Beat the egg white until stiff, fold into the mixture and pour into the pastry case. Decorate the top in a lattice pattern with the remaining pastry strips. Brush with milk and sprinkle with a little sugar. Bake at 200°C (400°F) for approximately 30 minutes. Serves 6.
*nearest equivalent can size.

Coconut Slice

250g (8oz) coffee biscuits, crushed
grated rind 2 lemons
1 cup desiccated coconut

½ cup condensed milk
125g (4oz) butter or margarine

Combine the biscuits, rind and coconut in a bowl, mix well, set aside. Gently heat the condensed milk and butter in a saucepan until mixture has melted then pour over the dry ingredients. Mix well and place the mixture into a greased 20cm (8") slab tin. Refrigerate until set, then ice with lemon icing and cut into small squares. Makes 20.

Strawberry Cream Tartlets

1 cup flour
pinch salt
60g (2oz) butter or margarine
1 egg yolk
1 tablespoon water
1 teaspoon arrowroot

1 x 425g (14oz) can* strawberries drained,.a little juice retained
squeeze lemon juice
pinch cinnamon
whipped cream for decoration

Make the pastry by sifting the flour and salt into a bowl. Rub in the butter then add the egg yolk and a little water if necessary. Knead lightly then roll out and cut into small circles and use to line patty tins. Prick the base and bake blind at 190°C (370°F) for 15 minutes, or until cooked. Allow to cool. Stir the arrowroot into the reserved juice in a saucepan, add lemon juice and cinnamon and gently bring to the boil. Stir until the mixture clears, cool. Spoon a few strawberries into the tartlets, glaze with a little of the syrup and decorate with whipped cream. Serves 4-6.
*nearest equivalent can size.

Fruity Cornflake Cookies

A tasty treat for afternoon tea.

3 cups cornflakes
1¼ cups self-raising flour, sifted
155g (5oz) butter or margarine
½ cup brown sugar
1 egg

1 teaspoon grated orange rind
1 cup coconut
⅓ cup glace cherries, chopped
¾ cup raisins

Crush cornflakes finely and combine with the flour. Cream the butter and sugar together until light and fluffy then beat in the egg. Add the orange rind, coconut, cherries and raisins, and stir in the dry ingredients. Place heaped teaspoons of mixture onto greased baking sheets and bake at 180°C (350°F) for 10-15 minutes. Cool before storing. Makes approximately 32.

APPLE PIE (RECIPE PAGE 107)

"DREAM STORY", ABORIGINAL ROCK PAINTINGS NOURLANGIE ROCK, CENTRAL AUSTRALIA

Fruit and Nut Bars

2 eggs
¾ cup caster sugar
4 cups Rice Bubbles, crushed
1 teaspoon baking powder
1 cup pitted dates, coarsely chopped
1 cup mixed nuts
⅓ cup dried peaches, chopped

Beat the eggs until light and fluffy, then gradually add the sugar, beating until the mixture thickens. Combine with the Rice Bubbles, baking powder, dates, nuts and peaches. Press into a greased 23cm (9") x 23cm (9") slab tin and bake at 180°C (350°F) for 20-25 minutes. Mark into bars before allowing to cool.

Makes approximately 32.

Ginger Snaps

Everyone loves crunchy ginger snaps, a special treat for those who love the spicy flavour of ginger.

125g (4oz) butter or margarine, melted
1 cup sugar
2 tablespoons golden syrup
1 egg
2½ cups self-raising flour
1 tablespoon ground ginger
mixed peel

Combine melted butter, sugar, golden syrup and egg in a bowl. Add flour and ginger, stir well to combine. Roll into small balls and either place onto greased baking sheets and flatten with a fork, or roll in mixed peel prior to baking. Bake at 180°C (350°F) 15-20 minutes or until cooked.

Makes approximately 30.

Chocolate Crisps

These crisps are best eaten the day they are made.

185g (6oz) butter or margarine
185g (6oz) caster sugar
1 egg beaten
2 cups self-raising flour, sifted
1 tablespoon cocoa, sifted
½ cup puffed wheat

Cream the butter and sugar until light and fluffy then beat in the egg. Combine the flour and cocoa, stir into the creamed mixture together with the walnuts and puffed wheat. Place heaped tablespoons of mixture onto greased baking sheets. Bake at 180°C (350°F) for 12-15 minutes. Cool for a minute before transferring to a cooling rack.

Makes approximately 40.

Chocolate Afghans

Afghans are a favourite with most Australians, and are worthy of inclusion in this section.

220g (7oz) butter or margarine
90g (3oz) caster sugar
185g (6oz) flour, sifted
1 tablespoon cocoa, sifted
2½ cups crushed Weet-Bix
chocolate icing, (optional)

Cream the butter and sugar until light and fluffy. Stir in flour, cocoa and weet-bix. Place teaspoons of mixture onto greased baking sheets pressing down slightly with a fork. Bake at 180°C (350°F) for 12-15 minutes. Ice when cold, if desired.

Makes approximately 30.

Pecan Bix Cookies

125g (4oz) butter or margarine
½ cup sugar
1 egg
1 cup flour
3 tablespoons cornflour
6 Weet-Bix crushed
1 teaspoon baking powder
pecan halves

Cream the butter and sugar together until light and fluffy, then add all the dry ingredients with the exception of the pecans. Roll into balls and place on greased baking sheets, pressing a pecan half into the centre of each cookie. Bake at 180°C (350°F) for approximately 15 minutes.   Makes approximately 32.

Honey Peach Jam

1kg (2lb) peaches
½ cup water
1½ cups sugar
½ cup honey

Peel, halve, stone, and slice peaches and place in a saucepan with water, sugar and honey. Stir over a low heat until sugar dissolves. Bring to the boil and continue boiling 45 minutes or until jam jells. Pour into hot, sterilised jars. Seal and store.

**FANTASY OF THE SQUARE RIGGER,
DARLING HARBOUR, SYDNEY, NEW SOUTH WALES**

Preserved Oranges

6 firm oranges, halved
3 cups water
¼ teaspoon bicarbonate of soda
2 cups white vinegar
2 cups sugar
1 teaspoon whole cloves
2 cinnamon sticks

Slice oranges, remove seeds and place in a saucepan with water and bicarbonate of soda. Bring to the boil, reduce heat, simmer 5 minutes. Drain oranges, reserving 1 cup of liquid. Place all remaining ingredients into pan with reserved liquid. Bring to boil, stirring until sugar has dissolved; simmer 10 minutes. Place orange slices into hot sterilised jars. Strain syrup and pour over oranges. Seal, store in a cool place. Keep 2 weeks before using.

Fig Jam

750g (1½lb) dessert figs, roughly chopped
1½ cups fresh orange juice
¼ cup fresh lemon juice
3½ cups sugar

Place figs, fruit juices and sugar into a large saucepan. Stir over a medium heat until sugar has dissolved. Bring to the boil and continue boiling 25 minutes or until jam jells. Pour into sterilised jars, seal and store.

Citrus Marmalade

1 grapefruit
1 lemon
1 green apple
1 orange
4 cups water
6 cups sugar

Roughly chop unpeeled citrus fruits and remove seeds. Purée grapefruit and lemon in a food processor and transfer to a large saucepan. Peel, quarter and core apple; finely chop in the food processor with the orange. Add to pan with water and sugar. Stir over low heat until sugar dissolves, then increase heat and boil rapidly uncovered for approximately 45 minutes or until marmalade jells. Pour into hot, sterilised jars. Seal while hot and store.

PHOTOGRAPH   PAGE 106

Orange Carrot Marmalade

1 orange halved, sliced
1 lemon halved, sliced
4 cups water
3 cups sugar
2 cups grated carrot

Place the orange and the lemon into a large saucepan with the water. Bring to the boil, reduce heat and simmer covered until fruit is tender; approximately 20 minutes. Add sugar and carrot. Stir until sugar dissolves. Bring to boil and continue boiling uncovered 45 minutes or until marmalade jells. Pour into hot, sterilised jars. Seal and store.

Diet Marmalade

grated rind 1 lemon
1½ cups water
3 teaspoons gelatine
1 tablespoon lemon juice
2 tablespoons sugar

Soak lemon rind in water for 24 hours. Sprinkle the gelatine over and stir to combine. Bring to the boil, add lemon juice and sugar, and gently simmer for 10 minutes. Allow to cool, then pour into sterilised glass jar. Seal and store in the refrigerator. Will keep approximately 10 days, stored in the refrigerator.

DIET MARMALADE (RECIPE PAGE 116) ORANGE CARROT MARMALADE (RECIPE PAGE 116)

Grapefruit and Lemon Marmalade

3 grapefruits
4 lemons
8 cups water
1.5kg (3lb) sugar

Slice fruit, removing seeds. Place into a large saucepan with the water. Bring to the boil, reduce heat and simmer approximately 30-40 minutes or until fruit is tender. Add the sugar and stir over a low heat until dissolved. Bring to boil approximately 45 minutes or until a jell forms. Pour into hot, sterilised jars. Seal and store.

Quince Jelly

2kg (4lb) quinces
12 cups water
sugar

Wash the quince but do not peel or core. Roughly chop and place in a saucepan with 8 cups of water. Cover and simmer for 1 hour or until the fruit is tender, strain the liquid and reserve. Return the pulp to the saucepan, add remaining 4 cups water and simmer for 30 minutes, strain through a cheese cloth, twisting cloth to extract all juice. Combine the two liquids. Allow 500g (1lb) sugar to each 2½ cups liquid. Bring the juice to the boil, stir in the sugar, bring back to the boil. Boil rapidly until setting point is obtained. Skim well and pour into small hot jars, cover, label and store.

PHOTOGRAPH   PAGE 106

Lemon Butter

125g (4oz) butter
½ cup lemon juice
2 teaspoons grated lemon rind
1½ cups sugar
2 egg yolks
4 eggs

Melt the butter in a double saucepan over simmering water. Add the lemon juice, rind and sugar. Stir until sugar has dissolved. Beat egg yolks and extra eggs well together. Blend in a little of the hot butter mixture, then add the eggs into the hot butter, in the double saucepan. Cook while stirring until the mixture coats the back of a silver spoon. Refrigerate in a covered container. Lemon butter will keep for approximately 1 week.

Banana and Passionfruit Butter

This makes an excellent cake filling, or spread for scones.

2 medium bananas, peeled
2 passionfruit
grated rind and juice 2 lemons
250g (8oz) butter
⅓ cup sugar
¼ teaspoon salt
2 egg yolks, beaten
¼ cup orange liqueur

Mash the bananas. Halve the passionfruit and scoop out the pulp. Place all the ingredients into the top of a double saucepan and cook over a medium heat, stirring or whisking until thickened. Bottle in sterilised jars and seal.

RURAL WHEAT HARVEST, NEW SOUTH WALES

SCENIC VIEW OF WREST POINT CASINO AND CONVENTION CENTRE, HOBART, TASMANIA, AUSTRALIA

BREADS, CAKES & BISCUITS

Golden Grains to Put Fibre in Your Diet.

Australians are concerned with fibre like everyone else. And, the abundance of grain we produce − wheat, corn, rice, barley and oats − makes it easy to put fibre into our diets.

Thanks to the large number of Irish who came to Australia in the early days, porridge (what "The Yanks" call oatmeal) has been one of our breakfast staples. Porridge is a good source of fibre and definitely sticks to the ribs until lunch.

Another good source of fibre is bread. European migrants have made a significant contribution to the variety of Australian breads. In what was once strictly the land of white bread, you'll find rye, black bread, pita, wholemeal and milk bread − some of the best tasting breads in the world.

Damper, the traditional bush bread, is a homemade flatbread that's simple to make and unbeatable with a little butter and honey. In general, Australians are tending more toward homebaking and the following section gives you recipes for walnut, wholemeal, raisin and muesli breads. You'll also find other recipes that are nutritious and make fibre enjoyable to eat.

COOKING OF FAMOUS AUSTRALIAN DAMPERS

Oat Bran Porridge

A quick and healthy breakfast dish suitable for winter.

½ cup bran	*honey*
½ cup rolled oats	*1 tablespoon dried fruit*
1¾ cups hot water	*1 banana sliced*
milk	

Combine bran, oats and water in a saucepan, bring to the boil. Simmer 5 minutes adding extra water if necessary. Sweeten to taste with honey and serve with milk, sprinkled with dried fruits and banana.

Serves 4-5.

Warm-Up Porridge

For variety, add dried fruits to the oats when cooking.

1 cup rolled oats	*cream or milk*
2½-3 cups hot water	*honey*

Place oats and water in a saucepan, bring to the boil stirring constantly, then reduce heat and simmer 10-15 minutes until soft. For extra creaminess, use milk instead of water and add extra water or milk if the porridge becomes too thick. Serve hot with milk or cream. Add honey if desired.

PHOTOGRAPH   PAGE   131

Serves 4.

DATE LOAF (RECIPE PAGE 138) TOP LEFT; BANANA AND MUESLI LOG (RECIPE PAGE 138) TOP RIGHT; FRUIT LOAF (NO RECIPE) FRONT

Wholemeal Quick Bread

30g (1oz) butter or margarine	*½ teaspoon bicarbonate of soda*
1 tablespoon honey	*1 teaspoon salt*
½ cup boiling water	*1 cup milk approximately*
3 cups wholemeal flour	*cracked wheat*
1 cup wheatgerm	

Melt the butter and honey with the water in a saucepan. Cool, and add the remaining ingredients with the exception of the cracked wheat. Knead to a dough and place in a greased loaf tin, sprinkle with cracked wheat and bake at 230°C (450°F) for 30-45 minutes, or until cooked. Serve warm.

Scotch Oatmeal

5 cups cold water	*250g (8oz) coarse oatmeal*
2 teaspoons salt	

Combine water and salt in a medium size saucepan. When almost boiling sprinkle in oatmeal, stirring continuously. Simmer 10-15 minutes. Cover and let stand for 4-5 hours or overnight. Gently re-heat when required.

Serves 4-6.

Oatmeal Rolls

250g (8oz) rolled oats	*60g (2oz) butter, melted*
2 cups milk	*1 teaspoon salt*
15g (½oz) compressed yeast	*2 cups flour*
¼ cup warm water	*egg and milk, for glazing*

Place rolled oats into a bowl, pour on the milk and leave to soak for at least 2 hours. Dissolve the yeast in warm water and add this to the oats. Add the melted butter, salt and enough flour to make a smooth dough. Knead thoroughly for about 10 minutes. Replace in the bowl, cover with a cloth and leave to rise for 1 hour. Break down the dough and knead again. Shape into rolls and mark an "X" on the top with a sharp knife. Place on a greased baking sheet and leave to double in size. Brush with beaten egg and milk and bake at 200°C (400°F) for 15-20 minutes or until golden brown.

Makes 12 rolls.

Cheesy Cottage Loaf

3 cups flour	*½ teaspoon sugar*
2 teaspoons salt	*1¼ cups warm milk*
1 tablespoon dry mustard	*egg and milk for glazing*
2 tablespoons grated Parmesan	*1 teaspoon sesame seeds*
cheese	*½ teaspoon mixed herbs*
20g (¾oz) fresh yeast	

Sift flour, salt and mustard together in a large bowl. Stir in the cheese. Place bowl over hot water and stir occasionally to allow the flour mixture to warm through. Blend yeast and sugar together until smooth and creamy, add warm milk and blend thoroughly into the yeast mixture. Make a well in the centre of the flour and stir in the milk to make a firm dough. Knead well on a floured board and return to a clean bowl. Cover with a damp cloth and allow to stand in a warm place for about 1 hour or until double the size. Knead lightly on a floured board. Remove a small portion of dough and set aside. Form remainder into a large ball. Roll small portion into a ball and place on top of the large one. Press the top onto the base by inserting the handle of a wooden spoon through the centre. Place on a baking sheet, glaze with egg and milk and sprinkle with sesame seeds and herbs and bake at 200°C (400°F) for approximately 30-40 minutes or until cooked.

Malt Bread

This is an old favourite, and always popular for afternoon tea.

1 teaspoon bicarbonate of soda	*1 tablespoon butter or margarine*
pinch salt	*1 tablespoon golden syrup*
2 cups self-raising flour	*1 teaspoon malt*
1 cup bran	*1¼ cups milk*

Add soda and salt to the flour and mix well with the bran. Rub in the butter. Melt the golden syrup and malt over a low heat and mix well into dry ingredients. Lastly add the milk. Pour into a well greased large nut loaf tin with lid on, or two small tins, and bake at 180°C (350°F) for approximately 45-60 minutes. Cool in the tin, and serve when cold; sliced and buttered.

AUSTRALIAN FARMER TESTING CROP OF WHEAT GROWN IN NEW SOUTH WALES

GREY GUM (EUCALYPTUS CAMALDULENSIS) TREES, CENTRAL AUSTRALIA

Raisin Bread

4 cups flour	30g (1oz) butter or margarine
2 teaspoons salt	1¼ cups milk
1 teaspoon cinnamon	30g (1oz) compressed yeast
1 teaspoon mixed spice	1 cup raisins
⅓ cup sugar	milk for glazing

Sift flour, salt, cinnamon, mixed spice and sugar together into a bowl, and rub in butter. Heat milk to lukewarm, add the yeast and stir until combined. Allow to cool and stir the milk mixture into the flour to make a soft manageable dough. Knead on a floured board and place in a lightly oiled bowl. Cover with a piece of plastic wrap and a tea towel. Stand in a warm place until dough doubles in size, approximately 30 minutes. Re-knead on a floured board kneading in the raisins and place in a greased 28cm (11") x 12cm (5") loaf tin. Cover and leave to prove in a warm place until dough doubles in size, approximately 30 minutes. Brush lightly with milk and bake at 220°C (440°F) for 35 minutes or until cooked.

Wholemeal Bread

30g (1oz) compressed yeast	2 tablespoons soya flour
2 teaspoons sugar	3 teaspoons salt
3-3½ cups warm water	2 tablespoons skim milk powder
7 cups wholemeal flour	3 tablespoons oil
¾ cup gluten flour	2 teaspoons sesame seeds

Combine yeast, sugar and 2 cups of the warm water in a warm bowl. Cover and stand in a warm place until the yeast froths, about 10 minutes. Sift flours, salt and milk powder together. Add oil to the yeast mixture with the rest of the warm water. Pour over the dry ingredients and mix to a soft dough. Turn out onto a floured board and knead until the dough is smooth, approximately 10 minutes. Place in an oiled basin, cover and leave in a warm place until dough has doubled its size. Punch down, divide the dough and form into loaves or buns. Place in greased bread tins or on greased trays. Cover and allow to rise in a warm place for 30-40 minutes. Glaze with milk, sprinkle with sesame seeds and bake at 220°C (440°F) for 25-30 minutes or until cooked. Makes 3 small loaves.

Muesli Loaf

A textured wholesome bread to serve fresh or toasted.

30g (1oz) compressed yeast	1 egg, lightly beaten
½ cup warm water	2 cups wheatgerm
2 teaspoons sugar	2 tablespoons skim milk powder
½ cup rolled oats	3 cups wholemeal flour
½ cup dried apricots, finely chopped	½ cup gluten flour
2 tablespoons brown sugar	2 tablespoons soya flour
2 teaspoons salt	1 cup flour
1 tablespoon oil	extra flour for kneading
2 cups boiling water	

Mix the yeast in the water and stir in the sugar until dissolved. Leave to stand in a warm place until frothy, about 10-20 minutes. Place the rolled oats, apricots, sugar, salt and oil in a large bowl. Pour the boiling water over these ingredients and allow to cool to lukewarm. Add the yeast, egg, wheatgerm and powdered milk to the lukewarm rolled oat mixture. Mix well. Sift the flours together and stir into the mixture. Place 1 cup extra flour onto a board and knead the dough for 10 minutes adding more flour if necessary. Place in a greased bowl, cover and allow to rise in a warm place until double in size, about 45-60 minutes. Punch down and form into loaves or buns. Place in greased tins or on greased trays and allow to rise in a warm place for 30-45 minutes or until well rounded and almost double in size. Bake at 200°C (400°F) for 10 minutes, then at 180°C (350°F) for a further 40 minutes. Brush with butter and cool on a wire rack. Makes 2-3 small loaves.

American Corn Bread

This bread with its coarse texture goes particularly well served with soups and stews.

30g (1oz) compressed yeast	½ cup cornmeal
¼ cup warm water	¼ cup water
½ cup warm milk	1 egg, beaten
60g (2oz) butter or margarine	3 cups flour
¼ cup sugar	melted butter for glazing
1 teaspoon salt	

Crumble yeast into water, stand 5 minutes. Combine milk, butter, sugar and salt in a large bowl, add yeast mixture, cornmeal, water and egg and gradually beat in flour. Knead dough on floured board until smooth and glossy. Place in greased bowl, brush top with butter, cover and refrigerate 48 hours. Punch down dough, roll in 20cm (8") square, fold in sides to meet centre and press together. Place in a greased 20cm (8") x 13cm (5")loaf tin seam down and brush with butter. Cover and stand in warm place for 30 minutes. Dough will not double in size. Bake at 200°C (400°F) for 15 minutes. Reduce heat to 190°C (375°F) and bake for a further 15-20 minutes. Turn loaf out of tin and brush with butter.

Potato Cakes

These are delicious served for breakfast, but just as nice served with a crisp salad.

125g (4oz) flour	30g (1oz) butter or margarine
½ teaspoon baking powder	250g (8oz) mashed potatoes
½ teaspoon salt	enough milk to moisten
½ teaspoon pepper	butter for frying

Sift flour, baking powder and salt into a bowl. Add pepper then rub in butter with finger tips. Make sure that the potatoes are very finely mashed, stir into the flour with enough milk to make a stiff dough. Turn on to a lightly floured board, roll out to about 5mm (¼") thick, cut into rounds about 5cm (2") in diameter. Pan fry in butter until golden brown on both sides, approximately three minutes each side and serve garnished with parsley.
Makes approximately 6-8.

Quick Corn Fritters

The food processor or blender will make quick work of the preparation.

2 cups canned corn kernels	½ cup milk
seasoning to taste	2 cups flour
1 egg	2 teaspoons baking powder
1 teaspoon oil	oil for frying

Purée the corn in a blender or food processor, season then add the egg, oil, milk, flour and baking powder. Heat oil in a deep fat fryer and cook tablespoons of the mixture until golden brown and cooked through. Drain and serve. Serves 6.

Open Soya Bean Sandwiches

1 x 430g (14oz) can* soya beans	½ teaspoon basil
1 Weet-Bix, crushed	finely chopped parsley
1 cup finely chopped celery	salt to taste
1 cup carrot, grated	⅓ cup gluten flour
2 onions, finely chopped	slices of rye bread
½ cup grated cheese	butter or margarine
2 eggs, beaten	lettuce leaves

Mash soya beans and combine with the Weet-Bix, vegetables, cheese, egg and seasoning. Mix in the flour. Press into a greased 30cm (12") x 10cm (4") loaf tin and bake at 190°C (375°F) for 1½ hours. Allow to cool, then refrigerate. Spread bread with butter, top with lettuce, then a slice of the loaf. Serves 8 to 10.
*nearest equivalent can size.

WHOLEMEAL PASTIES (RECIPE PAGE 133) LEFT

LEEK AND MUSHROOM QUICHE (RECIPE PAGE 130) RIGHT

THE BIG PINEAPPLE, NAMBOUR, QUEENSLAND

Oriental Chicken and Corn Soup

A very hearty soup, filled with lots of chicken and corn.

1 x No. 13 chicken	6 shallots, chopped
10 cups water	1 x 440g (14oz) can* corn niblets
½ cup water chestnuts, drained,	3 tablespoons cornflour
chopped	⅓ cup water
1 small onion, roughly chopped	1 tablespoon sweet sherry
2 rashers bacon, roughly chopped	2 teaspoons soy sauce
1 nob root ginger, finely chopped	1 egg

Place chicken into a large saucepan with the water. Bring to the boil and simmer for approximately 40 minutes or until chicken is cooked. Remove chicken from pan, allow to cool, reserving stock. Skim fat from the surface of the stock. Remove skin and bones from chicken, chop the flesh. Add all prepared ingredients to the reserved chicken stock together with the corn niblets. Bring to the boil. Mix cornflour and water to a smooth paste, add to soup, simmer, stirring 3 minutes. Add sherry and soy sauce. Lightly beat egg with a fork, and stir into the soup. Serve at once. Serves 10-12.
*nearest equivalent can size.

Tabouleh Salad

⅔ cup steamed, cracked wheat	1 onion, chopped
1½ cups parsley, chopped	¼ cup olive oil
¾ cup mint leaves, chopped	¼ cup lemon juice
1 clove garlic, crushed	seasoning to taste
3 tomatoes, chopped	

Combine all the ingredients together in a large bowl and serve as a salad or spooned into wholemeal pita bread.   Serves 8.

Diet Luncheon

A quick luncheon dish for those watching their "waist".

2 hard-boiled eggs	1 slice wholemeal bread buttered
2 slices Cheddar cheese	2 celery sticks
lettuce leaves	6 dried apricots

Cut eggs in half and sandwich together with two slices of cheese. Arrange lettuce leaves over the slice of wholemeal bread and top with the celery. Serve with the eggs and apricots.   Serves 1.
PHOTOGRAPH   PAGE 133

Steak and Cheese Pie

1 quantity basic wholemeal pastry	1 tablespoon Worcestershire sauce
(refer Basic Wholemeal Pastry recipe)	1 tablespoon chopped parsley
2 eggs, beaten	2 teaspoons salt
1 onion, chopped	1 cup fresh wholemeal breadcrumbs
½ cup milk	500g (1lb) minced steak
1 tablespoon dry mustard	6 slices tasty cheese
⅓ cup tomato puree	

Roll out pastry between two sheets of greaseproof and line a greased 23cm (9") pie plate. Combine all the remaining ingredients with the exception of the cheese and pour into pie shell. Bake at 200°C (400°F) for 45 minutes. Remove from the oven and arrange the cheese slices over the top of the pie. Continue cooking until cheese melts and serve garnished with parsley.

Serves 4

Farmhouse Slice

A tasty country luncheon slice.

½ quantity basic wholemeal pastry	4 eggs, separated
(refer Basic Wholemeal Pastry Recipe)	½ cup mayonnaise
1 onion, diced	1 cup grated tasty cheese
1 cup diced bacon	salt to taste
1 x 470g (15oz) can* corn niblets,	cayenne pepper to taste
drained	

Roll pastry out thinly and line a greased 18cm (7") x 27cm (11") slab tin. Bake blind at 190°C (375°F) for 5 minutes. Saute onion and bacon together until tender, add corn and allow to cool then spoon over pastry. Combine egg yolks, mayonnaise and cheese in a bowl. Beat the egg whites until stiff and fold through the mayonnaise mixture. Pour over the bacon filling, sprinkle with salt and cayenne pepper and bake at 190°C (375°F) for 30 minutes or until cooked. Cut into slices and serve either hot or cold.
Makes 18 slices.

*Nearest equivalent can size.

Leek and Mushroom Quiche

An excellent light luncheon or entree, which can be served either warm or cold, with a crisp salad.

1 quantity wholemeal pastry (refer	1½ cups milk
Basic Wholemeal Pastry recipe)	4 eggs, beaten
2 tablespoons oil	1 cup cream
1 leek, washed, finely sliced	¾ cup grated cheese
1 cup button mushrooms, finely sliced	freshly ground nutmeg
1 tablespoon cornflour	

Line a deep 23cm (9") quiche tin or a shallow 30cm (12") flan tin with the thinly rolled pastry and refrigerate for 30 minutes. Heat the oil in a frying pan and saute the leeks for 3-4 minutes. Add mushrooms and cook 1 minute. Spread over the base of the quiche. Blend cornflour with a little of the milk then add to remainder of the milk. Whisk in the beaten eggs and cream. Pour over the leeks and mushrooms. Sprinkle with cheese and nutmeg and bake at 190°C (375°F) for 40-45 minutes or until set. Serves 6.
PHOTOGRAPH   PAGES 128-129

WARM UP PORRIDGE (RECIPE PAGE 124)

VIEW OF ''FLINDERS RANGES'' SOUTH AUSTRALIA NOTED FOR IT'S GREAT SILVER GUMS (EUCALYPTUS TREES)

DIET LUNCHEON (RECIPE PAGE 130)

Wholesome Vegetable Pie

A textured pastry base, with a good combination of fresh vegetables makes this a nutritious pie.

The Pastry Base
1 cup All-Bran
½ cup milk
1¼ cups self-raising flour
pinch salt
125g (4oz) butter or margarine
Filling
1 tablespoon oil
2½ tablespoons wholemeal flour
425g (13oz) can* tomato juice
2 zucchinis, thinly sliced

2 carrots, grated
1 onion, chopped
1 clove garlic, crushed
¼ teaspoon mixed herbs
1 cup mushrooms, sliced
Topping
1 tablespoon butter or margarine, melted
1 clove garlic, crushed
1 cup wholemeal breadcrumbs
1 tablespoon chopped parsley

Make the pastry by pouring the milk over the All-Bran and set aside for 5 minutes or until milk is absorbed. Sift flour and salt into a basin and rub in the butter. Add the All-Bran mixture and knead until smooth, cover and refrigerate for 1 hour. Roll out and line a 23cm (9") pie plate. Prick base of pie with fork. Bake at 190° C (375°F) for 10 -15 minutes. Cool. Prepare the filling by heating the oil in saucepan and stirring in the flour. Gradually add the tomato juice. Bring to the boil, stirring constantly. Add the vegetables and herbs and simmer until tender. Allow to cool. Spoon into the pastry case and sprinkle with the combined topping ingredients. Bake at 190° C (375° F) for 15-20 minutes or until cooked.   Serves 6-8
*nearest equivalent can size.

Wholemeal Pasties

A healthy version of the traditional Cornish pastie.

1 quantity wholemeal pastry
(refer Basic Wholemeal Pastry Recipe)
1 cup left over cold meat, cubed
2 cups cooked vegetables, diced

1 teaspoon mixed herbes
seasoning to taste.
1 tablespoon wholemeal flour
a little milk for glazing
tomato sauce

Roll out pastry and cut into rounds using a large saucer as a cutter. Combine the meat, vegetables, herbs seasoning and flour and divide equally between the pastry. Moisten edges and shape into pasties, glaze with a little milk and bake at 200°C (400°F) for 30 -40 minutes or until cooked.
Serve with tomato sauce.   Makes 6.

PHOTOGRAPH   PAGES 128-129

Basic Wholemeal Pastry

The pastry with 100's of uses. For a softer pastry use a mixture of wholemeal and plain flour.

2 cups wholemeal flour
¼-½ teaspoon salt

125g (4oz) butter or margarine
½-²/₃ cup cold water

Sift dry ingredients together in a bowl and rub in the butter until mixture resembles breadcrumbs. Mix in sufficient water to make a firm but slightly moist dough. Turn out onto a floured surface, knead slightly and roll out to required size.
Makes 1 x 30cm (12") pie base.

BUSHY PARK AND HOP FIELDS, DERWENT VALLEY, TASMANIA

Anzac Biscuits

2 cups rolled oats
½ cup sugar
1 cup flour
125g (4oz) butter, melted

1 tablespoon golden syrup
1 teaspoon bicarbonate of soda
2 tablespoons boiling water

Combine the oats, sugar, flour and melted butter together. Then add golden syrup and lastly the soda dissolved in the boiling water. Place spoonfuls of mixture onto a greased sheet and bake at 180°C (350°F) for 15-20 minutes or until cooked.

Makes approximately 12-18.

Wholemeal Cheese Biscuits

Delicious spread with butter or peanut butter for afternoon tea.

1½ cups self-raising flour
½ cup wholemeal self-raising flour
¼ teaspoon salt
30g (1oz) butter or margarine

¾-1 cup milk
½ cup grated cheese
sesame seeds

Sift flours and salt together and rub in the butter. Heat the milk and add to the dry ingredients with the cheese and mix to a soft manageable dough. Turn onto a floured board and knead until smooth. Roll out 2cm (¾") thick and cut into rounds using a 6cm (2½") cutter. Place on a baking sheet, brush tops with milk and sprinkle with sesame seeds. Bake at 220°C (440°F) for 12-15 minutes or until golden.

Makes 12.

Honey and Sultana Biscuits

½ cup natural yoghurt
1 tablespoon honey
½ cup milk

3 cups self-raising flour
½ teaspoon salt
¾ cup sultanas

Combine the yoghurt and honey in a bowl, then beat in the milk, flour and salt. Stir in the sultanas. Knead dough on a lightly-floured board and shape into a round, approximately 2½cm (1") thick. Cut into rounds and place on a lightly greased baking sheet. Glaze with a little milk and bake at 200°C (400°F) for 10 minutes or until golden brown and cooked.

Makes approximately 16.

PHOTOGRAPH   PAGES 140-141

Parsley and Onion Biscuits

2 cups self-raising flour
seasoning to taste
2 tablespoons finely chopped parsley
½ onion, finely chopped

3 shallots, chopped
30g (1oz) butter or margarine
150ml (¼ pint) milk
extra milk for glazing

Combine the flour, seasoning, parsley, onion and shallots in a bowl, rub in the butter until the mixture resembles fine breadcrumbs then add sufficient milk to make a soft but manageable dough. Knead on a lightly-floured board, and shape into a round approximately 2½cm (1") thick. Cut into rounds and place on a greased baking sheet, glaze with a little milk and bake at 200°C (400°F) for 12-15 minutes or until cooked.

PHOTOGRAPH   PAGES 140-141

Makes approximately 12.

A SWEEPING VIEW OF WHEAT HARVESTING IN QUEENSLAND

THE THREE SISTERS, PART OF THE BEAUTIFUL BLUE MOUNTAINS, A POPULAR RETREAT IN NEW SOUTH WALES

Doughnuts

Delicious served with afternoon tea.

½ cup milk
2 teaspoons sugar
15g (½oz) compressed yeast
2 cups flour
1 teaspoon salt
30g (1oz) butter or margarine
oil for frying
1 teaspoon cinnamon
3 tablespoons sugar

Heat milk until lukewarm, add sugar and yeast and stir well until sugar has dissolved. Stand in a warm place until bubbles form on the surface, approximately 10 minutes. Combine the flour and salt in a bowl and rub in the butter, add the yeast mixture and work into a manageable dough adding a little extra milk if necessary. Knead on a lightly floured board, until dough forms a ball. Place in a lightly oiled bowl, rubbing the dough with a little oil. Cover, and sit in a warm place until doubled in size, approximately 30 minutes. Re-knead, cut into rounds, deep fry until golden brown and cooked, drain on absorbent paper and dust with the combined cinnamon and sugar. Makes approximately 10.

PHOTOGRAPH PAGES 140-141

Pikelets

Usually a popular addition to afternoon teas, but just as tasty served hot or cold for breakfast.

1 cup self-raising flour
¼ teaspoon bicarbonate of soda
pinch salt
2 tablespoons sugar
1 egg
¾ cup milk
1 teaspoon vinegar
2 teaspoons softened butter or margarine
extra butter or margarine

Combine flour, bicarbonate of soda, salt and sugar in a food processor. Add the egg, milk, vinegar and butter, blend until smooth. Drop tablespoons of batter into hot butter and cook on both sides until well browned. Served warm with butter and jam.

Makes approximately 30.

Muesli Squares

A tasty addition to any lunch box.

90g (3oz) butter or margarine
¼ cup brown sugar
1 egg, beaten
1 cup flour
pinch salt
1 teaspoon baking powder
1 cup muesli

Cream the butter and sugar together until light and fluffy. Add the egg and beat well. Sift flour, salt and baking powder together and gently stir into creamed mixture, alternately with the muesli. Roll out onto floured board and cut into squares or fingers. If the mixture is too sticky, refrigerate before rolling. Place squares on a baking sheet and bake at 160°C (325°F) for 15-20 minutes. Cool on rack and store in an airtight container. Makes approximately 24.

Fruit and Nut Wheatgerm Slice

2 large apples, peeled, finely chopped
⅓ cup water
½ cup brown sugar
1 cup raisins
1 tablespoon cornflour
1 ½ cups flour
1 teaspoon baking powder
½ teaspoon bicarbonate of soda
pinch of salt
1 cup brown sugar
1 cup finely chopped walnuts
1 cup wheatgerm
185g (6oz) butter or margarine

Place apples, water and brown sugar in a saucepan and simmer until the apples are tender, then add the raisins. Blend cornflour with some liquid from the apples, add to the pan and stir until thickened, allow to cool. Sift flour, baking powder, bicarbonate of soda and salt into a bowl, add brown sugar, walnuts and wheatgerm and rub in the butter. Press ⅔ of the mixture into the base of a 27cm (11") x 18cm (7") lamington tin. Place apple mixture over base and sprinkle over remaining crumb mixture. Bake at 190°C (375°F) for 40-50 minutes or until cooked.

Serve cold.

Date Loaf

125g (4oz) butter or margarine
1½ cups brown sugar
1 teaspoon vanilla essence
3 eggs, beaten

1½ cups wholemeal self-raising flour
3 cups pitted dates, chopped
1 cup walnuts, chopped

Melt the butter over a low heat and add sugar and vanilla essence. Stir until sugar dissolves. Cool slightly before adding the eggs. Sift the flour and gradually add to the butter mixture, beating well after each addition, stir in the dates and walnuts. Spoon into a greased loaf tin and bake at 180°C (350°F) for 30 minutes or until cooked.

PHOTOGRAPH   PAGE 124

Fruit Damper

A delicious bun for afternoon tea.

3 cups self-raising flour
½ teaspoon salt
1 teaspoon mixed spice
60g (2oz) butter or margarine
⅓ cup sugar
1 egg
¾ cup milk
¾ cup sultanas

Icing
1 cup icing sugar, sifted
1 tablespoon warm water
red food colouring
glace cherries
walnuts

Combine the flour, salt and spice in a bowl and rub in the butter until the mixture resembles fine breadcrumbs. Add the sugar, egg, milk and sultanas and mix into a soft manageable dough. Shape into a 15cm (6") round and mark with an "X" on the top. Place on a greased baking sheet, brush with milk and bake at 180°C (350°F) for 50 minutes or until cooked. Make the icing by combining the sugar and water and adding sufficient food colouring to obtain a pale pink colour. Drizzle over the bun and decorate with glace cherries and walnuts.

PHOTOGRAPH   PAGES 140-141

Fruit Crisp Cookies

1 cup self-raising flour
¾ cup coconut
¾ cup sugar
2 teaspoons mixed spice
60g (2oz) butter or margarine

1 tablespoon golden syrup
¼ teaspoon bicarbonate of soda
1 egg
1 cup cornflakes
½ cup currants

Combine flour, coconut, sugar and mixed spice in a bowl. Melt the butter and golden syrup over a low heat then stir in the soda; allow to cool. Add egg and melted butter mixture to dry ingredients together with cornflakes and currants. Place teaspoons of mixture onto lightly greased baking sheets, allowing room for spreading. Bake at 180° C (350° F) for 15-20 minutes or until golden brown, leave on trays 5 minutes before removing.

Makes approximately 40.

Rolled Oat Crust

This is a suitable base for baked cheese cakes or lemon meringue pies.

1 cup wholemeal flour
1 cup desiccated coconut
1 cup rolled oats
¼ teaspoon mixed spice

¼ cup warmed honey
125g (4oz) butter or margarine, melted
milk

Combine flour, coconut, oats and mixed spice in a bowl. Make a well in the centre. Pour in the honey and melted butter. Mix thoroughly, adding sufficient milk to make a manageable dough. Use as required. Makes 1 x 30cm (12") crust or 2 x 23cm (9") crusts.

Delicious Carrot Cake

The combination of carrot and raisins add a luscious flavour to this spiced cake.

125g (4oz) butter or margarine
½ cup honey
1 teaspoon vanilla essence
2 eggs, beaten
1½ cups grated carrot
½ cup chopped raisins
½ cup walnuts

¼ cups wholemeal flour
2½ teaspoons baking powder
½ teaspoon bicarbonate soda
1 teaspoon cinnamon
½ teaspoon allspice
¼ cup milk
2 teaspoons lemon juice

Cream butter, honey and vanilla together until light and fluffy then beat in eggs. Add carrot, raisins and walnuts and beat well. Add sifted dry ingredients alternately with milk and lemon juice. Spoon into a greased and lined 20cm (8") x 10cm (4") loaf tin. Bake at 160°C (325°F) for approximately 1¼-1½ hours. Cool in tin before turning out.

Banana and Muesli Log

A tasty combination of banana and muesli.

1¼ cups wholemeal self-raising flour
½ teaspoon salt
½ teaspoon bicarbonate of soda
75g (2½oz) butter or margarine
½ cup caster sugar
2 eggs, beaten

½ cup chopped walnuts
1 teaspoon finely grated lemon rind
2-3 bananas, mashed
½ cup muesli
lemon icing
banana for decoration

Sift flour, salt and soda into a bowl returning the remaining husks to the sifted ingredients. Cream butter and sugar until light and fluffy then add eggs gradually. Mix in the nuts, lemon rind and blend well then add the mashed banana, dried sifted ingredients and the muesli, alternately. Gently combine and spoon into a greased and lined 23cm (9") x 10cm (4") loaf tin. Bake at 180°C (350°F) for 50-55 minutes. Cool then slice and spread with butter or ice with lemon icing and decorate with banana.

PHOTOGRAPH   PAGE 124

Makes 1 Banana Log.

Seed Cake

375g (12oz) self-raising flour
½ teaspoon salt
185g (6oz) butter or margarine
185g (6oz) sugar
½ teaspoon lemon essence

3 eggs
2 tablespoons apricot jam
¾ cup milk
1 tablespoon caraway seeds

Sift the flour and salt into a bowl. Cream the butter, sugar and essence together until light and fluffy, then gradually add the lightly beaten eggs. Stir in the jam and add the flour alternately with the milk, then fold in the caraway seeds. Bake in a round 20cm (8") x 8cm (3") lined cake tin at 180°C (350°F) for 1 hour or until cooked.

Shortbread

250g (8oz) butter, cubed
⅓ cup caster sugar
½ teaspoon vanilla essence
2¼ cups flour

1 tablespoon cornflour
For Decoration
glace cherries or almonds

Cream butter, sugar and vanilla together until light and fluffy. Add flours, mix until ingredients are well combined. Press mixture into a 20cm (8") square cake tin and cut into small fingers. Prick each piece with a fork to form a pattern and decorate with a glace cherry or almond. Sprinkle with caster sugar and bake at 150°C (300°F) for 30-40 minutes or until cooked.

Makes 16 pieces

ABORIGINALS PLAYING THE DIDGERIDOO AND BODY PAINTING ACCORDING TO THE RULES OF A DREAMTIME DANCE, CENTRAL AUSTRALIA

FRUIT DAMPER (RECIPE PAGE 138) FAR LEFT; PARSLEY AND ONION BISCUITS (RECIPE PAGE 136) SECOND LEFT

Walnut Loaf

1 egg
¾ cup brown sugar
½ cup milk
1 cup flour

1 cup self-raising flour
pinch salt
½ cup chopped walnuts

Beat egg and sugar together then add the milk. Gradually blend in the sifted flours, salt and then the walnuts. Place in a well greased loaf tin and bake at 180°C (350°F) for 30-40 minutes. Serve when cold, sliced and buttered.

Wholemeal Fruit Slice

This slice is delicious served with tea or coffee.

1 cup raw sugar
1 cup wholemeal flour
1 cup desiccated coconut

1 cup mixed fruit
1 cup milk
12 dried apricots, finely chopped

Mix all the ingredients together and place in a greased lamington tin. Bake at 150° C (300° F) for 40-45 minutes or until cooked. Cut into fingers before the slice cools.   Makes 16 fingers.

Avocado and Walnut Spread

Use this in place of butter on bread; particularly good for asparagus rolls.

1 ripe avocado, peeled, mashed
1-2 tablespoons finely chopped walnuts
1-2 tablespoons lemon juice

salt to taste
1 shallot, finely chopped

Combine avocado with the lemon juice and salt, cover and chill. Stir in the walnuts and shallot. Adjust seasoning and serve with cracker biscuits.

Date and Peanut Butter Spread

Particularly tasty on fresh wholemeal bread.

1 cup pitted dates, roughly chopped
¾ cup water

salt to taste
smooth peanut butter

Place dates and water in a saucepan. Bring to the boil and cook 4-8 minutes, stirring frequently. Add a little salt to taste. Allow to cool, then stir in sufficient peanut butter to make a spreading consistency for sandwiches, rolls, etc.

DOUGHNUTS (RECIPE PAGE 137) THIRD LEFT; HONEY AND SULTANA BISCUITS (RECIPE PAGE 136) FRONT

Chick Pea Puree Dip

155g (5oz) chick peas
juice 2 lemons
2 cloves garlic, crushed
90g (3oz) sesame tahini paste
salt to taste

olive oil
paprika
finely chopped parsley
wholemeal pita bread

Soak peas for about 12 hours, then cook until tender. Use a
pressure cooker if desired. Strain and reserve liquid. Puree 4
tablespoons of chick pea liquid with the lemon juice, garlic and
chick peas in a blender or food processor. Add the tahini paste
and blend until smooth then add the remainder with a little extra
liquid if the mixture is too thick. Season and spoon into small
bowls and cover with thin layer of oil. Garnish with paprika and
chopped parsley and serve as a dip with pita bread.

Peanut Butter and Pineapple Spread

This spread is best used immediately.

¼ cup crunchy peanut butter
½ cup unsweetened crushed pineapple,
drained

Combine the peanut butter with the pineapple and use as a
spread on toast, rye breads, wholemeal muffins or in sandwiches
with lettuce or chopped parsley.

AN ABUNDANCE OF BREAD VARIETIES FROM AUSTRALIA'S RICH FARMLANDS

A ROMANTIC TOURIST MOTEL ''THE PENNY ROYAL'' IN HOBART, TASMANIA

The Australian way of
USING WINES

The Cooks Best Friend for 6,000 Years

Australia has come a long way in its attitude to wine. Not long ago, wine was called "plonk" and beer was one of the most important words in our vocabulary. Now, there is a true appreciation of wine both as a compliment to any meal and as a cooking ingredient. Savvy cooks know that wine adds a rich subtle flavour to their dishes.

Many people don't realize Australia is developing into one of the worlds great wine producing regions. Wines from the Barossa Valley, Hunter Valley and Mildura are "having a go" on the world market and doing quite well.

It was the thousands of European migrants after the war who encouraged production of dryer,

lighter wines, and now, 43% of grapes are made into wines of all varieties. In fact, vineyards occupy 30% of our total crop area. Not bad, when you consider that in America this would mean the entire states of Illinois, Nebraska, Ohio and Iowa would be vineyards.

In the Australian kitchen of today, it's no longer a bottle of sherry in the back of the cupboard. Instead, you're likely to find sherries, ports, marsala, reds and whites in plain view. We use these wines in everything from meat marinades to casseroles, seafood dishes, sauces and desserts.

Try the following recipes. They'll turn an ordinary dish into a real event and you'll see why wine has been the cooks best friend for over 6,000 years,

HARVEST TIME IN THE HUNTER VALLEY, NEW SOUTH WALES, WORLD RENOWNED FOR ITS QUALITY WINES

Deep Fried Pate Mushrooms

18 medium mushrooms, peeled, stalks removed
180g (6oz) butter or margarine
1 medium onion, chopped
1 clove garlic, crushed
500g (1lb) chicken livers
½ cup Orange Curacao
½ cup cream
1 teaspoon finely grated orange rind
salt, to taste
1 teaspoon ground black pepper
½ teaspoon nutmeg
2 large hard-boiled eggs, finely chopped
½ teaspoon garam masala
beaten egg, for coating
fresh breadcrumbs
deep oil for frying

Chop the mushroom stalks finely. Melt the butter in a frying pan and add the onion, garlic and stalks. Cook for 2 minutes then add the chicken livers and cook until they are pink in the centre. Remove from the heat and add the Orange Curacao, cream, orange rind, salt, pepper, nutmeg, eggs and garam masala. Blend or puree into a fine paste and set to one side to cool. Brush the inside of each mushroom with a little beaten egg and spoon enough pate into the cavity so that it may be smoothed to the rim of the mushrooms; refrigerate until pate is firm. Egg and crumb the mushrooms twice then leave them in the refrigerator for 1 hour before deep frying. Deep fry mushrooms at 180°C (350°F) until browned. Do not overcook. Drain on kitchen paper and serve decorated with a sprig of deep-fried parsley.   Serves 6.

Fish Pate

500g (1lb) fish fillets, skinned, boned
1 shallot, chopped
grated rind ½ lemon
½ cup dry white wine
1 chicken stock cube
60g (2oz) butter or margarine
salt
cayenne pepper
⅓ cup cream
2 teaspoons lemon juice

Place fish, shallot, lemon rind, wine and stock cube into a pan. Simmer gently for 5 minutes or until fish is just tender. Puree the fish with the stock cube, butter, salt, cayenne pepper, cream and lemon juice until smooth and spoon into a serving bowl or four individual moulds. Refrigerate several hours. Serve with melba toast or savoury biscuits.   Serves 4.

Pork Pate

60g (2oz) butter or margarine
750g (1½lb) pork liver, roughly chopped
3 rashers bacon, chopped
4 shallots, chopped
3 cloves garlic, crushed
350g (12oz) finely minced pork
seasoning to taste
pinch of nutmeg and oregano
1 tablespoon brandy
1 cup hot beef stock
4 teaspoons gelatine

Melt the butter in a frying pan and saute the liver with the bacon, shallots, garlic, pork and seasoning for 15 minutes, stirring occasionally. Remove from the heat and stir in the brandy and ½ cup beef stock. Puree until smooth in a food processor. Dissolve the gelatine in the remaining stock and stir into the meat mixture. Pour into a chilled wetted mould and refrigerate until set. Serve with crackers and crusty bread.   Serves 4.

PHOTOGRAPH   PAGE 151

Cream Anchovy Dip

1½ cups cream
2 x 45g (1½oz) cans* flat anchovies
3 cloves garlic, crushed
½ teaspoon ground black pepper
½ teaspoon chopped parsley

Pour the cream into a saucepan. Add the other ingredients and stir over a medium heat until the cream boils. Allow to reduce slightly. Cool and refrigerate. When the thickened dip has chilled completely, serve with crisp celery and water biscuits.
Makes approximately 1½ cups.
*nearest equivalent can size.

PHOTOGRAPH   PAGES 168-169

Chicken Liver and Hazelnut Pate

60g (2oz) butter or margarine
½ onion
1 clove garlic, crushed
500g (1 lb) trimmed chicken livers
150ml (¼ pint) cream
3 tablespoons dry sherry
3 hard-boiled eggs, chopped
1 teaspoon oregano
½ teaspoon marjoram
½ cup chopped hazelnuts
1 teaspoon chopped parsley
seasoning to taste

Melt the butter in a frying pan and saute the onion until cooked. Add the garlic and the livers and cook until the livers are just pink in colour. Remove the pan from the heat and stir in all the ingredients with the exception of the nuts. Puree in a food processor. Stir in the nuts and transfer to a pate pot. Sprinkle with extra chopped hazelnuts and refrigerate until required.

PHOTOGRAPH   PAGES 168-169   Serves 6.

Chicken Liver Pate

This pate is delicious served piped into mushroom caps or served with hot buttered toast.

½ onion, chopped
2 cloves garlic, crushed
90g (3oz) butter or margarine
500g (1lb) chicken livers
3 hard-boiled eggs
3 tablespoons dry vermouth
seasoning to taste
½ teaspoon chopped parsley
¾ cup cream
½ teapoon nutmeg and cinnamon

Saute the onion and garlic in the butter for 3 minutes. When cooked, add the livers and continue cooking until tender. Remove pan from the heat and add all the other ingredients. Puree in a food processor or blend until smooth. Transfer to a suitable dish and refrigerate until required.   Serves 4.

Sherry Liver Pate

125g (4oz) butter or margarine
1 small onion, finely chopped
500g (1lb) chicken livers
1½ cups chicken stock
¼ cup sherry
½ teaspoon paprika
¼ teaspoon allspice
¼ teaspoon salt
¼ teaspoon cayenne pepper
½ cup brandy
124g (4oz) cream cheese
5 teaspoons gelatine

Melt the butter in a frying pan, saute the onion and chicken livers for 15 minutes, stirring occasionally. Pour in three-quarters of stock with the sherry, paprika, allspice, salt and cayenne pepper and simmer for a further 5 minutes. Remove from heat, add the brandy and cream cheese then puree the mixture in a food processor until smooth. Heat the remaining stock and use to dissolve the gelatine. Add to the chicken liver mixture. Pour into a wetted mould and refrigerate until set. Turn out onto a serving platter and serve with fingers of hot buttered toast.   Serves 6-8.

PHOTOGRAPH   PAGE 151

Baked Mussels

30 mussels
2 shallots, finely chopped
1 sprig thyme
2 sprigs parsley
1 bay leaf
½ teaspoon salt
½ cup white wine
125g (4oz) butter or margarine, softened
1 tablespoon parsley, chopped
2 cloves garlic, crushed
1 tablespoon chives

Scrape beard, scrub and wash mussels thoroughly and place in a large saucepan with the shallots, thyme, parsley and bay leaf. Sprinkle over salt and then add the wine. Steam for 5 minutes or until the shells have opened. Open mussels and discard lids. Divide mussels in remaining half shells into four ovenproof dishes. Make a herb butter by combining butter, parsley, garlic and chives and place a generous portion on each mussel. Bake at 190°C (370°F) for approximately 3 minutes or until butter has melted.

PHOTOGRAPH   PAGE 166   Serves 4.

FIRST FLEET REINACTMENT, SHIPS ARRIVING AT SYDNEY HARBOUR (AUSTRALIA'S BICENTENARY) NEW SOUTH WALES

SEALING OF WINE CASKS, POKOLBIN NEW SOUTH WALES

Coconut Scallops

A very simple way to serve scallops but very delicious.

750g (1½lb) scallops
1 fresh coconut
1 tablespoon butter or margarine
3 tablespoons brandy

¾ cup cream
½ teaspoon salt
pinch cayenne pepper
4-6 cups cooked rice

Remove flesh from coconut and shred finely. Melt the butter in a frying pan, stir in the brandy and cream, increase the heat and add the coconut, salt and pepper. Stir until the sauce has reduced and thickened, approximately 30 seconds — 1 minute. Stir in the scallops and when just cooked spoon onto hot saffron rice and serve.   Serves 6.

Aspic Garnish

2 teaspoons gelatine
½ cup hot chicken stock
2 teaspoons lemon juice

1 tablespoon sherry
seasoning to taste

Dissolve the gelatine in the hot stock and stir in the remaining ingredients. Pour into the base of a wetted chilled mould and spoon in the pate of your choice. Refrigerate until set.

Fish Soup

1 onion, chopped
1 clove garlic, crushed
3 tablespoons oil
½ teaspoon thyme
½ teaspoon rosemary
500g (1lb) fish fillets, skinned, boned
seasoning to taste

2 tablespoons tomato paste
1 cup white wine
4 cups water
3 tablespoons brandy
1½ cups cream
3 tablespoons grated Parmesan cheese

Saute the onion and garlic in the oil until tender. Add the herbs and chopped fish. Stir fry for 5 minutes. Season and stir in the tomato paste, white wine and water. Simmer until the fish has cooked then stir in the brandy and cream; reheat and serve with the Parmesan cheese.   Serves 8-10.

Three Bean Bowl

1 tablespoon butter or margarine
125g (4oz) bacon pieces
2 large onions, chopped
1 clove garlic, crushed
1 x 140g (5oz) can* tomato paste
1¼ cups water

1 tablespoon vinegar
2 teaspoons brown sugar
2 teaspoons Worcestershire sauce
½ teaspoon dry mustard
2 x 440g (14oz) cans* three bean mix
1 tablespoon sherry

Melt butter in a saucepan and fry bacon, onions and garlic until tender. Add remaining ingredients, cover and simmer 20 minutes. Serve in deep soup bowls.   Serves 3-4.

*nearest equivalent can size.

PHOTOGRAPH   PAGE 154

Stuffed Cucumbers

2 cucumbers
250g (8oz) cream cheese, softened
¼ cup chopped pecans

dash of Tabasco sauce
¼ teaspoon salt

Skin the cucumbers, cut in half lengthwise; scoop out the seeds. Sprinkle with salt and leave to drain. Beat the cream cheese, pecans, Tabasco and salt together. Dry the cucumbers and spoon the cheese mixture into the centre of each half. Sprinkle with chopped parsley and refrigerate. When firm cut into slices to serve.   Serves approximately 12.

PHOTOGRAPH   PAGES 168-169

Stuffed Mushroom Bake

12 medium-sized mushrooms
500g (1lb) minced steak
seasoning to taste
4 shallots, chopped
1 teaspoon chopped basil
¼ teaspoon chopped sage

½ cup red wine
wheatgerm or flour for thickening
½ onion, finely chopped
2 sticks finely chopped celery
1 carrot, finely chopped
beef stock

Remove stalks from mushrooms and chop finely. Add to the steak with the seasoning, shallots, basil, sage and wine. Add sufficient thickening to make a firm mixture. With mushroom cap up, spoon in filling to form a dome shape. Scatter vegetables over the base of a casserole dish and place the mushrooms on top. Pour sufficient beef stock to half cover mushrooms. Cover and bake at 180°C (350°F) for 20 minutes. Remove mushrooms and thicken the stock with a little blended cornflour. Serve mushrooms with the sauce.   Serves 6.

PATE AND ASPIC
(PORK PATE RECIPE PAGE 148) (SHERRY LIVER PATE RECIPE PAGE 148)

Savoury Apricots in Port

A tasty accompaniment to lamb, pork, veal or beef.

1 x 825g (24oz) can* apricot halves
¼ cup apricot juice
½ cup cider vinegar
½ teaspoon ground cloves

1 cinnamon stick
¾ cup port
1 tablespoon arrowroot

Drain apricots, reserving ¼ cup of juice and place in an ovenproof dish. Heat vinegar with cloves and cinnamon in a saucepan and remove from heat. Blend the arrowroot and apricot juice together and stir in the port, add to the saucepan and return to the heat. Bring to the boil stirring constantly and allow to boil until mixture thickens. Pour over apricots and cook at 160°C (325°F) for 15-20 minutes. Serve with roast meats.
*nearest equivalent can size

LADY SELFOX AT DUSK, LAUNCESTON, TASMANIA

Whole Sole with Mushroom and Wine Sauce

125g (4oz) button mushrooms	1 cup dry white wine
60g (2oz) butter or margarine	30g (1oz) butter or margarine
4 shallots, finely chopped	1 tablespoon flour
2 sticks celery, finely chopped	½ cup milk
4 whole sole or flounder	¼ cup cream
seasoning to taste	2 teaspoons lemon juice

Remove stalks from mushrooms and finely chop. Melt butter in a frying pan, add mushroom caps and saute 2-3 minutes then remove from the pan. Add vegetables and saute 2 minutes. Place fish onto a buttered dish, large enough to hold the fish in a single layer. Season and spread with the mushroom mixture. Pour over the wine, cover with foil and bake 180°C (350°F)15-20 minutes until fish is just firm to touch. Drain cooking liquid from pan and reserve; keep fish warm. Make a sauce in the usual way with the butter, flour and reserved cooking liquid. Stir in the milk and cream. Bring to the boil and stir until the sauce thickens. Season, add lemon juice and pour over fish. Serve topped with mushroom caps.   Serves 4.

Barbecued Marinated Quail

This very small game bird is very tender and should therefore be cooked quickly. Delightful served as an appetizer or main course.

2 cups chicken stock	½ teaspoon salt
1 cup dry white wine	½ teaspoon cayenne pepper
2 whole cloves	1 tablespoon olive oil
1 small onion, chopped	6 quail
1 bay leaf, crushed	

Place all ingredients with the exception of quail into a saucepan and bring to the boil. Cut the birds in half and place in a large bowl and cover with the hot marinade. Cool and refrigerate overnight. Lift quail from the marinade and grill or barbecue basting constantly throughout the cooking time. The skin is deep brown and crisp when cooked. Serve with a side salad.   Serves 6.

THREE BEAN BOWL (RECIPE PAGE 151)

Smoked Turkey Terrine in Pastry

A rather attractive way of using filo pastry with the combination of smoked turkey.

1kg (2lb) smoked turkey breast	2 eggs
4 shallots, chopped	1 teaspoon cayenne pepper
3 tablespoons brandy	6 sheets filo pastry
2 cups cream	60g (2oz) butter or margarine, melted

Combine the turkey, shallots, brandy, cream, eggs, and seasoning in a food processor. Brush each sheet of pastry with melted butter and use to line terrine. Spoon the turkey mixture into the terrine and cover with the overlapping pastry. Cut slits in the top to allow the steam to escape. Brush with a little beaten egg. Bake at 190°C (370°F) for approximately 40 minutes or until cooked. When cool, cut into slices and serve.   Serves 6-8.

PHOTOGRAPH   PAGES 168-169

Duckling in Lemon Sauce

The flavour of sherry and lemon juice cuts through the richness of the duck, making this an excellent dish for a dinner party.

1 duckling	½ cup water
seasoning to taste	1 cup lemon juice
⅔ cup sugar	¼ cup dry sherry
2 tablespoons cornflour	

Wash and clean duckling under cold running water. Pat dry with paper towels and truss ready for roasting. Season. Place into a baking dish, cover with foil. Bake at 180°C (350°F) for 1½ hours, brushing occasionally with pan juices. Place the sugar and cornflour into a small saucepan and blend into a smooth paste with the water. Add lemon juice, sherry and seasoning, stir until sauce boils and thickens. Pour fat from baking dish and pour the sauce over the duck, continue cooking uncovered for a further 30 minutes or until duck is tender, basting continually with the lemon sauce.   Serves 2-4.

Rabbit and Pork Terrine

This would be wonderful packed in the picnic hamper as it travels well.

500g (1lb) rabbit	seasoning to taste
250g (8oz) belly pork	¼ cup claret
1 onion	¼ cup brandy
1 teaspoon chopped fresh thyme	2 rashers bacon
1 tablespoon chopped parsley	1 bay leaf
1 clove garlic, crushed	

Mince the rabbit with the pork and onion. Add herbs, garlic seasoning, wine and brandy and mix well. Press half the mixture into a greased terrine, cover with the bacon then top with remaining meat. Crumble the bay leaf over the top. Cover with foil and stand in a water bath, bake at 180°C (350°F) for 1½ hours. Cool, then refrigerate overnight.   Serves 6-8.

Chicken with Caraway Seeds

12 chicken thighs	3 finely chopped shallots
3 tablespoons caraway seeds	½ cup white wine
20g (⅔ oz) butter or margarine, melted .	seasoning to taste

Place thighs in a baking dish and brush with butter, sprinkle with caraway seeds and bake at 180°C (350°F) for approximately 50 minutes. Transfer to a serving dish and keep warm. Pour off excess fat, add shallots, wine; increase heat and boil for 3 minutes then add the remaining butter, stirring vigorously. Season and serve with the chicken.   Serves 6.

CHARMING CHATEAU YALDARA, BAROSSA VALLEY, SOUTH AUSTRALIA

Crunchy Chicken Bake

This is an economical tasty dish to serve at the weekend.

1 large cooked chicken
30g (1oz) butter or margarine
2 tablespoons flour
1¾ cups milk
1 teaspoon French mustard
2 sticks celery, sliced
1 green capsicum, de-seeded, quartered

1 onion, quartered
3 tablespoons lemon juice
2 tablespoons dry sherry
6 slices stale bread, crumbed
2 tablespoons finely chopped parsley
90g (3oz) butter
¼ cup Parmesan cheese

Skin and bone chicken and chop flesh. Make a sauce in the usual way with the butter, flour and milk. Stir in the mustard, combine the chicken with the sauce, vegetables, lemon juice and seasoning, then spoon into a greased ovenproof dish. Combine breadcrumbs and parsley and saute in the butter. Cool slightly then stir through the Parmesan cheese, sprinkle over the top of the casserole and bake at 180°C (350°F) for 30 minutes.

Serves 4-6.

Chicken Paprika

2 tablespoons butter or margarine
1.5kg (3lb) chicken pieces
2 teaspoons paprika
¾ cup white wine
1 onion, sliced
1 x 425g (13oz) can* tomatoes, drained

¼ cup sliced red pimento
bouquet garni
salt
1 tablespoon butter or margarine
1 tablespoon flour
¾ cup milk
3 cups hot cooked noodles

Heat butter in a heavy based saucepan and brown the chicken pieces. Remove and set aside. Add paprika and wine to the pan and stir to lift pan juices, then add the onions, tomatoes and pimento. Return the chicken to the pan together with the bouquet garni and salt, cover and simmer for 35 minutes. Transfer chicken to serving dish and keep warm. Puree the tomato sauce in a blender or pass through a sieve. Make a white sauce in the usual way with the remaining butter, flour and milk and stir in the tomato sauce. Reheat, adjust seasoning and spoon over the chicken. Serve with hot buttered noodles. Serves 4-6.
*nearest equivalent can size

Chicken and Cherries

The pale chicken with the red cherries makes this an elegant combination when entertaining.

6 large chicken fillets
flour
60g (2oz) butter or margarine
1 tablespoon oil

500g (1lb) white or red cherries
1 cup cream
½ cup white wine
seasoning to taste

Flatten the chicken fillets and dust in plain flour. Melt the butter and oil in a heavy-based frying pan and lightly saute the chicken fillets. Add the cherries, cream, wine and seasoning. Allow to boil, reduce heat then simmer for 10 minutes. The sauce should be quite thick. Serve with the sauce spooned over the chicken with the cherries on top.   Serves 6.

Cheesy Chicken

6 chicken breasts
seasoned flour
1 egg, beaten
dried breadcrumbs
oil for cooking
6 slices ham
250g (8oz) Mozzarella cheese, sliced
1 large onion, finely chopped
1 tablespoon butter

1 tablespoon flour
1 clove garlic, crushed
1 tablespoon chopped parsley
½ teaspoon oregano
1 teaspoon basil
1 x 425g (13oz) can* tomatoes, undrained
½ cup Riesling

Toss chicken breasts in seasoned flour. Dip into beaten egg and coat with breadcrumbs. Heat oil in a heavy pan, saute chicken until golden then transfer to an ovenproof dish. Top each piece with a slice of ham and cover with a slice of Mozzarella cheese. Bake at 180°C (350°F) for 15-20 minutes. Meanwhile make a sauce, saute the onion in the butter, stir in the flour, add garlic, parsley, oregano, basil and tomatoes and bring to boil. Simmer 15 minutes, then add wine and reheat. Serve chicken breasts coated with the sauce.   Serves 6.
*nearest equivalent can size.

Steak Provence

A favourite dish with everyone.

2 tablespoons oil
2 onions, chopped
2 green capsicums, sliced
2 red capsicums, sliced
1 tablespoon flour
1 tablespoon chopped parsley

1 x 425g (14oz) can* tomatoes
¼ cup Riesling
1 teaspoon basil
seasoning to taste
4 x 500g (1lb) thinly cut steaks
½ cup grated Parmesan cheese

Heat oil and saute the onion and capsicums until tender. Add flour, chopped parsley and tomatoes then stir in the wine, basil and seasoning. Simmer over a low heat while cooking the steaks. Serve the steaks with a little of the sauce poured over the top, sprinkled with Parmesan cheese.   Serves 4.
*nearest equivalent can size.

PHOTOGRAPH   PAGE 163

Cheese Topped Steaks

4 x 500g (1lb) rump steaks
2 tablespoons olive oil
125g (4oz) pepper cheese, sliced
1 clove garlic, crushed

1 tablespoon flour
½ cup white burgundy
2 tablespoons brandy

Heat oil in a heavy based frying pan and saute the garlic for a few minutes. Add the steaks and cook until required taste. Place cheese on top of the steaks, heat through then remove to a warm serving dish. Add the flour to the pan juices and brown. Stir in the burgundy and brandy; bring to the boil stirring until sauce thickens. Serve the steaks topped with the sauce.   Serves 4.

Chicken in Plum Sauce

The tasty plum sauce adds a special flavour to this dish and is very easy to prepare.

12 chicken thighs
1 cup water
1 cup white wine
1 bay leaf
500g (1lb) plums, seeds removed
¼ cup chopped onion

2 teaspoons chopped parsley
½ teaspoon garam masala
2 teaspoons soy sauce
seasoning to taste
chilli sauce to taste

Place the chicken in a baking dish with the water, wine and bay leaf. Cover and cook at 180°C (350°F) for 40 minutes. Strain the liquid from the chicken into a large saucepan, add the plums, onion, parsley, garam masala and soy sauce. Simmer until the plums are tender. Cool slightly then puree, return to saucepan and simmer until reduced and thickened. Season and stir in chilli sauce. Pour over the chicken and continue to cook at 180°C (350°F) until heated through. Serve with rice.   Serves 6.

Fillet of Beef Wellington

This is an elegant dish for a dinner party and quite easy to prepare.

1½kg (3lb) fillet of beef
seasoning to taste
60g (2oz) butter or margarine
¼ cup brandy
125g (4oz) peppered cream cheese

90g (3oz) liver pate
1 x 375g (12oz) packet frozen puff pastry
1 egg lightly beaten

Rub fillet with seasoning and melt the butter in a large frying pan. Sear the beef over a high heat until brown on all sides. Warm brandy, ignite and pour over beef, allow flames to subside. Remove meat from pan and cool, then arrange the cheese over the top of the fillet. Combine the pate with the pan juices and spread over the top of the cheese. Roll out the pastry into a rectangle large enough to encase the beef and place the fillet down one side. Brush edges with the egg. Fold pastry over, sealing the edges forming a neat parcel. Place seam side down on a large baking sheet. Slash the top of the pastry with a knife at intervals, glaze with remaining egg and bake at 220°C (440°F) for 15 minutes, then at 180°C (350°F) for 20-30 minutes. Serve cut into thick slices.

Serves 6.

Marinated Beef Pie

A very tasty good old fashioned family meal.

The Marinade
2 cups red wine
2 cups beef stock
½ cup olive oil
1 onion, chopped
1 stick celery, finely chopped
1 carrot, chopped
1 clove garlic, crushed
1 teaspoon marjoram

1 teaspoon salt
1 teaspoon crushed black peppercorns
For Cooking
1kg (2lb) beef, chuck or blade
flour
oil for frying
puff pastry sheet
1 egg, lightly beaten

Combine all the ingredients for the marinade in a saucepan. Bring to the boil and allow to cool. Cut the beef into bite-size pieces and place in a glass bowl. Cover with the marinade and marinate for at least 24 hours in the refrigerator. Drain meat, toss in flour and brown in hot oil. Transfer to a saucepan and pour in the marinade, simmer for approximately 1 hour or until tender. Spoon into a pie dish and cover with the pastry. Glaze with egg and bake at 200°C (400°F) for approximately 20 minutes or until the pastry is cooked.   Serves 4.

TASTING ONE OF AUSTRALIA'S FAMOUS RED WINES, HUNTER VALLEY, NEW SOUTH WALES

ONE OF THE MANY FASCINATING VAST CAVE SYSTEMS IN SOUTH AUSTRALIA

Tasty Mince Pie

375g (12oz) packet puff pastry
1 tablespoon butter or margarine
500g (1lb) lean minced steak
2 medium onions, sliced
1 medium green capsicum, sliced
1 cup red wine
2 tablespoons tomato paste

pinch basil
pinch marjoram
seasoning to taste
1 egg, lightly beaten
125g (4oz) Mozzarella cheese, grated
2 tomatoes, sliced

Use two-thirds of the pastry to line a 23cm (9") greased pie plate. Melt butter in a saucepan and brown the meat well. Add onions, capsicum, wine, tomato paste and seasoning. Simmer uncovered for 35 minutes or until most of the liquid has evaporated. Stir in the egg, reserving a little, and half the cheese. Spoon meat into the pie plate and top with the tomato slices then sprinkle with remaining cheese. Brush edge of pastry with a little water and cover pie with reserved pastry. Glaze with remaining egg mixed with a drop of milk and decorate with any leftover pastry. Bake at 190°C (370°F) for 20-25 minutes or until cooked.   Serves 4-6.

Beef and Mushroom Casserole

This delicious rich beef casserole is enhanced with the addition of good red wine.

1kg (2lb) round or topside steak
2 tablespoons oil
30g (1oz) butter or margarine
3 rashers bacon, roughly chopped
2 onions, roughly chopped
2 cloves garlic, crushed
2 tablespoons flour

1 cup beef stock
1½ cups red wine
1 bay leaf
½ teaspoon thyme
seasoning to taste
125g (4oz) mushrooms, sliced
¼ cup finely chopped parsley

Trim fat from meat and cut into cubes. Heat the butter and oil in a heavy based saucepan and brown the meat. Remove meat from the pan and saute the bacon, onion and garlic in the pan drippings. Stir in the flour and allow to brown. Remove from the heat, stir in stock, wine, bay leaf, thyme, seasoning. Return the meat to pan and simmer for approximately 1 hour or until meat is tender. Stir in the mushrooms; cook a further 15 minutes and serve sprinkled with parsley.   Serves 4-6.

VEAL ROLLS PROVOLONE (RECIPE PAGE 163)

Pork and Pear Bake

A delightful way of cooking pork chops. If fresh pears are not available, canned pears can be substituted. Just add 10 minutes before completion of cooking to heat through.

6 pork chops
3 firm pears
4 tablespoons lemon juice
¼ cup firmly packed brown sugar
¼ teaspoon ground cinnamon

¼ cup dry sherry
2 tablespoons butter or margarine
1 teaspoon cornflour blended with
1 tablespoon water

Brown pork chops in a frying pan in their own fat. Transfer to a large baking dish. Cut each pear in half lengthwise, remove core and stem and arrange pears, cut side up, around the chops. Sprinkle meat and fruit with lemon juice. Combine the brown sugar and cinnamon in a small bowl. Sprinkle over the meat and fruit, together with the sherry. Place a small nob of butter on each pear and bake at 160°C (325°F) for 30-40 minutes. Pour pan juices into a small pan, skim off fat then thicken with the cornflour. Serve with the chops and pears.   Serves 6.

Stuffed Pork Fillets in Apple Sauce

An ideal recipe which can be prepared ahead of time and cooked just prior to serving.

6 pork fillets
1 cup chopped dried apricots
¼ cup chopped shallots
6 thin slices of ham
flour
60g (2oz) butter or margarine

2 tablespoons apricot brandy
2 tablespoons Cognac
3 tablespoons tomato puree
3 apples peeled, thickly sliced
1 cup chicken stock

Slit the fillet lengthwise ¾ of the way through and open out onto a board. Pound to flatten a little. Combine the apricots and shallots and spoon some onto each fillet. Top with a slice of ham, roll and secure with string. Toss in flour and saute in the melted butter. Pour in the brandies, tomato puree, apples and stock. Simmer over a medium heat, stirring occasionally to avoid the rolls catching on the base of the pan and adjust seasonings. Remove string from pork rolls and serve with the sauce and vegetables of choice.   Serves 6.

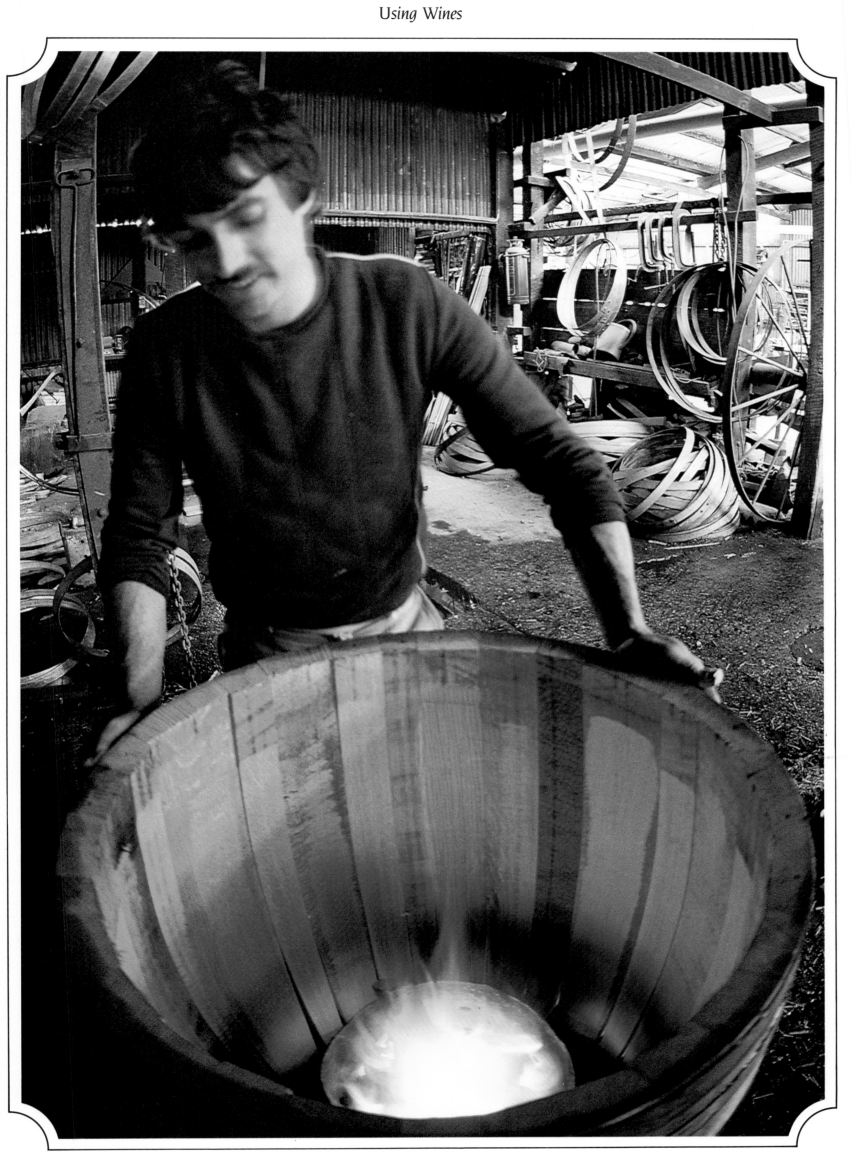

THE ART OF COOPERING, BAROSSA VALLEY VINEYARDS, SOUTH AUSTRALIA

STURT DESSERT PEA, AN UNUSUAL DESERT FLOWER IN FULL BLOOM, WESTERN AUSTRALIA

Tagliatelle Roma

An excellent dish for a party.

The Sauce	For Cooking
¼ cup olive oil	185g (6oz) green tagliatelle
1 clove garlic, crushed	185g (6oz) white tagliatelle
1 onion, chopped	½ cup claret
500g (1lb) minced steak	1 cup water
1 tablespoon chopped parsley	1 x 250g (8oz) can* tomato paste
1 teaspoon basil	½ teaspoon salt
½ teaspoon oregano	1 cup grated Parmesan cheese

Heat oil and saute the garlic and onion till tender. Add steak and saute till browned. Add parsley, basil, oregano, claret, water, tomato paste and salt. Cover and simmer for 35 minutes. Boil tagliatelle noodles together in boiling water till firm but tender. Drain and serve with the sauce poured over, top with the grated cheese.   Serves 4.

*nearest equivalent can size.

Veal Rolls Provolone

6 thin fillets veal	4 tablespoon olive oil
4 tablespoons soft white breadcrumbs	2 tablespoons flour
2 tablespoons grated Parmesan cheese	¼ cup sweet sherry
60g (2oz) grated Provolone cheese	1 tablespoon tomato paste
1 tablespoon chopped parsley	1¼ cups water
1 small clove garlic, crushed	½ teaspoon salt
1 egg, beaten	½ teaspoon basil
3 rashers bacon, halved	

Pound veal thinly. Combine breadcrumbs, cheeses, parsley, garlic and egg. Place a piece of bacon on veal fillets and spread with the cheese mixture, roll up and secure with toothpicks. Heat oil in a frying pan, add garlic and saute meat until brown. Drain off all but 1 tablespoon oil. Stir in flour, sherry, tomato paste, water, basil and salt. Stir until boiling. Return meat to pan. Cover and simmer 20 minutes. Serve with vegetables of choice.   Serves 3-6.

PHOTOGRAPH   PAGE 160

Lamb Hot Pot

1kg (2lb) lean lamb, cubed	1 tablespoon Worcestershire sauce
seasoned flour	1 teaspoon dry mustard
3 tablespoons oil	seasoning to taste
4 small onions, sliced	2 carrots, sliced
1 clove garlic, crushed	1 parsnip, sliced
1 x 440g (14oz) can* tomato soup	4 sticks celery, sliced
2 cups stock	1 red capsicum, sliced
2 tablespoons sherry	1 green capsicum, sliced
1 tablespoon brown sugar	2 tablespoons chopped parsley
1 tablespoon lemon juice	

Toss lamb in seasoned flour and brown in the oil with onion and garlic. Add remaining ingredients with the exception of the vegetables. Cover and simmer for 1 hour. Add vegetables, cover and simmer a further ½ hour or until vegetables are tender. Serve with crusty bread and mashed potatoes.   Serves 4-5.

*nearest equivalent can size

Roast Veal with Cheese Crust

1.5kg (3lb) piece veal	½ cup water
black pepper	90g (3oz) tasty cheese grated
1 onion, sliced	3 slices bread, crumbed
½ cup white wine	2 tablespoons finely chopped parsley

Place veal into a greased baking dish and sprinkle with black pepper; top with the onion and pour over the combined wine and water. Cover with foil and bake at 180°C (350°F) for 2½ hours, basting occasionally. While meat is cooking prepare crusty topping. Combine the cheese with the breadcrumbs and parsley. Press into the meat and bake uncovered a further 30 minutes or until the meat is tender.   Serves 6-8.

Veal and Mushroom Casserole

The veal is greatly enhanced in flavour with this tasty mushroom wine sauce.

2 tablespoons oil	1¼ cups chicken stock
8 veal chops	1 cup white wine
60g (2oz) butter or margarine	½ cup cream
8 shallots, chopped	seasoning to taste
185g (6oz) mushrooms, sliced	1 teaspoon fresh tarragon or
2 cloves garlic, crushed	½ teaspoon dried tarragon
3 tablespoons flour	

Heat oil in a frying pan and saute the veal until browned. Transfer to an ovenproof dish. Add 30g (1oz) butter to the pan and saute shallots, mushrooms and garlic for approximately 1 minute. Spoon on top of the chops. Melt the remaining butter, add the flour and stir over the heat for a few minutes then add the stock and wine. Stir until boiling then reduce heat, simmer 2 minutes. Add cream, seasoning and tarragon. Pour over chops, cover an bake at 180°C (350°F) for 40 minutes.   Serves 4.

STEAK PROVENCE (RECIPE PAGE 156)

Veal Marengo

A very tasty and economical dish to make. It can be made ahead and reheated when required.

1½kg (3lb) stewing veal	½ teaspoon thyme
3 tablespoons olive oil	½ teaspoon basil
1 onion, chopped	12 small white onions
1 x 140g (5oz) can* tomato paste	seasoning to taste
1 tablespoon flour	60g (2oz) butter or margarine
1½ cups chicken stock	250g (8oz) mushrooms
1 cup Riesling	4 tomatoes, skinned, halved
2 bay leaves	

Cut veal into cubes and brown in the oil. Stir in onion and tomato paste and cook for 2 minutes then blend in the flour, chicken stock and wine. Add bay leaves, thyme, basil, seasoning. Cover and simmer 1 hour. Meanwhile saute onions in butter till brown and tender, add mushrooms then stir into the veal. Stir in tomatoes and simmer a further 30 minutes. Serve with noodles tossed in butter and Parmesan cheese.   Serves 8.

*nearest equivalent can size

STRAWBERRY CREAM FREEZE (NO RECIPE) TOP LEFT; PINEAPPLE DELIGHT (RECIPE PAGE 168) MIDDLE LEFT; POACHED PEARS IN VERMOUTH (RECIPE PAGE 169) BOTTOM LEFT;

CHOCOLATE DIPPED STRAWBERRIES (NO RECIPE) MIDDLE; MERINGUE ORANGES (RECIPE PAGE 169) BOTTOM RIGHT

Blueberry Glazed Cheesecake

Any type of canned fruit may be used.

1 x 23cm (9") sponge	1½ tablespoons gelatine
2 eggs	½ cup water
125g (4oz) caster sugar	1¼ cups cream
500g (1½lb) ricotta cheese	**The Topping**
2 teaspoons grated lemon rind	2 teaspoons gelatine
2 tablespoons lemon juice	1 x 425g (13oz) can*
2 teaspoons vanilla essence	blueberries
2 tablespoons brandy	

Place the sponge in the base of a 23cm (9") spring form tin. Beat the eggs and sugar together until thick and creamy. Combine the ricotta cheese with the lemon rind, juice, vanilla and brandy. Dissolve the gelatine in the hot water and when cool beat into the ricotta cheese mixture. Combine the whipped cream with the egg mixture and stir into the ricotta cheese. Pour over the sponge layer and refrigerate until set. Make the topping by placing the fruit in a saucepan with the gelatine; stir until the gelatine has dissolved. Allow to partially set then pour over the cheesecake and refrigerate until firm. Slowly release spring on tin and remove from tin onto serving plate. Serves 6-8.

*nearest equivalent can size.

Peaches and Cream Cheesecake

The Crumb Crust	¾ cup sugar
250g (8oz) plain biscuits, crushed	500g (1lb) cream cheese, softened
125g (4oz) butter or margarine, melted	1 tablespoon brandy
1 teaspoon mixed spice	1 x 425g (13oz) can* peaches, drained
The Filling	1¼ cups cream, whipped
3 eggs	

Combine the biscuit crumbs with the butter and mixed spice in a bowl; press into the base and sides of 20cm (8") spring form tin. Refrigerate until firm. Make the filling for the cheesecake by beating the eggs and sugar together until thick and creamy. Beat the cream cheese and brandy together until smooth then combine with the eggs and pour half the mixture into the prepared crust and top with half the fruit. Carefully spoon over the remaining filling. Bake at 180°C (350°F) for 45 minutes or until firm. Turn oven off, and allow cheesecake to cool in the oven. Refrigerate until required. Serve decorated with whipped cream and remaining fruit. Serves 8-10.

*nearest equivalent can size

Normandy Tart (Apple Tart)

This recipe would also be delicious made with pears and served with custard.

1 packet shortcrust pastry	1 teaspoon lemon juice
6-8 medium cooking apples	1 tablespoon sugar
1 tablespoon water	**Apricot Glaze**
½ cup sugar	½ cup apricot jam
¼ cup brandy	1 tablespoon water
30g (1oz) butter or margarine	

Line a fluted 18cm (7") flan tin with pastry, prick well and chill 30 minutes. Bake blind at 200°C (400°F) for 10-12 minutes; allow to cool. Reserve two apples, peel, core and roughly chop the remainder. Place in a saucepan with the water, sugar, brandy and butter. Cover and simmer for about 20 minutes, stirring occasionally. Remove lid, increase heat and boil stirring until thickened; puree and allow to cool before spooning into the pastry case. Peel, core and thinly slice reserved apples, sprinkle with lemon juice and sugar and arrange over the top of the tart. Bake at 190°C (370°F) for 30 minutes or until cooked. Make the apricot glaze by heating the jam and water in a saucepan; stir until boiling. Strain onto the top of the tart and serve warm or cold with a bowl of whipped cream. Serves 4-5.

Apricot Pudding with Brandy Sauce

A steamed pudding is always a welcome winter dessert served with whipped cream.

125g (4oz) butter or margarine	⅓ cup milk
½ cup caster sugar	1 x 825g (28oz) can* apricot halves,
2 eggs	drained
1 cup self raising flour	2 tablespoons brandy
pinch salt	

Cream butter and sugar together until light and fluffy. Add the eggs one at a time beating well after each addition, then add sifted flour and salt and the milk. Grease a 5 cup pudding basin and cover the base with approximately eight apricot halves; spoon in the cake mixture, cover and steam for 1¼ hours or until cooked. Puree the remaining apricots with the brandy and heat in a small saucepan and serve with the pudding. Serves 6.

*nearest equivalent can size.

BAKED MUSSELS (RECIPE PAGE 148)

HARVESTING THE GRAPES, YARRA VALLEY VINEYARDS, VICTORIA

CREAM ANCHOVY DIP (RECIPE PAGE 148) BOTTOM RIGHT; CHICKEN LIVER AND HAZELNUT PATE (RECIPE PAGE 148) RIGHT

Maraschino Flan

1 quantity sweet shortcrust pastry
2 x 425g (13oz) cans* pitted dark cherries, drained syrup reserved

1 cup redcurrant jelly
2 tablespoons maraschino liqueur

Roll out pastry and use to line a 20cm (8") fluted flan tin. Bake blind at 190°C (370°F) for 20 minutes until cooked. Remove from the tin and allow to cool. Make the glaze by boiling the jelly with ½ cup of the syrup and the liqueur in a saucepan. Strain into a bowl. Arrange the cherries over the flan base then quickly brush with the hot glaze; refrigerate and serve with whipped cream. A variation of this recipe would be to sprinkle 3 tablespoons sugar over the drained cherries in the flan, place under a griller for 2-3 minutes to caramelize the sugar being careful that it does not burn. Heat ⅓ cup maraschino liqueur in a small pan, ignite and pour over the flan just before serving.   Serves 6.
*nearest equivalent can size

Pineapple Delight

.The pineapple can be macerated overnight and then drained thoroughly prior to stirring through the cream. Keep the pineapple shells if wished and serve the mixture in the shells for an attractive dessert.

1 medium pineapple
1 packet marshmallows, chopped
1 teaspoon nutmeg

½ cup brandy
½ cup sugar
1¼ cups thickened cream, whipped

Cut the pineapple in half lengthwise and scoop out the pulp with a sharp knife removing the core; roughly chop into cubes reserving as much juice as possible. Transfer to a large bowl and stir in the marshmallows, nutmeg, brandy and sugar. Cover and refrigerate for at least 4 hours. Stir through the whipped cream and serve.   Serves 4-6.

PHOTOGRAPH   PAGES 164-165

STUFFED CUCUMBERS (RECIPE PAGE 151) TOP MIDDLE; SMOKED TURKEY TERRINE PASTRY (RECIPE PAGE 154) BOTTOM LEFT

Meringue Oranges

This sophisticated dessert is extremely easy to prepare and looks most impressive.

6 medium-large oranges
2 tablespoons raisins
3 tablespoons brandy

1 tablespoon sugar
3 egg whites
4 tablespoons caster sugar

Cut the top from each orange and scoop out the pulp using a sharp knife. Retain the shells and dice the fruit into a glass bowl. Add the sugar, raisins and brandy and leave for 6 hours. Make a stiff meringue by stiffly beating the egg whites and gradually adding the sugar while beating continuously. Fill the shells with the fruit mixture and pipe some meringue on the top of each one. Bake at 230°C (475°F) for a few minutes until the meringue has browned.
Serve immediately.   Serves 6.

PHOTOGRAPH   PAGES 164-165

Poached Pears in Vermouth

6 large pears, peeled
grated rind 1 lemon
grated rind 1 orange

1 cup dry vermouth
1 cup caster sugar
¾ cup thickened cream, whipped

Place all the ingredients with the exception of cream into a saucepan. Add sufficient water to cover the pears, bring to the boil and simmer for 15 minutes. Remove from the heat, transfer to a bowl and refrigerate for at least 12 hours. Drain the pears and serve with the cream, decorate with sprig of mint.   Serves 6.

PHOTOGRAPH   PAGES 164-165

DARLING HARBOUR ENTERTAINMENT AND EXHIBITION CENTRE WITH MONORAIL TRANSPORT TO SYDNEY CENTRE, NEW SOUTH WALES

TROPICAL COOKING

What to Eat in a Tropical Paradise

If you're looking for a tropical paradise, this is it — brilliant sunshine, swaying palms, azure water, white sand and tropical fruit plantations. 45% of Australia lies in the tropics. This includes holiday islands dotting the Northern Coast and the Great Barrier Reef the eighth wonder of the world, enclosing 12,872 kilometres (8,000 square miles) . If you're going to "go troppo", the Northern Coast of Australia would be a great place to do it.

In our tropical areas the English heritage of eating meat and boiled potatoes, no matter how "bloody hot" it is, has given way to dishes using tropical fish

and crustaceans. We also enjoy luscious tropical fruits: avocadoes, mangoes, pawpaws, sugarbananas, rock melons, pineapples and passionfruit.

Of course tropical food is not confined to Northern Australia. Whether its Rockhampton or Rottnest, Darwin or Dimboola you can "tuck into" some cool enticing dishes.

This chapter is devoted to recipes like Piquant Lemon Whiting, Prawns in Coconut Sauce, Chilled Pawpaw Souffle, and Island Pineapple Rum — the things you'd eat in a tropical paradise.

BIRD SANCTUARY AT MICHAELMUS CAY, QUEENSLAND

Iced Cucumber Soup

1 large onion, sliced
sprig mint
1 teaspoon dill
seasoning to taste
5 cups chicken stock
2 large cucumbers, peeled, seeded, chopped

2 tablespoons cornflour
1 tablespoon water
1/3 cup sour cream
green food colouring — optional
extra cucumber slices and mint for garnish

Simmer onion with the mint, dill, seasoning and stock until tender. Add cucumbers and cook for a further 10 minutes. Puree mixture until smooth in a blender. Return to saucepan. Add cornflour blended with water and bring to boil and simmer 2-3 minutes. Remove from heat and allow to cool. Add sour cream and mint with green colouring if desired. Pour into a large serving bowl, cover and chill. Serve garnished with cucumber slices and mint.

Serves 10.

Cherry Soup

A rather nice chilled fruit soup, making excellent use of fresh cherries.

500g (1lb) fresh cherries with their stalks
3 cups white wine
grated rind 1 lemon
juice 1 lemon

1 cinnamon stick
1/3 cup sour cream
3/4 cup cream
1/3 cup Cherry Advokat liqueur

Stone the cherries and leave to one side. Crack the stones and put them into a saucepan together with the stalks, wine, rind, juice and cinnamon. Bring to the boil and cook for 5 minutes; remove from the heat and allow to stand for 20 minutes. Strain and pour the juices into a saucepan; bring to the boil and add the cherries. Cook for 1 minute then remove from the heat. Pour in the creams and liqueur. Stir well, cool and refrigerate. Serve well chilled.

Serves 6-8.

Chilled Melon Soup

A refreshing cold summer soup.

1 large rockmelon
2 teaspoons lemon juice
1/2 cup cold water
1 chicken stock cube, crumbed

1 tablespoon orange liqueur
freshly ground pepper
6 chives, chopped

Peel, seed and cube rockmelon. Place half the rockmelon into a food processor and puree. Repeat with remaining rockmelon and pour into a bowl. Combine rockmelon puree, lemon juice, cold water, crumbled stock cube, liqueur, pepper and nutmeg. Stir thoroughly. Place in the refrigerator and chill for several hours before serving. Sprinkle with finely chopped chives and serve.

Serves 6.

PHOTOGRAPH   PAGE 192

Crab and Avocado Supreme

A sumptuous luncheon dish to impress your friends.

1 egg yolk
1/2 teaspoon salt
pinch cayenne pepper
1 tablespoon tarragon vinegar
1/3 cup oil
1/4 teaspoon Tabasco sauce
1 teaspoon Worcestershire sauce
1/2 teaspoon lemon juice
1/2 cup cream, whipped

1/2 cup finely chopped capsicum
1/2 cup finely chopped shallots
1 x 170g (5oz) can* crabmeat, drained
1 avocado, peeled, sliced
1/4 cup finely chopped ham
1 clove garlic, crushed
1/4 cup chopped parsley

Combine egg yolk, salt, cayenne pepper and vinegar in a blender. Whisk together oil, Tabasco sauce and Worcestershire sauce and gradually add to egg mixture. Blend until thickened. Fold in lemon juice, cream, capsicum, shallots and crabmeat. Spoon mixture into four ramekins and arrange avocado on top. Combine ham, garlic and parsley and sprinkle over ramekins. Serve garnished with twists of lemon.

Serves 4.

*nearest equivalent can size.

FRENCH DRESSING (RECIPE PAGE 186)

THE TROPICAL CAPITAL, DARWIN, NORTHERN TERRITORY

SKINDIVING ON THE GREAT BARRIER REEF IN QUEENSLAND

Prawn Parcels

Delicious served as an entree or with cool summer drinks.

2 sheets frozen ready rolled puff
pastry, thawed
8 large green prawns, deveined,
butterflied
¾ cup desiccated coconut

¾ cup breadcrumbs
¼ cup chopped chives
lemon juice to moisten
seasoning to taste

Cut each sheet of pastry into four squares, place a prawn in the centre of each one. Combine the coconut, breadcrumbs, chives, lemon juice and seasoning and spread some of this mixture over each prawn. Fold prawn over to re-shape, moisten the edges of the pastry and fold to completely encase the prawn. Make an "X" on the top of each pastry parcel. Place on a baking sheet and bake at 180°C (350°F) for approximately 10 minutes or until cooked and golden.   Serves 8.

Prawns in Curried Coconut Sauce

¼ cup desiccated coconut
¾ cup milk
1 onion
1 clove garlic, crushed
1 teaspoon finely chopped root ginger
1 tablespoon curry powder
1 tablespoon butter or margarine

1 tomato, peeled, chopped
1 teaspoon salt
500g (1lb) cooked prawns, shelled
1 tablespoon chopped fresh mint
2 teaspoons cornflour blended in a
little cold milk

Simmer coconut in milk, then blend in a blender. Combine onion, garlic, ginger, curry powder and butter in a saucepan and cook 2 minutes over a low heat. Add tomato, salt, coconut milk, prawns and mint and heat. Add blended cornflour and stir over heat to thicken. Serve with boiled rice.   Serves 4.

Seafood Sauce

¼ cup mayonnaise
2 teaspoons tomato sauce
¼ cup cream

seasoning to taste
1 teaspoon Worcestershire sauce

Blend all ingredients together to make a smooth sauce.   Serves 2.

Pork Saute

2 tablespoons butter or margarine
500g (1lb) pork fillet, cut into strips
1 cup chopped shallots
1 cup strained fresh orange juice

½ cup green ginger wine
1 tablespoon cornflour
1 cup thinly sliced celery
¼ cup almond halves

Melt the butter in a heavy based frying pan. Saute pork and shallots for 5 minutes. Stir in orange juice. Cover and simmer for a further 5 minutes then blend in the ginger wine and cornflour. Stir until boiling then add celery and almonds and cook for 2-3 minutes. Spoon into serving dish and serve garnished with a few strips of orange rind.   Serves 4.

Sesame Seafood Nuggets

500g (1lb) fish fillets, skinned
2 tablespoons sesame seeds, toasted
1½ cups breadcrumbs
seasoned flour

2 eggs, beaten
125g (4oz) butter or margarine
4 cloves garlic, crushed
1 bay leaf, crumbled

Cut fish into bite-size pieces. Combine sesame seeds with breadcrumbs. Crumb fish pieces by tossing lightly in flour, dipping in egg, then finally tossing in sesame crumbs. Heat butter in a frying pan with garlic and bay leaf. Add fish and cook until crisp and golden. Drain and serve piled into a napkin lined basket.   Serves 4.

CRAB FISHERMAN, TOWNSVILLE QUEENSLAND

BEETROOT WITH SOUR CREAM AND CHIVES (RECIPE PAGE 186)

PINEAPPLE AND CHICKEN SALAD (RECIPE PAGE 181)

SPECTACULAR WINDSURFING AT MANLY BEACH, SYDNEY, NEW SOUTH WALES

Crunchy Salmon Logs

Delicious served on savoury biscuits for a summertime snack.

250g (8oz) cream cheese
¼ cup mayonnaise
2 teaspoons tomato paste
3 teaspoons Worcestershire sauce
¼ teaspoon Tabasco sauce
seasoning to taste
1 x 220g (7oz) can* red salmon,
drained, flaked

¾ cup fresh wholemeal breadcrumbs
½ cup toasted flaked almonds
1 tablespoon finely chopped onion
1 tablespoon chopped parsley

Beat the first six ingredients in a bowl until smooth and creamy, stir in the salmon and breadcrumbs. Refrigerate until mixture is firm. Combine the almonds, onion and parsley. Mould the salmon mixture into four even sized logs, wrap in plastic wrap and chill. When firm unwrap and roll in the breadcrumb mixture. Serve with biscuit crackers.
*nearest equivalent can size.

Pineapple and Chicken Salad

Chicken and fruit make an excellent combination for a summer salad.

1 pineapple
1 large cooked chicken
small nob root ginger, grated
1 small onion, sliced

1 red capsicum, sliced
¼ cup grapes
¼ cup chopped parsley
herbed French dressing

Slice pineapple in half lengthwise and carefully remove flesh taking care not to cut through the skin. Cut flesh into cubes. Bone chicken and cut flesh into bite-size pieces. Combine the ginger with the onion, capsicum, grapes and parsley and gently stir in the chicken. Spoon back into the pineapple shells, sprinkle with dressing and serve well chilled.   Serves 6.

PHOTOGRAPH   PAGES 178-179

Tropical Noodle Chicken

30g (1oz) butter or margarine
1kg (2lb) chicken portions
1 packet chicken noodle soup
1 x 425g (10oz) can* lychees,
undrained

1 x 425g (10oz) can* crushed
pineapple, undrained
1 tablespoon soy sauce
1 tablespoon cornflour
½ cup water

Melt the butter in a frying pan and saute the chicken pieces until brown; transfer to a casserole dish. Combine the soup mix, lychees, pineapple and soy sauce and pour over the chicken. Bake at 180°C (350°F) for approximately 20 minutes or until chicken is cooked. Combine the cornflour with the water, stir into the casserole and cook a further 15-20 minutes.   Serves 4.
*nearest equivalent can size.

Smoked Turkey and Melon with Pernod Dressing

Pernod Dressing
3 egg yolks
½ teaspoon salt
¼ teaspoon cayenne pepper
1½ cups oil
½ mango, peeled, sliced

2 tablespoons Pernod
For Serving
watercress
24 thin slices honeydew melon
24 slices smoked turkey breast

Make the Pernod Dressing by dropping the egg yolks into a food processor or blender with the salt and pepper. Process for 30 seconds and then add the oil in a continuous stream until a smooth consistency is obtained. Add the mango and Pernod and when smooth pour into a bowl and refrigerate. Alternate slices of melon and turkey on a serving platter and serve with the dressing.
Serves 6-8.

THE PINNACLES DESERT REGION, WESTERN AUSTRALIA

Avocado Turkey Salad with Kiwi Fruit Dressing

1 kiwi fruit, pureed
1 teaspoon curry powder
1 teaspoon mayonnaise
500g (1lb) smoked turkey breast,
sliced

2-3 medium ripe avocados, peeled,
sliced
6 sprigs of dill
kiwi fruit slices for garnish

Stir the kiwi fruit puree, and curry powder into the mayonnaise, mix well and refrigerate. Arrange the turkey breast and avocado slices alternately on a serving plate. Serve with the kiwi fruit mayonnaise and garnish with sprigs of dill and slices of kiwi fruit.
Serves 6.
PHOTOGRAPH   PAGE 188

Avocado with Prawn Filling

1 tablespoon finely chopped green
capsicum
1 tablespoon finely chopped red
capsicum
seasoning to taste
dash Tabasco sauce

1 quantity seafood sauce — (see recipe
2 avocados   page 117)
juice ½ lemon
125g (4oz) prawns, shelled, deveined
lemon slices
parsley

Stir capsicum, seasoning and Tabasco into seafood sauce. Halve and stone avocados and brush with lemon juice. Arrange prawns in the centre of each avocado, spooning some of the seafood sauce over the top. Serve garnished with lemon and parsley.
Serves 2-4

Island Fish Kebabs

8 small white fish fillets
4 firm bananas
1-2 teaspoons curry powder
¼ teaspoon nutmeg

1 x 170g (5oz) can* evaporated milk
2 tablespoons lemon juice
seasoning to taste

Peel the bananas and cut each into four. Thread two fish fillets and four pieces of banana onto skewers and place in a shallow dish. Combine the remaining ingredients and pour over the kebabs. Refrigerate for 1 hour. Grill kebabs, basting them with the marinade during cooking and serve with boiled rice and tossed green salad.   Serves 4.
*nearest equivalent can size

Tropical Kebabs

Sauce
3 tablespoons tomato sauce
1 tablespoon Worcestershire sauce
3 tablespoons Hoi Sin sauce
1 tablespoon lemon juice
2 tablespoons pineapple ji
1 onion, quartered

1 x 450g (16oz) can* ham, cubed
1 medium pineapple, cubed
250g (8oz) button mushrooms
1 green capsicum, de-seeded, quartered
1 red capsicum, de-seeded, quartered

Combine all the sauce ingredients together in a jug. Alternate onion, ham, pineapple, mushrooms and capsicums onto presoaked skewers, allowing approximately 2 skewers per person. Baste the kebabs with the sauce and barbecue; continue basting during cooking. Serve on a bed of rice, garnished with parsley.
*nearest equivalent can size   Serves 6.

Green and Gold Salad

A very colourful and refreshing salad.

2 avocados
2 teaspoons lemon juice
2 oranges
2 grapefruit

2 tablespoons oil
1 tablespoon vinegar
seasoning to taste
lettuce leaves, for serving

Cut avocados in half and carefully remove the seed. Sprinkle the cut surface with lemon juice to avoid discolouration. Remove skin and pith from the oranges and grapefruit and carefully segment. Mix the two fruits together with oil, vinegar and seasoning. Pile into avocados and chill for 1 hour. Serve on a bed of lettuce.
                                                      Serves 2-4.

Sunshine Pasta Salad

A refreshing colourful summer salad which takes only minutes to prepare.

1½ cups cooked macaroni
1 cup sliced green beans
½ red capsicum, finely sliced
½ cup celery, finely sliced

¼ cup chopped walnuts
¼ cup chopped shallots
4 tablespoons mayonnaise
shredded lettuce for serving

Combine all the ingredients in a large salad bowl and toss thoroughly. Chill until required. Serve on a bed of shredded lettuce.   Serves 2.

PHOTOGRAPH   PAGE 186

Meat Salad

750g (1½lb) assorted sliced meats, or salami
1 red capsicum, sliced

1 green capsicum, sliced
2 onions, sliced
¼ cup black olives

Place the sliced meat in a salad bowl and add the capsicums, onions and olives. Toss to combine and serve with French dressing or mayonnaise.   Serves 6.

Pork and Melon Salad

Leftover pork makes a tasty addition to a salad.

500g (1lb) cooked pork, finely shredded
250g (8oz) rockmelon, diced
250g (8oz) honeydew melon, diced
½ cup sliced celery
¼ cup chopped shallots
½ tablespoon curry powder

seasoning to taste
2 tablespoons Dry Vermouth
1 cup mayonnaise
For Garnish
slices of melon
lemon twists
alfalfa sprouts

Combine all the ingredients together with the exception of the mayonnaise and vermouth. Stir the vermouth into the mayonnaise and pour over the combined ingredients, toss together and leave 10 minutes prior to serving. Serve spooned into individual dishes and garnish with a slice of melon, twists of lemon and alfalfa sprouts.   Serves 6.

Pear and Avocado Salad

The delicate flavour of pears and avocados combine beautifully together.

⅓ cup oil
⅔ cup lemon juice
seasoning to taste

1 clove garlic, crushed
3 pears peeled, diced
3 avocados, peeled, diced

Make the dressing by combining the oil, lemon juice, seasoning and garlic. Carefully toss the pears and avocados in the dressing and spoon into lettuce cups to serve.   Serves 6.

Tossed Mixed Salad

1 lettuce
3 tomatoes
½ cucumber
1 onion, sliced
8 radishes, sliced

125g (4oz) button mushrooms
1 capsicum, sliced
3 sticks celery, sliced
French dressing

Wash and dry lettuce leaves and tear into bite-size pieces. Place into a large salad bowl with tomatoes cut into wedges. Score unpeeled cucumber with a fork and slice. Combine cucumber, onion, radishes, mushrooms, capsicum and celery in the bowl. Toss in French dressing and serve.   Serves 6-8.

Minted Orange and Pineapple Salad

A tangy mint dressing to accompany chilled fresh fruit.

6 oranges, peeled, halved, seeds removed
½ pineapple, peeled, cored, quartered

¼ cup mint leaves, chopped
2 teaspoons sugar
⅓ cup malt vinegar
2 tablespoons water

Slice the oranges and the pineapple into a serving bowl and chill. Combine the mint, sugar, vinegar and water together in a blender until smooth. Pour dressing over oranges, toss and serve.
                                                    Serves 8-10.

Savoury Rice Mould

¼ cup raisins, chopped
1 green capsicum, de-seeded, chopped
¼ cup parsley, chopped
¼ cup walnuts, roughly chopped
¾ cup canned pineapple pieces, drained, chopped

1 red apple, cored, chopped
1¼ cups long grain rice, cooked
½ cup oil
½ cup vinegar
2 teaspoons curry powder

Combine raisins, capsicum, parsley, walnuts, fruit and rice. Stir in the combined oil, vinegar and curry powder. Press mixture into a 20cm (8") ring mould and refrigerate for several hours. Unmould on to a plate, cut into wedges to serve.   Serves 6-8.

GREEN ISLAND ON THE GREAT BARRIER REEF, QUEENSLAND

CLOCKWISE: SPICED WINE PEARS (RECIPE PAGE 193) TOP LEFT; JAMAICAN BANANAS (RECIPE PAGE 195) BOTTOM LEFT

KIRSCH PINEAPPLE (RECIPE PAGE 193) TOP RIGHT; RICH CHOCOLATE CHEESE CAKE (RECIPE PAGE 270) BOTTOM RIGHT;

Beetroot with Sour Cream and Chives

This dish may be served hot as a vegetable accompaniment or cold as a salad.

4 *beetroot*
½ *cup sour cream*
2 *teaspoons lemon juice*

1 *teaspoon sugar*
seasoning to taste
8 *chives, chopped*

Cook whole beetroot in boiling salted water until tender, approximately 1 hour. Drain, cool and skin. Slice the beetroot into thin strips, place into a bowl and chill. Combine the sour cream, lemon juice, sugar and seasoning in a bowl. To serve, spoon sour cream mixture over beetroot and sprinkle with chives.   Serves 6.

Vegetable Cheese Pie

90g (3oz) *butter, melted*
1½ *cups cracker biscuit crumbs*
2 *eggs, lightly beaten*
⅓ *cup milk*
seasoning to taste

½ *teaspoon ground thyme*
1 *cup grated Edam cheese*
2 *small zucchini, finely chopped*
1 *tablespoon parsley, chopped*
1 *tablespoon Parmesan cheese*

Combine the melted butter and biscuit crumbs; press onto the base and sides of a 23cm (9") pie dish, chill until firm. Combine the eggs, milk, seasoning and thyme. Alternate layers of Edam cheese, zucchini in the pie shell. Sprinkle with parsley and pour over the liquid. Top with Parmesan cheese and bake at 180°C (350°F) oven for 20-25 minutes.   Serves 4-6.

French Dressing

3 *tablespoons white vinegar*
2 *tablespoons oil*
¼ *teaspoon powdered mustard*
¼ *teaspoon sugar*

1 *tablespoon chopped parsley*
½ *clove garlic*
seasoning to taste

Blend ingredients together in a food processor and use as desired.

PHOTOGRAPH   PAGE 174

Creamy Blue Cheese Dressing

This tangy dressing is delicious served with a crisp green salad.

6 *chives*
¼ *cup sour cream*
125g (4oz) *blue vein cheese*
2 *tablespoons mayonnaise*

3 *tablespoons milk*
½ *teaspoon prepared English mustard*
1 *teaspoon lemon juice*
seasoning to taste

Blend all the ingredients in a food processor until smooth and creamy.   Serve chilled.

Mayonnaise

A light fluffy dressing for all summer salads.

2 *egg yolks*
1 *tablespoon vinegar*
seasoning to taste

pinch dry mustard
1¼ *cups olive oil*

Beat the egg yolks, vinegar, seasoning, mustard together for 30 seconds. Add the oil in a continual stream until all the ingredients are combined. Serve chilled.

SUNSHINE PASTA SALAD (RECIPE PAGE 182)

PINEAPPLE AND CREME DE MENTHE SORBET (RECIPE PAGE 188)

LIME DAIQUIRI (RECIPE PAGE 195) LEFT; GRAND MARNIER COCKTAIL (RECIPE PAGE 195)

Strawberry and Orange Freeze

A delicious summertime dessert, making excellent use of fresh summer fruits.

3 teaspoons gelatine
¾ cup cold water
2 cups strawberries, hulled

4 oranges, peeled, sliced
sugar to taste

Sprinkle gelatine over water in a small saucepan and soften. Heat slowly, stirring constantly, until gelatine dissolves. Place the strawberries and oranges in a blender or food processor and blend until smooth. Add sugar, if desired, then combine with the gelatine mixture. Pour into an ice cube tray or shallow baking dish and freeze for 1½ hours, or until almost frozen. Remove from the freezer, place into a bowl and beat until fluffy. Re-freeze for a further 2 hours or until firm. Decorate with orange slices and strawberries.   Serves 6.

PHOTOGRAPH   PAGE 189

Fruit Salad Ice Cream

½ small pineapple, finely chopped
2 bananas, mashed
6-8 cherries, pitted, chopped
¾ cup orange juice
2 tablespoons lemon juice
¾ cup sugar
2 teaspoons gelatine

¼ cup water
2 cups cream, whipped
½ cup evaporated milk, chilled
overnight, whipped
1 teaspoon vanilla essence
4 passionfruit

Combine the fruits in a large bowl and stir in the fruit juices. Dissolve the sugar and gelatine in the water, in a saucepan over a low heat, allow to cool, then stir into the fruit. Combine the cream, evaporated milk, vanilla and passionfruit pulp, stir through the fruit and transfer to a 2 litre (½ gal) ice cream container and freeze. When semi-frozen, stir with a fork and re-freeze.   Serves 6.

AVOCADO TURKEY SALAD WITH KIWI FRUIT DRESSING (RECIPE PAGE 181)

Strawberry Cream Freeze

2 eggs, separated
¼ cup caster sugar
3 teaspoons gelatine
¼ cup hot water

2 tablespoons strawberry jam
1 cup, lightly whipped, cream
250g (8oz) strawberries, hulled

Combine egg yolks and sugar and beat until thick and creamy. Dissolve the gelatine in hot water and while still hot add to the egg and sugar mixture, beating until well combined. Stir the egg mixture and the strawberry jam into the cream. Whip the egg whites stiffly, fold into the mixture and spoon into a dish ready for freezing. Roughly chop the strawberries and swirl into the mixture. Freeze overnight and serve sliced with wafers.

PHOTOGRAPH   PAGE   194   Serves 6-8.

Pineapple & Creme De Menthe Sorbet

A brandy snap or sweet biscuit can be served with this dessert.

470g (15oz) can* pineapple, drained
1 tablespoon Creme de Menthe

1 tablespoon caster sugar
8 ice cubes

Place all ingredients with the exception of the ice cubes into a blender and blend until smooth. With motor running, remove cover and add ice cubes one at a time. Continue blending until the mixture is smooth. Pour into an ice-cream tray and freeze. Allow to soften slightly and serve in parfait glasses decorated with a mint leaf.   Serves 4.

*nearest equivalent can size.

PHOTOGRAPH   PAGE 187

STRAWBERRY & ORANGE FREEZE (RECIPE PAGE 188)

PORT DOUGLAS BEACH, MARLIN COAST, GATEWAY TO THE GREAT BARRIER REEF, QUEENSLAND

CHILLED MELON SOUP (RECIPE PAGE 174)

MACERATED FRUITS (RECIPE PAGE 195)

Vanilla Ice Cream

1 x 400g (13oz) can* condensed milk   pinch salt
1 cup water   1 cup whipped cream
2 teaspoons vanilla essence

Combine the condensed milk, water, vanilla and salt in a food processor; fold in the cream and transfer to a 1 litre (¼ gal) ice cream container; freeze until almost set. Return mixture to food processor to break down any ice which may have formed in the mixture. Re-freeze until required.   Serves 6.
*Nearest equivalent can size.

Rockmelon Mousse

This looks very attractive decorated with whipped cream and extra rockmelon balls.

1 medium rockmelon, cubed   2 tablespoons orange juice
3 teaspoons gelatine   ½ cup whipped cream
2 tablespoons boiling water   2 passionfruit

Puree the rockmelon in a food processor. Transfer to a bowl. Dissolve gelatine in boiling water, cool and add to rockmelon together with orange juice. Fold in the cream and passionfruit. Pour into one large serving dish or individual glasses. Refrigerate until set.   Serves 4-6.

Spiced Wine Pears

A very popular and elegant way to serve pears.

1 cup water   1 stick cinnamon
1 cup red wine   1 teaspoon whole allspice
2 tablespoons lemon juice   4-5 firm pears, peeled, stalks attached
1 cup sugar

Combine the water, red wine, lemon juice, sugar and spices in a saucepan and bring to the boil. Reduce heat and simmer gently for 5 minutes. Place the pears in an ovenproof dish, pour over the syrup and gently poach at 150°C (300°F) for approximately 20-25 minutes or until tender then pour a little of the syrup into the base of dessert glasses and place in the pears. Serve with whipped cream.   Serves 4.

PHOTOGRAPH   PAGE 184-185

Cointreau Ice Cream

3 eggs separated   2 tablespoons water
½ cup caster sugar   1⅓ cups cream, whipped
2 tablespoons Cointreau

Beat the egg yolks with the sugar, Cointreau and water in a double saucepan over simmering water until light and fluffy. Cool. Beat the egg whites until stiff. Fold into the Cointreau mixture with the cream and pour into a 20cm (8") square cake tin. Place in the freezer until partially set then break up the mixture gently with a fork. Re-freeze in the tin until set, about 4 hours.

Kirsch Pineapple

This is a delightful dessert which may be served hot or cold.

1 pineapple   ¾ cup caster sugar
¼ cup Kirsch   ⅓ teaspoon cream of tartar
3 egg whites   toasted coconut

Halve the pineapple lengthwise, cutting through the green top. Cut out the flesh in cubes without cutting through the skins. Macerate the pineapple cubes with the Kirsch in a shallow dish for 1 hour. Beat the egg whites until stiff, gradually adding the sugar and cream of tartar. Place the pineapple back in the shell and pipe over the meringue, sprinkle with the toasted coconut. Bake at 180°C (350°F) for approximately 10 minutes or until golden, serve at once.   Serves 6.

PHOTOGRAPH   PAGE 184-185

Poached Nectarines with Apricot Brandy Sauce

A rich delicious dessert.

12 medium nectarines, peeled   1 tablespoon wine
½ cup sugar   2 tablespoons Apricot Brandy
3 egg yolks

Poach the nectarines with ¼ cup sugar and sufficient water to cover. Make the sauce by combining the egg yolks, remaining sugar, wine and Apricot Brandy in the top of a double saucepan. Whisk over a medium heat until thick and frothy. Spoon over the nectarines and serve.   Serves 6.

FLAMBE FRUITS (RECIPE PAGE 195)

STRAWBERRY CREAM FREEZE (RECIPE PAGE 188)

Glazed Oranges

A splendid dessert for a hot summers day.

6 large oranges
3 tablespoons mandarin or orange liqueur
1½ cups sugar
½ cup water

Peel the oranges and cut the skin into julienne strips. Simmer in water for 10 minutes or until tender. Drain and dry on absorbent paper. Transfer to a small bowl and macerate in the liqueur. Remove pith from the oranges, cut a slice from one end so they will stand and arrange in a serving dish. Boil the sugar and water in a saucepan until a firm ball stage is reached. 120°C (250°F) using a jam thermometer. Add 3 tablespoons of the syrup to the orange peel and slowly glaze the oranges with the remaining syrup using a tablespoon at a time. Chill for several hours. Spoon the orange peel and marinade over the oranges and serve with whipped cream. *Serves 6.*

Lime Daiquiri

Daiquiris of all flavours can be made using the fruits of summer.

8 ice cubes
1 tablespoon rum
¼ cup lime juice
a little sugar, if required

Place all the ingredients into a blender and process until thick and frothy. Pour into a goblet and serve. *Serves 1.*

PHOTOGRAPH   PAGE 187

Banana Smoothie

1 banana
½ cup buttermilk or yoghurt
½ cup orange juice
1 tablespoon honey
1 tablespoon Amaretto
⅔ cup finely crushed ice

Blend all ingredients together in a food processor and pour into a tall milk shake glass. Serve with straws. *Serves 1.*

Island Pineapple Cocktail

1½ tablespoons white rum
1½ tablespoons Advokat
½ cup unsweetened pineapple juice
1 cup crushed ice

Shake all the ingredients together and strain into a chilled wine goblet. Garnish with spear of pineapple. *Serves 1.*

Iced Coffee Souffles

A rich, mouth-watering dessert.

60g (2oz) cooking chocolate, grated
1 tablespoon water
3 tablespoons Tia Maria
4 eggs, separated
2 tablespoons instant coffee
½ cup caster sugar
1¼ cups cream, whipped
1 teaspoon cocoa
1 tablespoon icing sugar

Melt the chocolate in the water with Tia Maria and allow to cool. Stiffly beat the egg whites, then beat the egg yolks, coffee and sugar together until well combined. Stir in the chocolate and fold in the egg whites and the cream. Spoon into individual serving dishes and refrigerate for at least 4 hours. Mix cocoa and icing sugar together. Sprinkle over each souffle before serving. *Serves 6.*

Grand Marnier Cocktail

8 ice cubes
4 tablespoons Grand Marnier
juice 8 oranges

Place 2 ice cubes in each glass, add 1 tablespoon of Grand Marnier and top up with orange juice. Decorate with a twist of orange and serve. *Serves 4.*

PHOTOGRAPH   PAGE 187

Macerated Fruits

1 cup port
2 teaspoons lemon juice
2 teaspoons sugar
3 bananas, sliced
1 cup strawberries, sliced
2 kiwi fruit, sliced
1 apple, sliced
½ pineapple, peeled, cored, sliced
1 pear, peeled, sliced

Combine the port, lemon juice and sugar together and pour over the fruit, cover and chill until required. Serve with delicate crisp biscuits. *Serves 6.*

PHOTOGRAPH   PAGE 193

Flambé Fruits

60g (2oz) butter
½ cup castor sugar
1 x 425g (13oz) can* peach halves, drained, syrup reserved
3 medium pears, peeled, thickly sliced
1 punnet strawberries, hulled
¼ cup Cognac

Melt butter in large frying pan. Stir in sugar, allow to dissolve then add ½ cup reserved peach syrup. Stir until boiling, then add pears, peaches and strawberries; allow to heat through. Heat the Cognac in a small pan or ladle, ignite and pour over the fruits. Serve immediately with scoops of ice cream or whipped cream. *Nearest equivalent can size. *Serves 6.*

Variations

Cherries. . . Use 2 x 425g (13oz) cans* pitted cherries. Add the syrup, substitute Maraschino liqueur instead of Cognac. Pineapple and Orange. . . Use 3 medium, peeled, sliced oranges and 1 x 425g (13oz) can* pineapple rings. Add the syrup, substitute Kirsch liqueur instead of the Cognac.

PHOTOGRAPH   PAGE 194

Choc-Raisin Ice Cream Crepe

2 litre (½gal) vanilla ice cream
2 tablespoons raisins
4 tablespoons chocolate peppermint liqueur
½ cup grated chocolate
2 tablespoons unsalted butter
¼ cup Tia Maria
6 crepes

Allow the ice cream to soften a little, then stir in the raisins and the liqueur. Re-freeze. Melt the chocolate, butter and Tia Maria in the top of a double saucepan over medium heat. Stir until all the ingredients are combined. Spoon some of the ice cream into the centre of each crepe; roll and place on a serving plate; coat with the chocolate sauce and serve immediately. *Serves 6.*

Jamaican Bananas

60g (2oz) dried apricots, finely chopped
½ cup orange juice
2 tablespoons dark rum
60g (2oz) butter or margarine
4 tablespoons soft brown sugar
4 bananas, diagonally sliced
Maraschino cherries

Macerate the apricots in the orange juice and rum for 2 hours. Melt the butter and sugar in a saucepan, add the apricots with their juice and the bananas and cook until heated through. Place into serving dishes and garnish with cherries. Serve warm. *Serves 4.*

PHOTOGRAPH   PAGE 184-185

Tropical Tea

A refreshing drink for the tropics.

4 cups orange juice
4 tea bags
¼ cup lemon juice
3 pieces cinnamon stick
8 whole cloves
dash ground nutmeg
4 lemon slices for garnish

Bring orange juice to the boil in a saucepan. Remove from heat and add all other ingredients with the exception of the lemon slices. Cover and let steep 5 minutes or until desired strength. Remove tea bags. Allow to cool then chill. Strain and serve in small goblets garnished with lemon. *Serves 6-8.*

FAMOUS TIAPUKAI ABORIGINAL DANCE GROUP IN TRADITIONAL DREAMTIME COLOURS, BLOWING THE DIDGERIDOO, QUEENSLAND

The Australian way of

THE MIGRANT VARIETIES

Around the World in 41 Recipes.

On the streets of many Australian cities, you're as likely to hear "buon giorno", "marhaba", "kalimera", or "zdravo" as you are a "G'day". Australia has become a great melting pot.

One of the benefits of our multi-national society is that our food is tastier and more interesting. Thousands of first generation Italians, Greeks, Yugoslavians, Chinese, Lebanese, Dutch, Maltese, Turkish and Hungarians have given our taste buds a new lease on life.

Typical Aussie "tucker" is no longer the meat pie, sausage roll and counter lunch at the local pub.

With cosmopolitan restaurants, delicatessens, take-away food bars, supermarkets, patisseries and open air markets you can get "stuck into" just about any kind of food you'd want.

Experimenting with international recipes in Australia is enjoyable because we have an abundance of meat, vegetables, produce, herbs and spices — any food or ingredient you need.

International dishes have become a part of our weekly menu. The following pages will give you some of our favourites and take you 'round the world in 41 recipes.

A RAPIDLY GROWING COSMOPOLITAN COUNTRY, ''AUSTRALIA''

Chicken & Oatmeal Soup

1 small chicken
8 cups chicken stock
2 carrots, roughly chopped
1 parsnip, roughly chopped
2 onions, roughly chopped
2 sticks celery, sliced
¼ cup chopped parsley
seasoning to taste
1 packet chicken noodle soup
¼ cup coarse oatmeal

Place the chicken in a saucepan with the stock and simmer over a low heat for 2-3 hours. Transfer to a bowl, allow to cool and refrigerate overnight. Skim off fat, remove skin and bone from chicken, and chop the flesh. Place the jellied stock, and chicken with all the remaining ingredients in a large saucepan and simmer until the vegetables are tender, approximately 1 hour. Serve in deep soup bowls with crusty bread.   Serves 10.

"THE WONDER OF SPICES" FROM PARAM'S INDIAN RESTAURANT, WOOLLAHRA, NEW SOUTH WALES

French Onion Soup

30g (1oz) butter or margarine
6 onions, sliced
6 cups beef stock
430g (14oz) can* beef consomme
pepper to taste
½ cup grated cheese

Melt butter in a saucepan, add onions and cook over a medium heat until tender and lightly browned. Add stock, beef consomme and pepper. Bring to the boil and simmer for 20 minutes. Serve hot, sprinkled with cheese.   Serves 6-8.
*nearest equivalent can size.

PHOTOGRAPH   PAGE 213

Rich Tomato Sauce

1 tablespoon oil
2 onions, finely chopped
3 cloves garlic, crushed
1 x 475g (16oz) can* tomatoes, coarsely chopped
¼ cup tomato paste
¼ cup red wine
1 teaspoon oregano
½ teaspoon basil
1 bay leaf
2 teaspoons sugar
seasoning to taste

Heat oil and saute onion until tender. Add garlic and cook for 1-2 minutes. Add tomatoes with their liquid and remaining sauce ingredients. Bring to the boil and then simmer uncovered for 1 hour, stirring occasionally. Remove bay leaf and adjust seasonings to taste. The sauce should be smooth and thick when cooked. When cool, sauce can be kept in refrigerator until required.
*nearest equivalent can size.

Gazpacho

The name gazpacho is derived from the Arabic for "soaked bread". Gazpacho is made throughout Spain, with variations in different regions.

1 cucumber, peeled, seeded, chopped
4 tomatoes, skinned, chopped
2 onions, chopped
1 green capsicum, chopped
2 cloves garlic, crushed
3 cups water
4 tablespoons red wine vinegar
2 teaspoons salt
2 tablespoons olive oil
2 cups bread crumbs, crust removed
Garnishes
chopped cucumber, onions, capsicum and hard boiled egg

Combine ingredients in a food processor until smooth. It may be necessary to process in two batches. Refrigerate for 2 hours and serve with garnishes.   Serves 4.

Brodetta

Brodetta is a very good accompaniment for Australian barbecue meals.

3 tomatoes, sliced
The Sauce
2 tablespoons cornflour
2 cups milk
1 tablespoon chopped basil
90g (3oz) grated tasty cheese
1 cup breadcrumbs

Grease a shallow ovenproof baking dish and arrange tomato slices over the base. Blend cornflour with a little milk, pour into a saucepan with the remaining milk, and basil. Bring to the boil and cook for 1 minute, stirring constantly. Remove from the heat and add three-quarters of the cheese. Pour over the tomatoes and sprinkle with breadcrumbs. Top with remaining cheese and bake at 200°C (400°F) for 10 minutes or until heated through and browned.   Serves 3.

PHOTOGRAPH   PAGE 208

Spinach Triangles

2 tablespoons butter or margarine
1 x 250g (8oz) packet frozen spinach, thawed
3 onions, finely chopped
¼ cup finely chopped shallots
3 eggs, beaten
250g (8oz) Feta cheese, chopped
2 teaspoons nutmeg
seasoning to taste
15 sheets filo pastry
125g (4oz) butter or margarine, melted

Melt butter, saute spinach, onions and shallots, remove from the heat. Add eggs, cheese, nutmeg, and seasoning, beating well until combined. Divide pastry in half lengthwise, then fold each sheet again in half, lengthwise and brush with melted butter. Place a tablespoon of filling on end of strip of pastry. Fold corner of pastry over filling to from a triangle. Continue to fold pastry over in triangles to the end. Repeat with remaining pastry and filling. Place onto a baking sheet, brush with butter and bake at 190°C (375°F) for 20-25 minutes, or until cooked. Makes 30 triangles.

CHICKEN & HAM CANNELLONI (RECIPE PAGE 207)

Borsch

A rich red coloured soup, made from beetroot, is the classic soup of Russia and Poland and is always served with sour cream.

10 *cups beef stock*
4 *beetroots, peeled, sliced*
2 *potatoes, finely chopped*
1 *large onion, finely chopped*
1 *clove garlic, crushed*

1 *tablespoon lemon juice*
freshly ground pepper
sour cream
chopped chives

Bring stock to the boil, add prepared vegetables and simmer 45 minutes or until beetroot is tender. Add lemon juice and pepper. Serve soup topped with a spoonful of sour cream and chives.
Serves 6-8.

Braised Fennel

A delicious vegetable with a delicate aniseed flavour which is often served as an accompaniment to fish.

4 *fennel bulbs, quartered*
2 *tablespoons olive oil*
1 *clove garlic, crushed*

freshly ground black pepper
2 *tablespoons tomato paste*
1 *cup white wine*

Wash and drain fennel and saute in the oil with the garlic, approximately 10 minutes. Season. Blend the tomato paste with the wine and pour over the fennel. Cover and simmer 15 minutes or until tender.
Serves 4.

"JAPANESE FESTIVAL", CHINATOWN, SYDNEY, NEW SOUTH WALES

Sauerkraut

2 *onions, chopped*
2 *tablespoons pork fat*
2 x 430g (14oz) *cans* sauerkraut, drained*
2 *cups apple, peeled, sliced*
1 x 430g (14oz) *can* beef consomme*

2 *tablespoons vinegar*
1 *tablespoon flour*
2 *tablespoons water*
1 *potato, grated*
pinch caraway seeds

Saute onion in a large frying pan with the pork fat until golden. Add sauerkraut, apples, consomme and vinegar and simmer uncovered for 15 minutes. Blend flour with water until smooth, then stir into the sauerkraut with the potato and caraway seeds. Cook over moderate heat, stirring until slightly thickened and potato has cooked.
Serves 4-6.
*nearest eqivalent can size.

Taboulleh

A very popular dish from the Middle East. The burghul gives a delicious nutty flavour and the dish is excellent served with pita bread.

½ *cup burghul (cracked wheat)*
1½ *cups chopped tomatoes*
¾ *cup finely chopped shallots*
1½ *cups chopped parsley*

1 *teaspoon salt*
⅓ *cup olive oil*
⅓ *cup lemon juice*
2 *tablespoons chopped fresh mint*

Soak burghul in luke warm water for 1 hour. Drain and spread on paper towel to dry. Combine burghul with tomatoes, shallots, parsley and salt. Whisk together oil, lemon juice and mint and combine the two mixtures. Refrigerate until well chilled and serve on a bed of lettuce.
Serves 4.

DOLMADES (RECIPE THIS PAGE)

COTTAGE PIE (RECIPE PAGE 212)

Dolmades

Dolmades-stuffed vine leaves are very popular throughout the Middle East.

The Tomato Sauce
1 onion chopped
oil/butter for frying
1 x 440g (14oz) can* tomatoes, drained, chopped
2 teaspoons brown sugar
1 tablespoon lemon thyme
1 tablespoon tomato paste
3 tablespoons red wine
chopped parsley

Vine Leaves
16 vine leaves
oil
2 cups cooked brown rice
1 tablespoon chopped fresh herbs
1 teaspoon grated nutmeg
seasoning to taste
2 tomatoes, chopped
1 tablespoon chopped parsley
2 shallots, finely chopped

Prepare the tomato sauce by sauteeing the onion in a little oil and butter until golden brown. Add the remaining ingredients and simmer on a low heat for approximately 20 minutes, stirring occasionally. Prepare the vine leaves by pouring some boiling water over them and leaving for a few minutes until softened. Drain thoroughly and brush each one with a little oil and place in a single layer on a chopping board. Combine the remaining ingredients and divide equally between the vine leaves. Fold into neat parcels and carefully transfer to the saucepan of tomato sauce, simmer on a low heat for 30 minutes. Serve on a bed of additional brown rice with some of the tomato sauce spooned over the top. Serves 4-6.

*nearest equivalent can size.

PHOTOGRAPH THIS PAGE

Spiced Rice Croquettes

60g (2oz) butter or margarine
1 onion, finely chopped
¼ cup flour
1 tablespoon curry powder
1 cup milk
½ teaspoon salt
pinch cayenne pepper

2 cups cooked brown rice
1½ cups minced steak, cooked
seasoned flour
1 egg
1 tablespoon water
dried breadcrumbs

Melt the butter in a frying pan and saute the onion. Add the flour and curry powder and cook 1 minute then stir in the milk, salt and cayenne pepper. Bring to boil, stirring constantly, then add the rice and meat; allow to cool. Shape into croquettes and roll in seasoned flour, dip in the combined egg and water and coat with breadcrumbs. Deep fry until golden brown 2-3 minutes and serve garnished with parsley. Makes approximately 6-8.

Stuffed Eggplant

4 small eggplants, halved
250g (8oz) lamb, cubed, fat removed
1 medium onion, quartered
1 clove garlic
oil for frying
2 tomatoes, quartered

1 tablespoon tomato paste
1 teaspoon sugar
few drops Tabasco sauce
seasoning to taste
1 egg
½ cup grated cheese

Sprinkle eggplants with salt, leave for 15 minutes, then rinse and pat dry. Mince the lamb with the onion and garlic. Heat the oil in a frying pan, add meat and saute until well browned. Puree the tomatoes with the tomato paste, sugar, Tabasco sauce, and seasoning. Add half the tomato mixture to the meat with ¼ cup of water. Cover and simmer for 20 minutes. Heat oil and shallow fry eggplant, flesh side down until golden brown. Drain on paper towelling. With a spoon, scoop out flesh and combine with the meat mixture and the egg, mixing well together. Spoon into shells and arrange in a greased ovenproof dish, top with remaining tomato mixture. Sprinkle with grated cheese and bake at 180°C (350°F) for 30 minutes.
Serves 8 as an entree or 4 as a main meal.

PHOTOGRAPH PAGE 206

Italian Risotto

An Italian rice dish, usually made with thick short grained Italian rice, flavoured with numerous vegetables and served generously with Parmesan cheese.

1½ tablespoons butter or margarine
2 onions, chopped
1 cup raw rice
1 cup sliced mushrooms
2 cups chicken stock
1½ cups white wine

1 clove garlic, crushed
pinch saffron
seasoning to taste
1 bay leaf
3 tablespoons Parmesan cheese
1 tablespoon butter or margarine

Melt the butter and saute onion until tender. Stir in rice and cook for 2-3 minutes. Add mushrooms, saute lightly. Add the stock, 1 cup of wine, the garlic, saffron, seasoning and bay leaf. Simmer until rice is tender, stirring occasionally and adding the remaining wine as the rice absorbs the liquid. When rice is tender, remove from heat and adjust seasonings. Sprinkle with Parmesan cheese, dot with butter, cover pan and leave for 5 minutes. Stir lightly and serve. Serves 4.

"BLESSING OF THE FLEET" — FREMANTLE, WESTERN AUSTRALIA

STUFFED EGG PLANT (RECIPE PAGE 203)

Hot Meat Curry

The ever popular curry may be hot or mild. Served with suitable accompaniments it is a most enjoyable meal.

1kg (2lb) lean lamb or mutton chops
4 dried chillies
2 tablespoons ghee or clarified butter
1 small nob root ginger, finely chopped
3 cloves garlic, crushed

3 large onions, chopped
2 tablespoons curry powder
1 cup water
seasoning to taste
lemon juice
cooked rice

Trim and cut meat into small cubes. Soak the chillies in a little hot water for 5 minutes. Strain, then chop finely, removing the seeds. Heat the ghee and saute the meat with the ginger and garlic. Reduce heat, add the onions, curry powder, chillies and water. Cover and simmer for about 2 hours. Season and add lemon juice to taste. Serve with hot cooked rice and a selection of the following accompaniments:- chutney, sliced bananas, apples or tomatoes, dried fruits, peanuts or cashews, cucumber, coconut.

Serves 4-6.

Curried Chicken Wings

750g (1½lb) chicken wings
1 tablespoon flour
1 tablespoon mild curry powder
little butter, oil or ghee
1 onion, roughly chopped

1 cup chicken stock
seasoning to taste
250g (8oz) potatoes, cubed
3 large carrots, sliced
garnish: papadams, sliced lemon

Toss chicken wings in the combined flour and curry powder. Melt butter in a large saucepan and brown the wings with the onion. Add the stock, seasoning, potatoes and carrots. Bring to the boil, reduce heat and simmer for approximately 45 minutes or until the potatoes are tender and the chicken wings are cooked. Serve with papadams, sliced lemon and any other curry accompaniments.

PHOTOGRAPH   PAGE 215
Serves 4.

Chicken & Ham Cannelloni

Stuffed pasta shells with the richness of tomato and cheese sauces.

Filling
250g (8oz) minced chicken
125g (4oz) ham, minced
¼ cup chopped parsley
4 shallots, chopped
2 sticks celery, sliced
seasoning to taste
1 egg
Tomato Sauce
1 x 440g (14oz) can* tomatoes
2 cloves garlic, crushed

½ teaspoon basil
seasoning to taste
1 teaspoon sugar
Cheese Sauce
60g (2oz) butter or margarine
3 tablespoons flour
2 cups milk
½ cup cream
¾ cup grated cheese
For Cooking
15 cannelloni shells, pre-cooked

Combine all the filling ingredients together in a bowl. Make the tomato sauce by pureeing the undrained tomatoes with garlic. Transfer to a saucepan and add the seasonings and sugar. Simmer uncovered for 10 minutes. Make the cheese sauce by melting the butter in a saucepan. Add flour and cook for 1 minute. Gradually add milk and stir until sauce boils and thickens. Stir in cream and half of the cheese. Stir ½ cup of cheese sauce into the chicken filling and use to fill the cannelloni shells. Spoon a thin layer of tomato sauce over the base of a greased ovenproof dish, large enough to take the cannelloni in a single layer. Place cannelloni in dish and cover completely with the remaining cheese sauce. Top with the tomato sauce and sprinkle with the grated cheese. Bake at 180°C (350°F) for 40 minutes.

Serves 6.

*nearest equivalent can size.

PHOTOGRAPH   PAGE 201

Chilli Con Carne

The popular Texan dish with a Mexican flavour has become popular throughout the world.

1kg (2lb) minced steak
2 onions, finely chopped
2 cloves garlic, crushed
3 tablespoons oil
500g (1lb) tomatoes, pureed
1 cup beef stock
3 tablespoons tomato paste

2 teaspoons – 2 tablespoons chilli powder to taste
1 teaspoon cumin
¼ teaspoon oregano
seasoning to taste
1 x 450g (15oz) can* red kidney beans, drained

Combine meat with onions and garlic. Heat oil in a frying pan and saute meat over a high heat until well browned. Add tomatoes, stock, tomato paste and seasonings. Bring to the boil, reduce heat and simmer covered for 30 minutes. Rinse beans, drain and add to the meat mixture. Simmer covered for a further 30 minutes.

Serves 4-6.

*nearest eqivalent can size.

CREOLE GUMBO (RECIPE THIS PAGE)

Creole Gumbo

This is a traditional Creole dish and is a cross between a stew and a soup.

½ cup vegetable oil
1 chicken, jointed
⅓ cup flour
6 cups cold water
500g (1lb) Polish or French garlic smoked sausage, sliced
250g (8oz) lean ham steaks, cubed
2 cups chopped onions

½ cup chopped capsicum
½ cup chopped shallots
2 tablespoons chopped parsley
2 cloves garlic, crushed
1 teaspoon dried thyme
3 whole bay leaves, crumbled
seasoning to taste

Heat oil in a large saucepan and brown the chicken pieces. Remove from pan, stir in the flour and cook until lightly browned. Gradually add a little water to make a gravy. Add sausage, ham and vegetables. Return chicken to the pan with remaining water, herbs and seasoning. Cover and simmer for approximately 1 hour or until chicken and vegetables are tender. Serve in deep bowls over cooked rice.

Serves 6-8.

PHOTOGRAPH   THIS PAGE

Lasagne

One of the most popular of all the pasta dishes. The precooked lasagne sheets are now readily available making preparation time so much simpler.

The Meat Sauce	**The White Sauce**
3 tablespoons oil	2 tablespoons butter or margarine
1 onion, finely chopped	2 tablespoons flour
125g (4oz) bacon, diced	2⅓ cups milk
250g (8oz) minced steak	pinch nutmeg
¾ cup red wine	seasoning to taste
2 x 425g (13oz) cans* tomatoes,	extra butter
roughly chopped	1 cup water
⅓ cup tomato paste,	1 x 200g (16oz) lasagne noodles
diluted in 1 cup water	250g (8oz) Mozzarella cheese,
½ teaspoon basil	thinly sliced
½ teaspoon oregano	½ cup grated Parmesan cheese
1 tablespoon sugar	
seasoning to taste	

Prepare the meat sauce by heating the oil in a frying pan and sauteeing the onion until tender. Add the bacon and minced steak and continue cooking until browned. Pour in wine, tomatoes and tomato paste mixture. Bring to the boil and add the remaining ingredients. Reduce heat and simmer for approximately 1 hour. Meanwhile make the sauce in the usual way with the butter, flour and milk, add the nutmeg and season to taste. Remove from heat and set aside. Grease an ovenproof oblong dish, add the water and a layer of meat sauce. Arrange the lasagne strips slightly overlapping the mixture. Cover with the meat sauce, white sauce and Mozarella cheese. Continue layering until all the mixture has been used, ending with a layer of sauce. Sprinkle with Parmesan cheese and bake at 210°C (415°F) for 40-45 minutes. Serve garnished with parsley.   Serves 6-8.
*nearest equivalent can size.

BRODETTA (RECIPE PAGE 200)

Tacos with Chilli Beef

This is probably one of the most popular Mexican recipes and is a natural inclusion in this section.

500g (1lb) minced steak	½ teaspoon cumin
1 onion, finely chopped	seasoning to taste
1 clove garlic, crushed	1 packet taco shells
1½ tablespoons oil	¾ cup grated cheese
250g (8oz) tomatoes, pureed	2 tomatoes, roughly chopped
½ cup beef stock	4 lettuce leaves, shredded
2 tablespoons tomato paste	1 onion, roughly chopped
1 teaspoon chilli powder	

Combine meat with onion and garlic. Heat oil in a frying pan and saute meat over a high heat until meat is well browned. Add tomatoes, stock, tomato paste and seasonings. Bring to the boil, reduce heat and simmer covered for 30 minutes. Place taco shells onto a baking sheet and heat through in the oven at 180°C (350°F) for 5 minutes. Spoon some grated cheese into taco shells, top with meat, tomatoes, lettuce and onion.   Serves 6.

PHOTOGRAPH   PAGE 215

Quiche Lorraine

The most famous of all Quiches with its filling of eggs, cream and bacon.

Rich Short Crust Pastry	**Filling**
2 cups flour	3 rashers bacon, chopped
pinch salt	125g (4oz) Gruyere cheese, grated
150g (5oz) butter or margarine	3 eggs
1 egg yolk	1 cup cream
squeeze lemon juice	pepper
2 tablespoons water	nutmeg to taste
	½ teaspoon dry mustard

Make the pastry by sifting the flour and salt together into a bowl. Rub in the butter. Beat the egg yolk, lemon juice and water together and add to the dry ingredients to make a firm dough. Wrap and chill for 30 minutes. Roll out the pastry and line a 20cm (8") quiche dish. Bake blind at 220°C (440°F) for 10 minutes. Remove paper and bake for a further 3 minutes. Allow to cool. Cook bacon until crisp and drain. Sprinkle over pastry base and top with grated cheese. Combine eggs, cream and seasonings. Carefully pour into the pastry case. Bake at 190°C (375°F) for 45 minutes or until golden brown.   Serves 6-8.

Pizza

A crusty bread base and toppings of your choice covered with tomato sauce and Mozzarella cheese.

The Base	**The Topping**
1½ cups flour	prawns
½ teaspoon salt	anchovies
teaspoon sugar	pepperoni slices
1 sachet dried yeast	strips of capsicum
½ cup luke warm water	chopped onions
3 tablespoons oil	chopped bacon
1 cup Tomato and Garlic Sauce	sliced mushrooms
250g (8oz) Mozzarella cheese, grated	
2 tablespoons grated Parmesan cheese	

Sift flour into a large bowl and mix in salt, sugar and yeast. Pour water and oil into centre of dry ingredients and mix to form a dough. Turn onto a lightly floured board and knead until smooth and elastic. Cover dough and stand in a warm place to double in size for approximately 10-15 minutes. Roll dough out to fit a 25cm (10") oiled pizza plate. Spread sauce over dough, sprinkle with topping ingredients, ending with the cheese. Allow pizza to stand again in a warm place for 15 minutes. Bake at 230°C (450°F) for 15-20 minutes.

PHOTOGRAPH   PAGE 214

CREPES SUZETTE (RECIPE PAGE 220)

NATIONAL FOLKLORE FESTIVAL, (ITALIAN GROUP), SYDNEY

Cottage Pie

The traditional cottage pie was made with left over cold meats. It is now usually made with minced steak to be enjoyed at any time.

3 tablespoons oil
750g (1½lb) minced steak
2 onions, finely chopped
1 large carrot, finely chopped
½ cup red wine
1 beef stock cube
½ teaspoon mixed herbs

seasoning to taste
2 sticks celery, finely chopped
2 shallots, chopped
750g (1½lb) potatoes cooked, drained
30g (1oz) butter or margarine
¼ cup of milk
1 egg

Heat oil in a large saucepan and saute meat, onions and carrot over a high heat until golden brown. Add wine, crumbled stock cube, mixed herbs, seasoning, celery and shallots; simmer gently for 5 minutes. Spoon into greased ovenproof casserole. Mash potatoes with butter and milk and spoon onto meat. Brush with lightly beaten egg and bake at 200°C (400°F) for 30 minutes.

PHOTOGRAPH   PAGE 203   Serves 4-6.

SCALLOPS NEAPOLITAN (RECIPE PAGE 214)

Meat Balls Italiana

500g (1lb) beef, veal or pork, minced
2 rashers bacon, chopped
1 onion, finely chopped
1 egg
pinch oregano
pinch nutmeg
seasoning to taste

1 cup fresh breadcrumbs
2½ cups stock
1 tablespoon seasoned flour
oil for frying
cooked pasta
Rich Tomato Sauce (Recipe page 200)

Combine the meat, bacon and onion with the egg, oregano, nutmeg, seasoning and breadcrumbs. Mould into small balls, adding a little stock if mixture is too dry. Toss in seasoned flour and fry in hot oil until golden brown. Remove and poach in the heated stock for approximately 10-15 minutes. Drain and serve with pasta and Tomato and Garlic Sauce.   Serves 4.
Variations: Add finely grated Parmesan cheese to meat mixture. Add a few finely chopped or minced anchovies to meat mixture.

Beef Bourguignonne

A traditional French dish, flavoured with good wine, has a wonderful aroma.

2 cups red wine
1 carrot sliced
2 onions, sliced
½ cup chopped parsley
2 cloves garlic, crushed
2 tablespoons oil
1 bay leaf
pinch thyme
seasoning to taste

1½kg (3lb) chuck or round steak, cubed
2 tablespoons butter or margarine
1 tablespoon flour
½ cup consomme
2 doz small white onions
125g (4oz) salt pork, diced
1½ cups sliced mushrooms

Combine wine, carrot, onions, parsley, garlic, oil and seasonings in a deep bowl. Add the beef and marinate for 4 hours, turning the meat occasionally. Remove the meat and drain well on paper towelling. Strain the marinade and set aside. Heat the butter in a large frying pan. Add the meat and brown well on all sides. Add the flour, stir and cook for 2 minutes, then stir in the consomme and reserved marinade. Cover and bring to the boil. Lower heat and simmer covered for 2 hours. Saute onions and salt pork for 10 minutes or until brown. Pour off the fat and add the pork and onions to the meat mixture with the mushrooms. Cover and simmer for 45 minutes or until meat is tender.   Serves 6-8.

Spring Rolls

A small stuffed pancake, belonging to Chinese cooking. There are many varieties of fillings which range from chicken, fish, pork etc. They are extremely popular not only in South East Asia but Australia also.

250g (8oz) pork mince
¼ small cabbage, shredded
6 shallots, finely chopped
1 stick celery, finely chopped
¼ cup water chestnuts
2 tablespoons soy sauce
1 teaspoon salt

1 teaspoon sugar
pepper
1 tablespoon cornflour
¼ cup water
250g (8oz) packet spring roll wrappers
oil for frying

Combine pork with vegetables, water chestnuts, soy sauce, salt, sugar and pepper, mixing well. Combine cornflour and water, stirring till smooth. Spread approximately 2 tablespoons of pork mixture evenly across the corner of the spring roll wrapper. Brush edges with cornflour mixture and roll up in an envelope shape, making sure edges are well sealed. Heat oil and deep fry spring rolls a few at a time until golden brown and cooked through. Drain on absorbent paper and serve.   Makes 20.

PHOTOGRAPH   PAGE 220-221

Chinese Beef

3 tablespoons oil
1 kg (2lb) rump, partially frozen, sliced very thinly
1 onion, sliced
4 sticks celery, sliced
6 shallots, chopped
230g (7oz) can* whole bamboo shoots, drained, sliced
1 red capsicum, seeded, sliced

3 cloves garlic, crushed
1 small nob root ginger, sliced
2 cups beef stock
2 tablespoons soy sauce
2 tablespoons sweet sherry
1½ tablespoons sugar
seasoning to taste
6 spinach leaves
3 tablespoons cornflour

Heat oil in a wok or frying pan and stir fry ½ the meat until well browned. Remove from the pan and stir fry the remaining meat. Add all sliced vegetables and meat to the pan and stir fry for a further 2 minutes. Add stock, soy sauce, sherry, sugar, seasoning and spinach leaves torn into pieces. Mix cornflour with sufficient water to make a smooth paste and add to meat and vegetables, stirring well until mixture boils and thickens. Simmer approximately 5 minutes or until meat and spinach leaves are tender. Serve with rice.   Serves 4-6.

*nearest equivalent can size.

FRENCH ONION SOUP (RECIPE PAGE 200)

PIZZA (RECIPE PAGE 208)

Fish with Grape Sauce

4 shallots, finely chopped	2 tablespoons flour
1kg (2lb) fish fillets	3 tablespoons grape juice
1 cup white wine	1 cup cream
seasoning to taste	1 x 250g (8oz) can* seedless white
1 tablespoon butter or margarine	grapes

Grease an ovenproof casserole dish and sprinkle with the shallots. Arrange fish on top and pour over the wine. Season and bake at 180°C (350°F) for 12-15 minutes or until fish is tender. Transfer to a serving dish and keep warm. Strain liquid from casserole into a saucepan and reduce by half. Melt the butter in a saucepan, add flour and cook for 1 minute. Add the grape juice to the fish stock and stir into the roux to make a smooth sauce. Simmer gently for 7 minutes. Add cream, reheat but do not boil. Add grapes and spoon over fish. Serve hot, garnished with lemon and parsley.
*nearest equivalent can size.   Serves 6-8.

Fish with Sweet 'n' Sour Sauce

1 tablespoon oil	2 tablespoons sugar
1 red capsicum, seeded, sliced	1 tablespoon soy sauce
3 medium carrots, sliced	1 cup chicken stock
½ cucumber, sliced	2 tablespoons sherry
2 medium onions, sliced	4 medium snapper
1 small pineapple, peeled, cored, sliced	soy sauce
2 tablespoons cornflour	cornflour for coating
4 tablespoons vinegar	oil for frying

Heat the oil in a saucepan. Add the vegetables and pineapple and cook for 3 minutes. Stir in cornflour, vinegar, sugar, soy sauce, stock and sherry. Bring to boil, stirring continuously until sauce thickens. Simmer 3 minutes. Score the fish on both sides diagonally with a knife. Rub with soy sauce, coat lightly in cornflour, shake off excess. Pan fry fish in a small quantity of oil until well browned and cooked on both sides. Serve hot with pineapple sauce.   Serves 4.

Scallops Neapolitan

500g (1lb) scallops	4 peppercorns
¼ cup lemon juice	1 tablespoon wine vinegar
1 cup tomato puree	¼ cup finely chopped onion
1 clove garlic, crushed	1 capsicum, finely sliced
1 teaspoon salt	½ cup mushrooms, finely sliced

Place the scallops in an ovenproof dish with the lemon juice and bake at 180°C (350°F) for 5 minutes. Combine all the remaining ingredients in a saucepan and bring to the boil. Reduce heat and simmer for 5 minutes. Pour the sauce over the scallops, return to the oven and cook a further 15 minutes.

PHOTOGRAPH   PAGE 212

Kourabiethes

These lovely delicacies are traditional sweets of Greece, served for Christmas and New Years Day.

250g (8oz) unsalted butter	3 cups flour
1 cup icing sugar, sifted	½ teaspoon baking powder
1 egg yolk	whole cloves
1½ tablespoons brandy	¾ cup icing sugar, sifted

Cream the butter and sugar together, until white and fluffy. Add egg yolk and brandy. Gradually stir in flour and baking powder. Mix to a soft dough. Shape teaspoons of mixture into balls and slightly flatten in palms of hands. Pinch with thumb and finger twice. Place a clove in the centre of each one. Bake on greased baking sheets at 180°C (350°F) for 20 minutes. While still warm, roll in icing sugar and sift any remaining icing sugar over the top.
                                    Makes 20-25.

Dim Sims

125g (4oz) minced pork	2 tablespoons soy sauce
4 shallots, finely chopped	few drops sesame oil
1 cup shredded cabbage	¼ teaspoon salt
10 shelled prawns, finely chopped	wanton wrappers
1 tablespoon cornflour	oil for frying
1 egg	

Combine pork with chopped ingredients, with cornflour, egg, soy sauce, sesame oil and salt, mixing well. Place a teaspoon of mixture into centre of each wanton wrapper, pinch the wanton skin together at the top to form a small package. Heat oil and deep fry until golden brown. Drain and serve with soy sauce or sweet and sour sauce.   Makes approximately 30.

PHOTOGRAPH   PAGE 214

Sauerbraten

One of Germany's most celebrated dishes and an excellent way of tenderising tough meat.

1½kg (3lb) piece fresh silverside	2 cloves garlic, crushed
1 cup water	1 tablespoon butter or margarine
1 cup vinegar	2 onions, chopped
2 tablespoons brown sugar	1 carrot, diced
seasoning to taste	2 tablespoons chopped parsley
8 peppercorns	1 tablespoon flour
2 cloves	½ cup sour cream
1 bay leaf	

Place meat in a bowl with the water, vinegar, brown sugar, seasoning, peppercorns, cloves, bay leaf and garlic. Cover and leave in refrigerator for 3-4 days, turning meat daily. Remove meat from marinade, drain well and pat dry. Reserve marinade. Melt butter and brown meat on all sides. Add half marinade with onions, carrot and parsley. Cover and bring to the boil. Simmer gently for 2½ hours adding the remainder of the marinade if necessary. Remove meat to a platter and keep hot. Blend flour with a little water and add to liquid, bring to the boil and simmer for 2 minutes, stirring constantly. Add sour cream, check seasoning and strain into a sauce boat. Slice the meat and serve with the sauce.   Serves 6-8.

CURRIED CHICKEN WINGS (RECIPE PAGE 207)

TACOS WITH CHILLI BEEF (RECIPE PAGE 208)

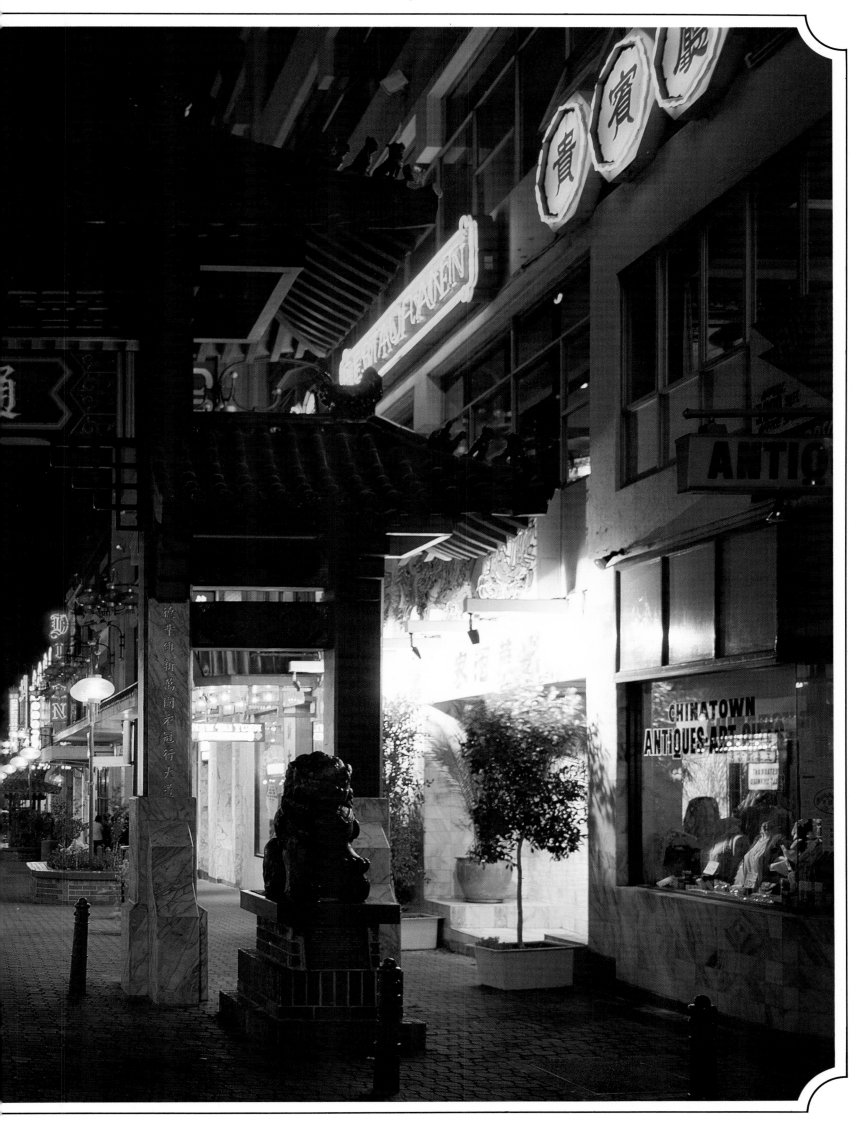

"CHINATOWN", DIXON STREET, SYDNEY, NEW SOUTH WALES

A LATVIAN BEAUTY WEARING TRADITIONAL DANCING DRESS

AUSTRALIAN FOLKLORE FESTIVAL, SYDNEY, NEW SOUTH WALES

Dutch Cherry Cheesecake

The Biscuit Crust
250g (8oz) sweet biscuits, crushed
125g (4oz) butter, melted
The Filling
500g (1lb) cream cheese
½ cup caster sugar

2 teaspoons gelatine
1 x 425g (13oz) can* dark cherries, drained, syrup reserved
3 tablespoons Cherry Advokat
1¼ cups cream, whipped

Prepare the crust by combining the biscuit crumbs with the butter and pressing into the base and sides of a 20cm (8") springform tin. Refrigerate until firm. Soften the cheese and gradually beat in the sugar. Melt the gelatine in ½ cup of the reserved cherry syrup and fold into the cheese, together with the liqueur and the cherries. Pour into the prepared tin. Refrigerate for at least 8 hours, preferably overnight. Serve decorated with cream.
*nearest equivalent can size. Serves 6-8.

Almond Cake

A traditional Austrian cake.

185g (6oz) butter or margarine
1 cup caster sugar
4 eggs
2 cups flour
3 teaspoons baking powder

1 teaspoon salt
½ cup milk
1 teaspoon vanilla essence
⅓ cup slivered almonds
½ cup grated chocolate

Cream butter and sugar together until light and fluffy. Add eggs one at a time, beating well after each addition, then fold in the sifted dry ingredients, alternately with the milk and vanilla. Arrange almonds over the base of a greased and floured 20cm (8") ring tin. Place ⅓ of the cake mixture over almonds and sprinkle with half of the chocolate. Repeat this process until all the mixture has been used, ending with a layer of cake mixture. Bake at 180°C (350°F) for 1 hour. Cool in tin for 15 minutes before turning out. Serve dusted with icing sugar.

Sicilian Cheese and Almond Pudding

1 tablespoon butter or margarine
1 tablespoon dry white breadcrumbs
2 tablespoons rum
1 tablespoon sultanas or seedless raisins
2 tablespoons mixed peel
500g (1lb) Ricotta cheese

4 eggs
¾ cup ground almonds
½ cup slivered almonds
pinch cinnamon
1 tablespoon grated lemon rind
1 tablespoon sugar

Grease a large square ovenproof dish and sprinkle with breadcrumbs. Pour rum over fruit and leave for 10 minutes. Sieve cheese and beat into the eggs. Stir in fruit, almonds, cinnamon, lemon rind and sugar. Spoon into the dish and bake at 180°C (350°F) for 45 minutes or until the top has lightly browned. Allow to cool, then refrigerate, cut into squares and serve with cream. Serves 6-8.

Chinese Fried Ice Cream

From the Cantonese provence of China, a dessert traditionally served with caramel sauce.

3 cups cake crumbs
2 tablespoons Tia Maria or suitable liqueur
6 scoops ice cream
¼ cup cornflour

1 egg, beaten
2 tablespoons milk
½ cup breadcrumbs
oil for frying

Combine cake crumbs and Tia Maria. Roll each scoop of ice cream in cake crumbs. Re-freeze until firm. Roll in cornflour. Dip in egg and milk mixture, then toss in breadcrumbs and deep fry in hot oil for 5 seconds only. Serve immediately. Serves 4-6.

SPRING ROLLS (RECIPE PAGE 212) LEFT

Crepes Suzette

This beautiful dessert from France, always looks so intricate to prepare, therefore is usually only eaten in French restaurants. Try them at home for yourself, they really are quite simple to make.

The Crepe Batter
1 cup flour
1 egg
1 egg yolk
1 cup milk
2 tablespoons orange liqueur

The Sauce
125g (4oz) butter, softened
1/3 cup icing sugar
1 tablespoon grated lemon rind
grated rind and juice 1 orange
6 tablespoons orange liqueur
1 orange, peeled, thinly sliced
4 tablespoons Cognac

Make the batter by sifting the flour into a large bowl. Make a well in the centre and add the egg and yolk. Gradually whisk in the milk and liqueur to make a smooth batter. Cover and refrigerate for 1 hour. Make crepes in the usual way, using a 15cm (6″) crepe pan. Stack the crepes and keep warm. Make the sauce by creaming the butter and icing sugar together until light and fluffy. Beat in lemon and orange rind, orange juice, 4 tablespoons of the liqueur and melt in a large frying pan. Simmer for 5 minutes. Dip each crepe in the hot butter mixture and fold into quarters. Push to edge of pan. Add the sliced orange and sprinkle with a little extra icing sugar. Combine remaining liqueur with the Cognac in a small pan or ladle, heat, ignite and pour over the crepes. Serve as soon as flames subside.   Serves 4.

Brioche

A popular breakfast bread in France and gaining popularity in Australia.

2 cups flour
30g (1oz) yeast
1/4 cup warm water
extra warm water
1/2 teaspoon salt

2 teaspoons sugar
3 eggs, beaten
125g (4oz) butter or margarine, softened
egg or milk for glazing

Combine 1/2 cup flour with the crumbled yeast. Mix to a soft dough with the warm water, lightly knead in the bowl and make a shallow cross on the top with a sharp knife. Leave to prove, in a warm place until dough doubles its size. Sift remaining flour into a basin with the salt and sugar. Make a dough with the eggs and a little extra warm water if necessary and then knead on a floured board until it is soft and pliable. Knead the butter and flour dough into the yeast dough until well combined and dough is smooth and elastic (about 10-15 minutes). Transfer to an oiled bowl. Cover and set aside to prove, until doubled in size. Knead lightly, break off small pieces and fill greased brioche or muffin tins. Press a hole in the top of each piece of dough and insert another smaller piece so that when cooked, the brioche resembles a "hat". Allow to rise again, then brush with egg or milk and bake at 230°C (450°F) for 20 minutes, approximately.   Serve hot.

PHOTOGRAPH   PAGE 209

DIM SIMS (RECIPE PAGE 214) RIGHT

Baklava

A very popular sweet pastry form the Middle East.

250g (8oz) almonds, finely chopped
250g (8oz) walnuts, finely chopped
4 tablespoons sugar
3 teaspoons mixed spice
500g (1lb) filo pastry
500g (1lb) butter or margarine

The Syrup
2 cups water
½ cup lemon juice
1 cup sugar
1 cup honey
1 x 5cm (2") cinnamon stick

Combine almonds and walnuts in a bowl. Add sugar and spice, mixing well. Grease a large baking dish or slab tin and cover the base with six sheets of filo pastry, brushing each sheet with melted butter. Sprinkle over quarter of the nut mixture and repeat process with the next six sheets of filo pastry. Repeat until all the nut mixture and pastry have been used, finishing with filo pastry. Score the top sheets of pastry into diamond shaped serving pieces. Bake at 210°C (410°F) for 15 minutes, then reduce heat to 180°C (350°F) and bake for a further 15 minutes. Make the syrup by placing the remaining ingredients into a saucepan. Stir until sugar has dissolved and boil until thick and syrupy. Strain and cool, pour over the hot baklava and allow to stand until the syrup has been absorbed. Cut into pieces and serve cold.

Zabaglione

A traditional Italian dessert.

3 egg yolks
¼ cup caster sugar
½ cup Marsala

Beat egg yolks and caster sugar in the top of a double saucepan, until thick and creamy. Stir in Marsala and continue beating until mixture thickens, 8-10 minutes approximately. Serve warm with sponge fingers and strawberries.

Serves 4.

SCENIC MOUNT WARNING, NEW SOUTH WALES

The Australian way of

USING NATURES HEALTH

Cooking that Comes Naturally

Vegetables are playing a bigger part in everyone's diet. And here in "godzone", we're luckier than most because our land is so generous. On the outskirts of Australian cities, you'll still find grazing cattle, market gardens and roadside stalls with fresh eggs and just-picked fruit and vegetables.

Migrants from Europe and Asia have introduced different varieties of vegetables and new ways of cooking them. In general, there is a growing awareness of nutrition and a search for alternatives

to grandma's recipe for greens — a teaspoon of salt, a teaspoon of bicarbonate and boil the brussels sprouts 'til they're gray. "Vegies" have become more than an overcooked sidedish for meat.

Cooking with dairy products also offers lots of variety. Dairy foods are versatile and are part of favourites such as fondue, quiche and the old standard — egg and bacon pie.

We hope the following recipes, using the bounty of the Australian countryside, will inspire you to some good natural eating.

ABORIGINAL WOMAN GRINDING GRASS SEEDS, NORTHERN TERRITORY

Minted Pea Chowder

A quick and easy soup, making good use of nutritious fresh vegetables.

2 onions	seasoning to taste
1 carrot	2 cups frozen peas
2 sticks celery, trimmed	2 tablespoons flour
2 potatoes	2 tablespoons chopped mint
3 tablespoons butter or margarine	½ cup cream
6 cups water	

Chop all fresh vegetables roughly. Melt butter in a large saucepan. Add chopped vegetables and sauté for 5 minutes. Add water, seasoning and bring to the boil. Simmer gently for 20 minutes. Add peas and continue simmering for 10 minutes. Strain the vegetables and purée in a food processor or through a coarse sieve. Gradually blend flour with a little of the hot vegetable stock to form a smooth paste and stir into the vegetables with the remaining stock. Return to the saucepan with the mint and bring to the boil. Cook for two minutes. Swirl in the cream and serve garnished with sprigs of mint.   Serves 8.

PORTOBELLO CAFE (OPERA HOUSE WALK) SYDNEY HARBOUR, NEW SOUTH WALES

PINK MULLA MULLA WILDFLOWERS, NORTHERN TERRITORY

Leek and Tomato Soup

Leeks have a delightful flavour and are a good combination with tomatoes.

3 leeks, washed, finely chopped	1 teaspoon salt
5 cups chicken stock	½ teaspoon lemon pepper
1kg (2lb) tomatoes, skinned and chopped	1 teaspoon chopped basil

Place the finely chopped leeks in a saucepan and cover with the chicken stock. Bring to the boil. Cook for a further five minutes, then add tomatoes. Simmer until the tomatoes are tender, about 30 minutes. Remove from the heat, add seasonings and serve.

Serves 6.

Carrot and Honey Cream Soup

500g (1lb) baby carrots	salt
4 cups vegetable stock	mace
¼ cup honey	150ml (¼ pint) cream
3 cloves garlic, crushed	chopped parsley

Slice carrots into a saucepan with the vegetable stock, honey, garlic, salt and mace. Bring to the boil, reduce heat and simmer 30 minutes or until carrots are tender. Adjust seasonings to taste. Purée in a blender or food processor and gently reheat, then stirr in the cream. Continue to heat gently but do not boil. Serve sprinkled with chopped parsley.   Serves 6.

PHOTOGRAPH   PAGES 230-231

Minestrone Soup

A hearty, filling soup, good for lunch on the run.

2 tablespoons butter or margarine	3 ltr (6 pints) beef stock
4 carrots, sliced	1 x 220g (7oz) can* red kidney beans
4 sticks celery, sliced	1 x 440g (14oz) can* peeled
2 potatoes, roughly chopped	tomatoes
3 onions, roughly chopped	¾ cup macaroni
2 cloves garlic, crushed	¼ cup chopped parsley
3 rashers bacon, roughly chopped	seasoning to taste

Melt the butter in a large saucepan and sauté the vegetables and bacon for 5 minutes. Rinse and drain the beans and add with the stock and tomatoes. Bring to the boil, cover and simmer for 30 minutes. Add macaroni and simmer, uncovered, until tender, about 25 minutes. Serve in deep bowls, sprinkled with parsley.
*nearest equivalent can size.   Serves 10-12.
PHOTOGRAPH   PAGES 230-231

Brussels Sprouts Soup

2 tablespoons butter or oil	4 cups chicken stock
1 onion, finely sliced	¼ cup cream
1kg (2lb) brussels sprouts	

Melt the butter in a saucepan and sauté onion until tender. Add brussels sprouts and stock and bring to the boil. Reduce the heat and simmer for 10-20 minutes or until cooked. Puree in a food processor or through a sieve. Reheat and serve with a swirl of cream.   Serves 4.

PHOTOGRAPH   PAGES 230-231

Pumpkin Vichysoisse

500g (1lb) peeled, seeded pumpkin	cayenne pepper to taste
250g (8oz) chopped, washed leeks	½ cup of cream or yoghurt
8 cups chicken stock	½ teaspoon paprika
1 teaspoon salt	

Place all ingredients except the seasoning and cream into suitably sized saucepan. Bring to the boil and cook until the pumpkin is tender. Remove from the heat, add seasonings, blend in a blender until smooth. Refrigerate until well chilled. Just before serving swirl in a cream and garnish with chopped parsley or chives.   Serves 6.
PHOTOGRAPH   PAGE 229

BOTTLE BRUSH, A RUGGED BUT BEAUTIFUL AUSTRALIAN WILDFLOWER

SASHA & SYLVIA SUNBATHING, PATONGA BEACH, NEW SOUTH WALES

Tomato Refresher

This is a quick and easy "no cook" soup that could also be served as a drink with the addition of a splash of vodka.

1 large orange, peeled, chopped
1 red apple, peeled, cored, diced
500g (1lb) ripe tomatoes, peeled, chopped
1 small onion, diced
2 cloves garlic, crushed
½ teaspoon salt
1 cup chicken stock
1 tablespoon lemon juice

Blend all the ingredients together in a food processor until smooth. Pour into a large bowl and chill until required.   Serves 4.

Macaroni Slaw Salad

1⅓ cups cooked macaroni
1 cup grated cabbage
¼ cup grated carrot
¼ grated capsicum
90g (3oz) ham, chopped
2 hard boiled eggs, sliced
1 tablespoon mayonnaise
1 tablespoon cider vinegar
1 tablespoon tomato sauce
¼ teaspoon tarragon
2 lettuce cups
sprigs of herbs to garnish

Combine the macaroni with the cabbage, carrot, capsicum, ham and eggs. Combine the mayonnaise with the vinegar, tomato sauce and tarragon. Pour over the macaroni and toss together thoroughly. Serve, spooned into the lettuce cups and garnish with sprigs of herbs.   Serves 2.

Sweet Potato and Snow Peas Sauté

A unique and tasty way to serve this vegetable.

3 tablespoons vegetable oil
1 large sweet potato, peeled, thinly sliced
1 leek, washed, sliced
2 teaspoons sesame seeds
seasoning to taste
150g (5oz) cup snow peas
1 teaspoon dill

Heat the oil in a frying pan or wok and sauté the potato and leek until tender. Add sesame seeds, seasoning, snow peas and dill. Cook for 1 minute, then serve immediately. Do not overcook the snow peas.   Serves 3-4.

PHOTOGRAPH   PAGES 236-237

Cheese and Parsnip Bake

500g (1lb) parsnips, roughly chopped
1 egg
1 tablespoon flour
seasoning to taste
1 shallot, chopped
15g (½oz) butter or margarine
60g (2oz) grated cheese

Simmer parsnips in boiling, salted water for approximately 5 minutes or until tender. Drain. Purée the parsnips with the egg, flour seasoning, shallot and butter in a food processor. Transfer to a small, greased, ovenproof dish and top with cheese. Bake, uncovered, at 180°C (350°F) for 15 minutes or until the cheese has browned and melted.   Serves 4-6.

Stir-Fried Vegetables

Serve this colourful dish as a main course or with Chinese noodles. Delicious!

3 tablespoons vegetable oil
1 nob root ginger, peeled, finely sliced
1 clove garlic, crushed
2 sticks celery, diagonally sliced
½ red capsicum, seeded, sliced
1 cup peas
1 zucchini, thinly sliced
6 brussels sprouts, quartered

1 carrot finely sliced
1 cup button mushrooms, sliced
1 leek, finely sliced
1 cup bean shoots
1 cup raw cashews
½ cup water
3 teaspoons soy sauce
2 teaspoons cornflour

Heat the oil in a frying pan or wok, add the ginger and garlic and cook for 30 seconds. Stir in the remaining vegetables and nuts and stir fry for a few minutes. Combine the water, soy sauce and cornflour and add to the vegetables. Allow to simmer for a few minutes, then serve.   Serves 2-4.

PHOTOGRAPH   PAGES 236-237

Crunchy Vegetable Stir Fry

The macadamia nuts add a lovely texture and crunch to these vegetables.

2 tablespoons vegetable oil
1 onion, finely sliced
1 carrot, sliced
1 parsnip, peeled, sliced

1 zucchini, sliced
1 teaspoon dill
½ cup macadamia nuts

Heat oil in a frying pan or wok and sauté the onion, carrot and parsnip for 2-3 minutes. Add zucchini, dill and macadamia nuts and continue cooking for a further 3-4 minutes. Do not overcook. Serve immediately.   Serves 3-4.

PHOTOGRAPH   PAGES 236-237

Broccoli Ham Flan

A delicious luncheon dish made with tasty Cheddar cheese.

1½ sheets ready rolled shortcrust pastry
1 packet frozen broccoli
8 slices ham
4 eggs
1 x 375ml can* (1½ cups) evaporated milk

1 cup tasty Cheddar cheese, coarsely grated
1 stock cube, crumbled
⅛ teaspoon cayenne pepper
⅛ teaspoon grated nutmeg
1 tablespoon chopped chives

Line a lightly greased 25cm (10") fluted flan tin or pie plate with pastry, trim edges, then crimp. Bake blind at 190°C (375°F) for 15 minutes then remove from the oven. Cook frozen broccoli as directed on packet, drain thoroughly and wrap a slice of ham around each piece. Arrange in the base of the pastry case. Beat eggs, evaporated milk, ½ cup cheese, the stock cube and seasonings together and carefully pour over the broccoli. Sprinkle with the remaining cheese and bake at 200°C (400°F) for 10 minutes, then reduce oven temperature to 180°C (350°F) and continue baking for further 45 minutes or until custard is firm. Serve hot or cold as a luncheon dish.   Serves 8.
*nearest equivalent can size.

Garlic Flavoured Leeks

1 tablespoon finely chopped onion
1 clove garlic, crushed
3 tablespoons butter or margarine

6 leeks, washed, trimmed, cut in half lengthwise
seasoning to taste

Lightly sauté onion and garlic in a little of the butter until softened. Place leeks into boiling salted water and reduce heat to simmer and cook 2-3 minutes. Drain and refresh in cold water. Place in a greased shallow casserole dish, dot with butter, sprinkle over the sauteed onions, and garlic and seasoning. Cover with a lid or foil and cook at 180°C (350°F) for 20 minutes. Serve hot as a side dish for roast meats.

PHOTOGRAPH   PAGES 246-247

PUMPKIN VICHYSOISSE (RECIPE PAGE 226)

BRUSSELS SPROUTS SOUP (RECIPE PAGE 226) LEFT

MINESTRONE SOUP (RECIPE PAGE 226) CENTRE; CARROT & HONEY CREAM SOUP (RECIPE PAGE 226) RIGHT

ABORIGINAL ROCKPAINTING, "DREAMTIME"

Mushroom and Zucchini Bake

60g (2oz) butter or margarine
250g (8oz) mushrooms, sliced
½ teaspoon salt
1 clove garlic, crushed
pepper
¼ teaspoon oregano

3 large zucchini, coarsely grated
¼ cup soft breadcrumbs
4 tablespoons Parmesan cheese, grated
1 tablespoon cream
4 eggs, beaten

Melt butter in a large saucepan add mushrooms and cook until most of the liquid has evaporated. Add salt, garlic, pepper and oregano. Combine zucchini, breadcrumbs, 2 tablespoons Parmesan cheese and mushroom mixture and spoon into an ovenproof dish. Pour combined cream and eggs over zucchini mixture and bake at 180°C (350°F) for 25-30 minutes. Cut into squares and top with remaining cheese. Serve with a salad of your choice. Serves 6-8.

PHOTOGRAPH   PAGES 246-247

Spiced Zucchini Crêpes

The Filling
1 tablespoon butter
1 leek, washed, chopped
500g (1lb) zucchini, sliced
½ teaspoon ground allspice

1 egg, lightly beaten
8 x 18cm (7") crepes
(refer recipe for Crêpe Suzette) page 220
seasoning to taste

Melt butter in a saucepan. Add leek and zucchini and sauté until tender. Purée in a food processor or through a sieve. Season and beat in the egg. Divide the filling between the crêpes, fold and place in a dish. Reheat at180°C (350°F) for 20 minutes covered with foil, or in the microwave for 2-3 minutes. Serves 8.

Mushroom Souffle

60g (2oz) butter or margarine
250g (8oz) button mushrooms, chopped
½ cup chopped shallots
3 tablespoons orange liqueur

30g (1oz) butter or margarine
2 tablespoons flour
1 cup milk
seasoning to taste
5 eggs, separated

Melt the 60g (2oz) of butter in a frying pan and sauté the mushrooms and shallots until tender. Pour in the liqueur and ignite, and when the flames have subsided, remove from heat. Make a white sauce in the usual way, with the remaining butter, flour and milk. Stir in the mushrooms and seasoning, then add the beaten egg yolks. Whisk the egg whites until stiff and fold into the mushroom mixture. Grease a large soufflé dish and carefully spoon in the mixture. Bake at 180°C (350°F) for 40 minutes or until cooked. Serve immediately. Serves 4.

Orientale Fondue

500g (1lb) mature Cheddar cheese, grated
2 tablespoons flour
1 clove garlic, crushed
¼ cup chopped shallots
¼ cup chopped gherkins
2 teaspoons soy sauce

2 teaspoons brown sugar
1 teaspoon ground ginger
1¼ cups dry white wine
1 x 425g (13oz) can* crushed pineapple, drained
seasoning to taste

Combine cheese and flour in a plastic bag. Bring garlic, shallots, gherkins, soy sauce, brown sugar, ginger and wine to a simmer in fondue pot, then stir in cheese, a handful at a time. Allow to dissolve between each addition until fondue is bubbling and smooth. Stir in the pineapple and seasoning and keep warm over burner. Serve with some lightly cooked cubes of pork or steak, crusty bread and whole mushrooms. Serves 4-6.
*nearest equivalent can size.

NIGHTLIFE WITH THE FESTIVAL THEATRE IN ADELAIDE, SOUTH AUSTRALIA

Cheese Fondue

Fondue makes a lovely after theatre supper or a snack on a winter's evening. As you can see, the basic recipe can be varied in a number of ways.

500g (1lb) Swiss cheese, grated
3 tablespoons flour
2 cloves garlic, halved

1½ cups dry white wine
seasoning, nutmeg to taste
2-3 tablespoons kirsch

Toss cheese and flour together in a plastic bag. Rub a fondue pot with garlic. Discard and pour in the wine. Bring to simmering point, then stir in cheese, a handful at a time, over low heat. Allow to dissolve completely between each addition. Stir till fondue is bubbling and smooth. Season generously then add the kirsch. Keep fondue hot over burner and serve with cubes of crusty bread or crudites of vegetables. Serves 4-6.

Asparagus Fondue

1 x 310g (10oz) can* asparagus cuts, drained, liquid reserved
1 clove garlic, crushed

500g (1lb) Cheddar cheese, grated
3 tablespoons cornflour
seasoning to taste

Add sufficient water to asparagus liquid to make 1 cup of liquid. Pour into the fondue pot with the asparagus and garlic. Bring to simmering point. Toss cornflour and cheese together in plastic bag. Stir in a handful at a time, allowing to dissolve between each addition. Season generously and keep fondue hot over burner. Serve with chunks of crusty bread, peeled and de-veined prawns or lightly grilled bacon cuts. Serves 4-6.
*nearest equivalent can size.

Simple Cheddar Souffle

3 tablespoons butter or margarine
¼ cup flour
1 cup milk
125g (4oz) Cheddar cheese, grated
¼ teaspoon dry mustard
pinch cayenne pepper
1½ teaspoons salt
3 eggs, separated

Melt the butter in a saucepan and blend in flour. Cook 1-2 minutes, then whisk in the milk. Stir constantly over moderate heat until smooth and thickened. Remove from heat and briskly beat in cheese and seasonings. Cool a little then beat in egg yolks. Whisk egg whites until stiff, then fold into the sauce. Pour into a medium sized, greased souffle dish. Bake at 160°C (325°F) for 50-60 minutes. Serve immediately with a tossed salad and hot, crusty bread.

Serves 4.

Mozzarella Melters

125g (4oz) butter or margarine, softened
seasoning to taste
1-2 cloves garlic, crushed
8 slices bread
8 slices salami
2 tomatoes, sliced
1 onion, finely sliced
8 olives, stoned, chopped
250g (½lb) Mozzarella cheese, thinly sliced

Cream butter, seasoning and garlic together till creamy. Spread evenly over both sides of bread, taking care to spread to the edges. Place bread on a baking sheet and top each piece with slices of salami, tomatoes, onion and olives. Top with the cheese and bake at 190°C (375°F) for 20 minutes. Cut in half diagonally and serve hot.

Serves 8.

TOMATO BACON QUICHE (RECIPE THIS PAGE) TOP LEFT; EGGS EN COCOTTE (RECIPE PAGE 238) TOP RIGHT; EGG AND BACON PIE (RECIPE PAGE 238) BOTTOM

Tomato Bacon Quiche

The Pastry
3 tablespoons butter or margarine
1 cup flour
¼ teaspoon salt
2 tablespoons iced water
The Filling
4 rashers bacon, chopped
4 shallots, chopped
4 eggs
1 tablespoon cornflour
¼ teaspoon lemon thyme
1½ cups cream
½ cup milk
⅔ cup grated tasty cheese
seasoning to taste
1 large tomato, sliced
1 tablespoon chopped parsley

Make the pastry by rubbing the butter into the flour and salt then add water and mix to a firm dough. Knead lightly and chill for 30 minutes. Line a 20cm (8") quiche tin with the pastry and bake blind at 200°C (400°F) for 8 minutes. Cool. Sauté bacon and half the shallots, until bacon is cooked. Beat together the eggs, cornflour and lemon thyme and add cream, milk and seasoning. Pour into prepared quiche tin and sprinkle with cheese. Arrange tomato slices over mixture, sprinkle with remaining shallots and parsley. Bake at 180°C (350°F) for 20-25 minutes or until set. Serve either hot or cold.

Serves 4-6.

PHOTOGRAPH THIS PAGE

Herbed Tomato Quiche

1 cup flour
pinch salt
60g (2oz) butter or margarine, cubed
2-3 tablespoons water
3 tablespoons Parmesan cheese
1 tablespoon parsley, chopped
2 tablespoons oil
1 large onion, finely chopped
2 cloves garlic
4 tomatoes, chopped
1 tablespoon tomato paste
1 teaspoon basil
1 teaspoon sugar
2 eggs
seasoning to taste

Make a pastry in the usual way, with the flour, salt, butter, water, 1 tablespoon of Parmesan cheese and the parsley. Knead lightly together until smooth, roll out onto a floured board and use to line a 20cm (8") quiche tin. Prick pastry well, with a fork and refrigerate for 10 minutes. Bake at 180°C (350°F) for 15 minutes or until pastry is pale, golden brown. Heat oil in frying pan and sauté the onion and garlic until tender. Remove pan from heat and stir in the tomatoes and remaining ingredients. Pour into prepared case and bake at 180°C (350°F) for approximately 40 minutes or until cooked.

Serves 4-6.

FOOTBALL (AUSTRALIAN RULES), SYDNEY SWANS VERSUS CARLTON, BATTLING FOR THE BALL

STIR-FRIED VEGETABLES (RECIPE PAGE 229) TOP LEFT; SWEET POTATO AND SNOW PEAS SAUTE (RECIPE PAGE 228) BOTTOM

CRUNCHY VEGETABLE STIR FRY (RECIPE PAGE 229) RIGHT

Egg and Bacon Pie

The Pastry	**The Filling**
185g (6oz) self-raising flour	4 eggs
60g (2oz) flour	seasoning to taste
½ level teaspoon salt	6 tablespoons milk
125g (4oz) butter or margarine	185g (6oz) bacon, chopped
5 tablespoons cold water	beaten egg for glazing

Sift together flours and salt and rub butter into flour mixture. Make a well in the centre, add water and stir into the flour, mix to firm dough. Turn out onto a floured board, shape into a ball and halve. Roll each piece to ½cm (¼") thickness to fit a 20cm (8") pie plate. Line the plate with one half of the pastry, and whisk the eggs and seasoning and milk. Arrange the bacon in the bottom of the pastry case and pour over the egg mixture. Cut remaining pastry into strips and lattice the top of the pie. Glaze with beaten egg and bake at 200°C (400°F) for 15 minutes. Reduce to 175°C (340°F) and cook for a further 15-20 minutes or until set.   Serves 4-6.

PHOTOGRAPH   PAGE 234

Eggs en Cocotte

2 tablespoons butter or margarine	4 eggs
6 shallots, chopped	seasoning to taste
125g (4oz) mushrooms, sliced	4 tablespoons cream or yoghurt
½ cup chopped ham or salami	grated Parmesan cheese

Melt butter in pan and sauté shallots until soft. Add mushrooms and ham and cook a further 2 minutes. Spoon mixture evenly between four individual ramekins and break an egg into each one. Season. Spoon 1 tablespoon of cream or yoghurt over each egg and sprinkle with grated Parmesan cheese. Cook at 180°C (350°F) for 12-15 minutes or until eggs are set. Serve accompanied with hot buttered toast.   Serves 4.

PHOTOGRAPH   PAGE 234

TOSSED GREEN SALAD WITH YOGHURT DRESSING (NO RECIPE)

Country Quiche

This recipe could also be adapted for individual quiches for lunchboxes or picnics.

The Pastry	2 rindless rashers bacon, chopped
125g (4oz) butter or margarine	2 onions, sliced
1½ cups flour, sifted	3 eggs
1 egg yolk	1¼ cups milk
1 tablespoon water	½ cup grated Parmesan cheese
squeeze lemon juice	seasoning to taste
The Filling	chopped parsley
2 tablespoons butter or margarine	

Make the pastry by rubbing the butter into the flour until the mixture resembles fine breadcrumbs. Combine the egg yolk with the water and lemon juice and work into the flour to form a firm dough. Knead, cover and rest in the refrigerator for 30 minutes. Use the pastry to line a deep 23cm (9") quiche tin. Melt the butter in a frying pan and sauté the bacon and onions until tender. Spoon over the base of the pastry case. Beat the eggs, milk, Parmesan cheese and seasonings together and carefully pour into the flan. Place onto a baking sheet and bake at 200°C (400°F) for 10 minutes. Reduce to 180°C (350°F) and bake a further 30 minutes before removing from the tin. Garnish with chopped parsley and serve.   Serves 6.

Bacon Buns with Egg

6 soft hamburger buns	1 onion, sliced
3 tablespoons butter or margarine	seasoning to taste
2 teaspoon Worcestershire sauce	250g (8oz) processed Cheddar cheese,
6 eggs	grated
3 rashers bacon, chopped	

Cut a slice from the top of each bun and reserve. Hollow out each bun, leaving a thick shell. Melt the butter in a saucepan and stir in the Worcestershire sauce. Brush inside of buns with butter mixture and carefully break an egg into each one. Sauté bacon and onion in frying pan, drain well and spoon over the eggs. Season, top with cheese and replace lids. Brush with remaining butter. Bake at 200°C (400°F) for 15 minutes or until the egg has cooked. Serve hot or cold.   Serves 6.

Chicken with Parsley Dumplings

	Dumplings
1½kg (3lb) chicken jointed, skin removed	2 cups self-raising flour
1 cup white wine	1 tablespoon butter or margarine
water or stock to cover chicken	½ teaspoon salt
1 small onion, sliced	1 tablespoon chopped parsley
3 sprigs parsley	1 cup milk
2 sticks celery, sliced	3 tablespoons cornflour
1 bay leaf	seasoning to taste
5 peppercorns	paprika
2 teaspoons salt	parsley sprigs for garnish
seasoning to taste	
paprika	

Place chicken in a shallow baking dish. Add wine, water, onion, parsley, celery, bay leaf, peppercorns and salt. Cover and bake at 120°C (250°F) for 1½-2 hours or until chicken is cooked. Skim off fat. While chicken is cooking, prepare the dumplings. Sift the flour and rub in the butter. Add the salt and parsley and milk. Drop the dumplings in on top of the chicken, (they should not sink). Cook for 20 minutes or until dumplings have risen and browned. Remove chicken and dumplings and keep warm. Strain liquid and blend cornflour with a little water or wine and add to the liquid. Combine and season. Bring to the boil and pour gravy over chicken and dumplings. Dust with paprika and garnish with parsley.   Serves 4.

PHOTOGRAPH   PAGE 244

"NATURE AT ITS BEST", FRESH FOODS A' PLENTY

WHEAT IN SUNNY, RURAL AUSTRALIA

Chicken Pie

1 tablespoon butter or margarine
1 onion, finely sliced
2 rashers bacon, sliced
1 cup mushrooms, finely sliced
¼ cup finely chopped parsley
2 tablespoons butter or margarine
2 tablespoons flour

1 cup chicken stock
1 tablespoon white wine
seasoning to taste
500g (1lb) cooked, diced chicken
1 sheet ready rolled puff pastry
beaten egg for glazing

Melt 1 tablespoon butter and sauté onion until soft. Add the bacon, mushrooms and parsley. In another pan make the sauce by melting 2 tablespoons butter, adding flour and making a roux. Add chicken stock stirring continuously and cooking until thick and boiling. Reduce heat, add wine and season to taste. Mix together bacon, mushroom mixture and chicken. Add to sauce and spoon into pie dish. Cover with pastry, decorate and glaze with beaten egg. Bake at 200°C (400°F) for 5 minutes, reduce temperature to 180°C (350°F) for remaining 20 minutes. Serve hot with vegetables or your favourite salad.   Serves 4.

PHOTOGRAPH   PAGE 244

Chicken Puff Kiev

90g (3oz) unsalted butter or margarine
1 clove garlic, crushed
2 shallots, chopped
1 tablespoon parsley, chopped
2 teaspoons Worcestershire sauce

¼ teaspoon black pepper
4 whole breasts of chicken, skinned, boned
2 sheets ready rolled puff pastry
milk or cream for glazing.

Cream the butter, garlic, shallots, parsley, Worcestershire sauce and pepper together and shape into a 28cm (11") oblong. Wrap in foil and freeze until firm. Pound out chicken breasts until very thin with a meat mallet or rolling pin. Cut frozen butter mixture into 4 equal portions. Place one portion in the centre of each chicken breast and fold chicken over butter so that it is completely encased and makes a roll shape. Cut pastry sheets in half and place a chicken roll on each strip of pastry. Roll up firmly. Place seamside down on a baking sheet. Glaze with milk or cream and bake at 230°C (450°F) for 20-25 minutes or until pastry is golden brown. Serves 4.

SUNSET FROM MOUNT NELSON, HOBART, TASMANIA

"THE ROCK", AYERS ROCK, NORTHERN TERRITORY

CHICKEN WITH PARSLEY DUMPLINGS (RECIPE PAGE 238) TOP; CHICKEN PIE (RECIPE PAGE 240) BOTTOM

Chicken Cabbage Rolls

This mixture can also be used with vine leaves as a filling for dolmades; to be served with drinks.

1kg (2lb) chicken mince	*1 teaspoon wheatgerm*
3 shallots, chopped	*½ cup chicken stock*
1 teaspoon salt	*6 large cabbage leaves, blanched*
1 teaspoon green peppercorns	

Combine the chicken with shallots, salt and green peppercorns. Add wheatgerm to make a firm mixture. Open out the cabbage leaves and divide chicken mixture evenly over each one. Roll up and secure and place in a baking dish. Add the chicken stock cover with foil and bake at 180°C (350°F) for approx. 20 minutes or until cooked.   Serves 6.

Lamb and Zucchini Casserole

1.5kg (3lb) leg lamb, boned, cubed	*1½ cups beef stock*
2 tablespoons seasoned flour	*seasoning to taste*
4 tablespoons butter or margarine	*½ cup rice*
2 onions, chopped	*3 zucchini, sliced*
60g (2oz) Hungarian salami, chopped	*125g (4oz) Cheddar cheese, grated*
2 cloves garlic, crushed	*2 tablespoons grated Parmesan cheese*

Toss meat in flour and brown in 3 tablespoons of the butter. Add onion, salami and garlic and sauté 2 minutes. Stir in stock and bring to simmering point. Spoon into a large casserole. Cover and bake at 180°C (350°F) for 30 minutes. Season and stir in rice. Cook for a further 15 minutes. Sauté the zucchini in remaining butter, stir the casserole and arrange the zucchini on top. Sprinkle with the cheeses and bake a further 5-10 minutes.   Serves 4-6.

Beef and Bacon Pie

3 tablespoons butter or margarine	*125g (4oz) can* golden butter beans, drained,*
2 tablespoons prepared mustard	*125g (4oz) matured Cheddar cheese, cubed*
250g (8oz) blade steak, cubed	*1 x 375g (12oz) packet frozen puff pastry, thawed*
4 rashers bacon, chopped	*1 egg yolk*
1 onion, sliced	*1 tablespoon milk*
2 tablespoons flour	
½ cup liquid reserved	

Melt the butter with the mustard in a heavy based frying pan. Add meat, bacon and onion and sauté for 3-4 minutes. Stir in flour and cook for 2 minutes. Add reserved bean liquid, stir constantly and bring to the boil. Add mushrooms and beans and simmer for a further 5 minutes. Add the cheese. Roll half the pastry out and use to line a 20cm (8") pie dish. Spoon in filling, moisten edges with a little water. Roll out remaining pastry and use to cover the pie. Trim edges, seal well and decorate. Refrigerate for 15 minutes. Combine egg yolk with milk and glaze the pie. Bake at 200°C (400°F) for 25-30 minutes or until pastry is golden brown.   Serves 6.
*nearest equivalent can size.

Roast Veal with Mushroom Cream Sauce

1.5kg (3lb) leg veal boned	*250g (8oz) mushrooms, thinly sliced*
4 rashers bacon	*2 tablespoons flour*
¼ cup brandy	*1 teaspoon dried basil*
The Sauce	*1¼ cups cream*
½ cup chopped shallots	

Form veal neatly into a roll. Wrap bacon rashers around it, securing with wooden toothpicks. Place in a greased baking dish. Pour over brandy and cover with foil. Bake at 180°C (350°F) for 1½ hours. Remove foil and bake for a further hour or until veal is sufficiently cooked. Keep warm on a serving dish while preparing sauce. Skim excess fat from dish. Add shallots and mushrooms and sauté for 2-3 minutes. Blend in flour and basil and cook 1 minute. Remove from heat and stir in the cream. Return to a low heat and stir constantly until sauce thickens. Carve the meat and serve accompanied with the sauce.   Serves 6.

THE NEW NATIONAL TENNIS CENTRE WITH MOVABLE ROOF, MELBOURNE, VICTORIA

MUSHROOM & ZUCCHINI BAKE (RECIPE PAGE 233) BOTTOM

Stuffed Baked Apples

6 cooking apples
12 cloves
12 dates
18 sultanas

1 teaspoon cinnamon
3 teaspoons brown sugar
2 tablespoons butter or margarine
2 cups water

Core apples and peel 1cm (½") around the top. Slit skin. Insert 2 cloves and stuff each apple with 2 dates and 3 sultanas. Sprinkle with cinnamon. Top with brown sugar and dot with butter. Place water in an electric frying pan with lid off and set at 120°C (250°F). Bake apples with lid on and vent closed for 15-20 minutes or until apples are cooked but still firm. Serve hot or cold with either whipped cream, yoghurt or custard. Serves 6.

Peach and Cherry Compote

3 tablespoons butter or margarine
½ cup brown sugar
1 x 425g (13oz) can* cherries, drained,

½ cup liquid reserved
1 x 425g (13oz) can* peach halves,
drained, ½ cup liquid reserved

Melt butter in a frying pan and stir in the sugar and cherry liquid. Stir over a medium heat for 5 minutes. Add remaining fruit and liquid and continue cooking for a further 2 minutes until fruit has heated through. Serve hot with ice cream. Serves 4-6.
*nearest equivalent can size.

Plaited Plum Strudel

A lovely, light pastry dessert in which fresh plums may be used as an alternative, when in season.

125g (4oz) butter or margarine
2 cups fresh wholemeal breadcrumbs
2 tablespoons brown sugar
1 tablespoon finely grated lemon rind

1 x 825g (24oz) can* dark plums,
drained, stoned, liquid reserved
6 sheets filo pastry
¼ cup flaked almonds

Melt half the butter in a medium sized saucepan. Add the breadcrumbs and stir over heat until golden brown. Cool slightly then stir in the sugar and lemon rind. Remove ¼ cup of the crumbs and set aside for topping. Combine the remaining crumbs with the plums. Melt the remaining butter in a separate pan and brush 1 sheet of pastry with butter. Place another sheet directly on top and brush with butter. Spread ⅓ of the plum mixture along the centre and gently shape into a roll, brush with more melted butter immediately. Repeat with the remaining pastry and filling. Place the 3 rolls side by side on a baking sheet and plait together. Tuck ends underneath. Brush the top with any remaining butter and sprinkle with reserved crumbs and flaked almonds. Bake at 200°C (400°F) for 20 minutes and serve dusted with icing sugar, with cream or custard. Serves 6.
*nearest equivalent can size.

GARLIC FLAVOURED LEEKS (RECIPE PAGE 229) TOP

Strawberry Ice

A healthy ice, making good use of natural yoghurt and fresh strawberries.

2 teaspoons gelatine
2 tablespoons boiling water
1 punnet strawberries, hulled
1 carton natural yoghurt
2 egg whites
¼ cup caster sugar

Dissolve gelatine in boiling water and pour into a blender with the strawberries and yoghurt. Blend until smooth. Pour into a shallow dish or ice cream container and freeze until a border of ice crystals form around the edge. Beat mixture with a fork to break up ice crystals. Whisk egg whites until soft peaks form, then gradually add sugar and beat to a firm meringue. Carefully fold into the strawberry mixture and freeze for several hours until just firm. Spoon into chilled serving bowls and serve decorated with fresh strawberries. Serves 6-8.

Choc-Rum Delights

These are delicious served with coffee.

1 x 400g (13oz) can* condensed milk
1 x 100g (3oz) block dark chocolate
1 tablespoon gelatine
2 tablespoons water
2 tablespoons rum

Combine condensed milk and chocolate in a saucepan and heat gently until chocolate melts. Dissolve gelatine in hot water and stir into the chocolate mixture with the rum. Pour into a wetted 18cm (7") square cake tin and refrigerate overnight. Cut into squares and serve decorated as desired, by tossing in toasted ground almonds, sifted icing sugar or chopped unblanched almonds.
*nearest equivalent can size. Makes 36.

CATTLE DROVING, WOLLOGORANG CATTLE STATION, QUEENSLAND

EATING ON THE MOVE

Something to Liberate the Busy Cook.

Like most people living an urbanised western lifestyle, Australians can't seem to find enough time in the day, (Australia is one of the most urbanised societies in the world – most of us live in large cities on the coast). Anything that saves time, especially when it comes to preparing a meal, is welcome. Enter the microwave.

It's easy to see why the microwave is becoming the cooks "best mate". To begin with, cooking time is reduced by a third. You can defrost frozen foods easily and reheating takes a matter of minutes. Food doesn't stick to the inside of the oven or to dishes and utensils. And, you can almost throw away that oven mitt – microwaves stay cool even though the food is hot. The microwave also uses about half the energy of conventional cooking.

Whether it's a simple meal or a banquet, the microwave is perfect for Australians "living in the fast lane" (as the Americans say). The following are recipes that will liberate the busy cook.

JILLAROO (FEMALE JACKAROO) WITH SHEEPDOG PILLION RIDER TAKING LAMBS BACK TO MUM

Plum and Sultana Compote

A delicious way to serve plums; quick and easy cooked in the microwave. Serve with breakfast cereals.

500g (1lb) plums, washed
¼ cup water

¼ cup sugar
1 cup sultanas

Leave plums whole, but pierce each one with a fine skewer and place in a 5 cup casserole dish. Add water and sprinkle with sugar. Cover and microwave on HIGH for 8 minutes. Stir in the sultanas and allow to cool.   Serves 4.

WINDSURFING AT SUNSET, PATONGA, NEW SOUTH WALES

Fruit Kebabs

A wonderful way to serve a quick fruity breakfast.

small cubes ham
pineapple chunks
small apples, cored, thickly sliced

oranges, cut into segments with skin intact
bananas, thickly sliced
melted butter

Thread ham with the fruit alternately onto skewers. Brush with melted butter and grill to heat through. Remove from skewers and serve with cottage cheese.

Herbed Scrambled Eggs

Fresh herbs add that special touch and flavour to scrambled eggs.

2 eggs
2 tablespoons milk
¼ cup chopped fresh herbs-parsley,
thyme, chives

15g (½oz) butter or margarine
seasoning to taste

Beat the eggs with the milk, seasoning and herbs. Melt the butter in a small 2 cup dish on HIGH for 30 seconds, then pour in the egg mixture. Microwave on MEDIUM for 1-1½ minutes, stirring frequently. Do not overcook. Allow to stand before serving on hot buttered toast or muffins.   Serves 1.

Hot Fruit Muesli

½ cup rolled oats
1-2 tablespoons raw sugar or honey
⅓ cup toasted slivered almonds
2 tablespoons wheatgerm
cinnamon or nutmeg to taste
1 orange, peeled, chopped

1 banana, peeled, sliced
⅓ cup raisins
½ apple, cored, roughly chopped
3-4 tablespoons yoghurt
cinnamon or nutmeg for garnish

Place the oats, raw sugar, almonds, wheatgerm and cinnamon in a bowl. Microwave on HIGH for 2 minutes and stir. Add the chopped orange with the banana, raisins and apple and microwave on HIGH for a further 30 seconds-1 minute. Spoon into individual bowls, placing a tablespoon of yoghurt on top of each serve. Sprinkle with a little cinnamon or nutmeg and serve hot.
Serves 3-4.

Omelettes

A good omelette deserves a good pan. Keep your omelette pan for omelettes only, and never wash it. Just wipe clean with a damp cloth or paper towel and some salt. There are many types of omelettes and a great variety of fillings.

Basic Omelette
4 eggs
1½ tablespoons cold water

seasoning to taste
1 tablespoon butter or margarine

Break eggs into a basin and beat well with a fork. Add the water and seasoning. Melt butter in an omelette pan. When frothing, pour in egg mixture and leave for about 10-15 seconds, then stir. Lift up the edge of the omelette to let any raw egg run to the edge of the pan. Add the filling; tilt the pan away from you and fold the omelette over the filling. Gently slide on to a hot serving plate.   Serves 2.

Suggested Fillings
2 tablespoons grated cheese
Sliced mushrooms, sauteed in butter
Finely chopped cold chicken
Chopped bacon and onion, sauteed

Chopped prawns and shallots
Chopped ham
Cold cooked fish, flaked and mixed with
lemon

Poached Eggs with Caviar

Ideal for a special breakfast or Sunday lunch.

⅔ cup hot water
½ teaspoon vinegar
2 eggs
seasoning to taste

caviar
chives
buttered toast

Combine water and vinegar and pour into the base of 2 ramekins. Microwave on HIGH for 40 seconds, then break an egg into each one. Pierce the yolks carefully with a pin and season. Cover with plastic wrap and microwave on MEDIUM for 1-2 minutes approximately. As soon as the yolks start to change colour, stop cooking. Stand for 1 minute, then remove eggs with slotted spoon. Garnish with some caviar and chives and serve with fingers of toast.   Serves 2.

PHOTOGRAPH PAGE 260

HOT DOGS WITH A FOSTERS BEER (RECIPE PAGE 259)

Cinnamon Banana Muffins

A breakfast suggestion for those with a sweet tooth.

butter or margarine
2 English muffins, halved
creamed honey

small bananas, finely sliced
cinnamon

Butter the muffins and spread with creamed honey. Top 2 halves with the banana and sprinkle liberally with cinnamon. Cover with remaining muffin. Place on a plate and microwave on MEDIUM-HIGH for 1½ minutes.
Serves 2.

Savoury Muffins

Ideal for breakfast or as a midday snack.

2 English muffins, halved
4 slices salami
4 slices cheese

1 firm tomato, finely sliced
butter or margarine
seasoning to taste

Butter the muffins and top with the salami, cheese and tomato, season to taste. Place on a plate and microwave on MEDIUM-HIGH for 1½ minutes.
Serves 2.

Spanish Rice

1 cup long grain rice
3 cups water
1 onion, finely chopped
1 bay leaf
15g (½oz) butter or margarine
1 chicken breast

extra butter
2 bratwurst sausages
250g (8oz) scallops
125g (4oz) salami, diced
1 medium green capsicum, diced
2 tomatoes, sliced into wedges

Place rice, water, onion, bay leaf and butter into an 8 cup casserole, cover and microwave on HIGH for 10 minutes, so the rice is slightly undercooked. Place chicken breast in a small dish, rub with butter, add two tablespoons of water, cover and microwave on HIGH for 5 minutes, turning once. Allow to stand 3 minutes then dice. Pierce sausages, place in a 4 cup casserole, cover with water and plastic wrap and microwave on HIGH for 3 minutes. Slice sausages diagonally, removing the skin. Clean and wash scallops, place in a small dish, cover with a little water, plastic wrap and microwave on MEDIUM for 2 minutes. Combine all ingredients with the rice and microwave on HIGH for 2 minutes. Remove bay leaf before serving.
Serves 4.

Stuffed Capsicums

These capsicums are also delicious with tuna or salmon filling in place of meat.

30g (1oz) butter or margarine
1 onion, finely chopped
½ teaspoon oregano
125g (4oz) minced steak
125g (4oz) sausage mince
1 cup fresh breadcrumbs
2 tablespoons finely chopped parsley

1 small capsicum, finely diced
2 shallots, finely chopped
1 carrot, grated
1 egg, lightly beaten
seasoning to taste
4 medium-sized green capsicums.

Place butter, onion and oregano in a bowl, cover and microwave on MEDIUM-HIGH for 2 minutes. Add steak and sausage mince and microwave on HIGH for 5 minutes. Break cycle and stir. Allow to stand 5 minutes and drain off any excess fat. Add all other ingredients with the exception of the green capsicums, and combine thoroughly. Season to taste. With a sharp knife, carefully cut tops from the green capsicums, removing seeds. Spoon stuffing mixture into each capsicum and replace tops. Place capsicums into a baking dish or glass pie plate with 1 tablespoon of water. Cover and microwave on MEDIUM-HIGH for 7 minutes. Allow to stand 5 minutes before serving, or cool and serve cold.
Serves 4.

Mango Apricot Sauce

This sauce is an excellent accompaniment to seafood or poultry dishes.

2 mangoes, peeled, stoned
1¾ cups apricot or orange juice

1 tablespoon mint

Puree the mangoes with the juice and the mint in a food processor. Transfer to a casserole or jug and microwave on HIGH for 3 minutes.
Serves 4-6.

PHOTOGRAPH   PAGES 256-257

SPEEDY CHOW MEIN (RECIPE PAGE 260)

Speedy Spuds

A hearty lunch time snack that makes an ideal weekend treat.

4 medium potatoes
3 rashers bacon, chopped
1 onion, finely chopped
3 tablespoons sour cream

¼ cup grated cheese
1 tablespoon grated cheese (reserved),
seasoning to taste
4 shallots, chopped

Scrub potatoes and pierce the skins in several places. Microwave on HIGH for 10 minutes, then allow to cool. Microwave bacon and onion for 3 minutes. Slice top from potatoes, scoop out centres leaving a 2½cm (1") wall. Combine potato centres with the bacon, onion, sour cream, grated cheese and seasoning. Fill cavities of potatoes with bacon mixture, sprinkle with reserved cheese and shallots and reheat for approximately 2 minutes.
Serves 4.

CLASSIC STEAM TRAIN TRAVELLING THROUGH A PICTURESQUE VALLEY NEAR MUDGEE, NEW SOUTH WALES

Cauliflower Soup

A light tasty soup which may be served as an entree or main course.

1 small cauliflower	1 teaspoon Worcestershire sauce
3 tablespoons chopped shallots	2 tablespoons flour
2 tablespoons water	seasoning to taste
2½ cups hot chicken stock	½ cup grated tasty cheese
1 cup milk	2 tablespoons chopped shallots

Trim stalks and break cauliflower into small florets. Combine cauliflower, shallots and water. Cover and microwave for 5 minutes, drain off liquid. Add to the combined stock, ¾ cup of the milk and the Worcestershire sauce. Blend the remaining milk with the flour and stir into the liquid. Cover, microwave until boiling, approximately 10 minutes. Season and pour over the cauliflower. Top with cheese and reheat 3-4 minutes. Serve garnished with shallots.   Serves 3-4.

Hearty Vegetable Casserole

Suitable for vegetarian lunch.

2 carrots, sliced	1 x 440g (15oz) can*, cream of
250g (8oz) florets broccoli	chicken soup
4 small potatoes, sliced	1 cup sweet corn kernels
½ medium onion, finely chopped	1 cup grated tasty cheese
2 tablespoons water	2 teaspoons caraway seeds
2 medium zucchinis, sliced	½ cup breadcrumbs
	1 egg, beaten

Place the carrots, broccoli, potatoes and onion with the water into the base of a 5 cup casserole. Cover and microwave on HIGH for 8 minutes. Add the zucchini and microwave for a further 2 minutes. Combine the soup, corn, cheese, caraway seeds, breadcrumbs and beaten egg, in a large bowl. Drain the vegetables and add to the soup mixture. Cover and microwave on HIGH for 4 minutes. Allow to stand 3 minutes before serving.
*nearest equivalent can size.   Serves 4.

Tomato and Mushroom Casserole

For a crispy brown topping, place under a conventional preheated grill for 3-4 minutes or until browned.

30g (1oz) butter or margarine	seasoning to taste
1 onion, sliced	mixed herbs
1 shallot, chopped	½ teaspoon raw sugar
500g (1lb) ripe tomatoes, sliced	¾ cup wholemeal breadcrumbs
½ cup sliced mushrooms	¼ cup Parmesan cheese

Place half the butter in a 4 cup casserole with the onion and shallot and microwave on HIGH for 2 minutes. Add tomatoes, mushrooms, seasoning and herbs. Sprinkle with sugar, breadcrumbs and Parmesan cheese. Dot with the remaining butter, cover and microwave on HIGH for 6 minutes.   Serves 3-4.

Baked Avocado with Prawn Filling

Crabmeat or red salmon could be used in place of the prawns if preferred.

30g (1oz) butter or margarine	1 tablespoon sherry
2 tablespoons flour	1 shallot, finely chopped
¾ cup milk	1 x 220g (7oz) can* prawns, drained
1 tablespoon white wine	seasoning to taste
1 teaspoon French mustard	3 large avocadoes, halved
1 teaspoon Worcestershire sauce	1 tablespoon grated Parmesan cheese
4 teaspoons Tabasco sauce	paprika
2 teaspoons lemon juice	

Melt the butter in a medium sized bowl in the microwave for 1 minute on HIGH. Add flour, stir well and return to microwave for 20 seconds on HIGH. Stir in milk, wine and seasonings and microwave for a further 3-4 minutes, stirring occasionally. Add sherry, shallot, prawns, season to taste and allow to cool. Divide the mixture evenly between six avocado halves. Sprinkle with grated Parmesan cheese and a little paprika. Place in a baking dish and microwave on MEDIUM-HIGH for 6 minutes.   Serves 6.
*nearest equivalent can size.

MANGO APRICOT SAUCE (RECIPE PAGE 254) TOP LEFT

GLAZED CHICKEN WINGS (RECIPE PAGE 265) BOTTOM

GUM TREES IN MURRAY RIVER, VICTORIA

Pineapple Ham Steaks

2 *tablespoons brown sugar*
2 *tablespoons pineappple juice*
6 *cloves*
1 *teaspoon French mustard*
1 *teaspoon Worcestershire sauce*
4 *ham steaks*
4 *slices pineapple*

Place sugar, juice, cloves, mustard and sauce in a small bowl and microwave on HIGH for 4 minutes. Arrange ham steaks in a square baking dish with a slice of pineapple on each one. Glaze with the sauce and microwave on MEDIUM-HIGH for 5 minutes.

Serves 4.

PawPaw and Mango Beef Rolls

For those who love meat and fruit combinations, this makes an excellent main course, and can be served hot with the sauce or cold with the accompanying fruit.

6 *thinly sliced pieces topside steak*
1 x 175g (6oz) *jar pawpaw and mango chutney*
2 *cups wholemeal fresh breadcrumbs*
½ *teaspoon oregano*
½ *teaspoon marjoram*
seasoning to taste
60g (2oz) *butter or margarine*
1 *onion, finely chopped*
1 *shallot, finely sliced*
1 *tablespoon oil*
The Sauce
2 *tablespoons tomato paste*
1 *tablespoons cornflour*
1 *cup beef consomme*

Place steaks on a chopping board and pound, using a meat mallet. Spread with ⅔ of the pawpaw and mango chutney. Combine breadcrumbs, herbs and seasoning in a bowl. Melt the butter in the microwave on HIGH for 1½ minutes. Add the onion and shallot and microwave on HIGH for 2 minutes, then stir into the breadcrumb mixture. Sprinkle over the steaks and chutney, roll up and secure with toothpicks. Brush with oil and place in a shallow dish. Cover and microwave on HIGH for 6 minutes, turning occasionally, then on MEDIUM-HIGH for 4 minutes. Allow to stand. Combine the tomato paste, cornflour and remaining chutney in a 4 cup bowl and gradually mix in the beef consomme, cover and microwave on MEDIUM for 6-8 minutes or until it boils and thickens. Remove toothpicks from rolls and pour over the sauce; serve with pineapple wedges and fresh pawpaw or mango.

Serves 6.

Hot Dogs

Everyone loves a hot dog and those served straight from the microwave will certainly be a family favourite.

4 *frankfurters*
2 *tablespoons water*
4 *hot dog rolls*
mustard or tomato sauce

Pierce the frankfurters with a skewer or sharp knife and place in a shallow casserole. Add water, cover and microwave on MEDIUM for 3½ minutes. Allow to stand. Warm the rolls on HIGH for 30 seconds. Split, and fill with the frankfurters and your choice of mustard or sauce.

Serves 4.

PHOTOGRAPH PAGE 253

Tasty Hamburgers

These hamburgers could also be served in pita bread with shredded lettuce, tomato and cucumber.

500g (1lb) *minced beef*
1 *onion, finely chopped*
½ *cup dried breadcrumbs*
1 *egg, lightly beaten*
1 *tablespoon tomato sauce*
1 *tablespoon Parmesan cheese*
1 *teaspoon Worcestershire sauce*
1 *tablespoon evaporated milk*
1 *tablespoon lemon juice*
2 *tablespoons chopped parsley*
seasoning to taste
1-2 *tablespoon oil*

Combine the ingredients, with the exception of the oil, and make six hamburgers. Brush hamburgers with a little oil then arrange around the edge of a large plate. Cover with paper towel and microwave on medium high for 12-15 minutes. Allow to stand 3-4 minutes, then serve with your favourite sauce.

Serves 6.

PHOTOGRAPH PAGE 262

Curried Sausage Hot Pot

A quick and easy dish which will cope with emergencies.

500g (1lb) *thin sausages, pierced*
1 *packet curry soup*
3 *cups water*
½ *cup frozen peas*
1 *onion, finely chopped*
1 *carrot, finely chopped*
2 *large potatoes, cubed*
½ *cup sweet corn kernels*
1 *cup diced celery*
1 *tablespoon lemon juice*
1 *tablespoon chopped parsley*
boiled rice for serving

Place a double layer of paper towelling on a plate and place the sausages on top. Cover with plastic wrap and microwave on MEDIUM-HIGH for 3 minutes. Allow to cool, then remove the skins and cut into chunks. Mix the soup with a little water to make a paste and combine with all the other ingredients with the exception of the parsley and rice, in an 8 cup casserole dish. Microwave on HIGH approximately 10-12 minutes, stirring occasionally during the cycle, then microwave for a further 10 minutes on MEDIUM-HIGH, stirring halfway during the cooking cycle. Allow to stand for 10 minutes, serve on a bed of boiled rice, garnished with chopped parsley.

Serves 4-6.

JAFFA NUT CAKE (RECIPE PAGE 266)

Swedish Meatballs

These meatballs may be served with whole boiled potatoes or buttered noodles.

3 slices bread, crusts removed
1 egg, beaten
½ cup water
60g (2oz) butter or margarine
1 large onion, finely diced
750g (1½lb) minced beef

seasoning to taste
3 tablespoons cornflour
1½ cups water
⅔ cup evaporated milk
1 teaspoon soy sauce

Soak the bread in the combined egg and water. Melt half the butter with the onion in a container and microwave on HIGH for 3 minutes. Stir into the bread mixture. Add the mince, season and form into approximately 3 dozen balls. Cook in three batches allowing approximately 10 minutes for each batch, then transfer to a deep, nine cup casserole. Prepare the sauce by melting the remaining butter in a container on HIGH for 1 minute. Add cornflour and combine until smooth. Microwave for a further 1 minute on HIGH. Gradually stir in water, microwave on HIGH for 3 minutes, stirring frequently during cooking. Add evaporated milk, soy sauce and seasoning, stir and pour over meatballs. Cover and cook on MEDIUM for approximately 12-15 minutes. Serve hot, sprinkled with paprika and chopped parsley.   Serves 4-6.

Glazed Meat Loaf

Meat loaf makes an excellent, economical buffet or luncheon dish. Leftovers can be thinly sliced and used as sandwich fillings.

750g (1½lb) minced beef
⅔ cup dried breadcrumbs
150 ml (¼ pint) evaporated milk
1 egg
1 onion, finely chopped
2 tablespoons tomato sauce
1 tablespoon Worcestershire sauce

½ teaspoon mustard
2 beef stock cubes, crumbled
seasoning to taste
The glaze
¼ cup tomato sauce
1 tablespoon brown sugar
1 teaspoon mustard

Combine all the ingredients for the meat loaf and press into a loaf dish. Cover and microwave on high for 10 minutes, drain off fat and excess juices and continue to microwave, uncovered, a further 5 minutes on MEDIUM-HIGH, allow to stand. Combine the ingredients for the glaze in a small bowl and microwave for 4 minutes on MEDIUM-HIGH. Turn meat loaf out onto a serving dish and brush with the glaze, return to the microwave and cook on HIGH for 2 minutes. Serve hot or cold with fresh vegetables and a garnish of fresh herbs.   Serves 6-8.

POACHED EGGS WITH CAVIAR (RECIPE PAGE 252)

Easy Bolognaise Sauce

Serve over hot spaghetti with a bowl of Parmesan cheese.

30g (1oz) butter or margarine
1 onion, chopped
2 cloves garlic, crushed
1 carrot, finely chopped
1 stick celery, finely chopped
2 rashers bacon, finely chopped
500g (1lb) minced beef

1 tablespoon oil
1 x 425g (13oz) can* tomatoes,
  drained and chopped
3 tablespoons tomato paste
150ml (¼ pint) red wine
Parmesan cheese for serving

Place butter, onion, garlic, carrot, celery and bacon in a medium sized casserole dish. Cover and microwave on HIGH for 5 minutes, stirring occasionally. In separate dish, microwave meat on HIGH for 8 minutes. Stir in the vegetables, tomatoes, tomato paste, bay leaves and wine. Cover and microwave on HIGH for 5 minutes, then MEDIUM for a further 5 minutes.   Serve 4-6.
*nearest eqivalent can size.

Speedy Chow Mein

This speedy Chow Mein is delicious served with crusty bread or toast and garnished with spring onions.

500g (1lb) minced beef
1 onion, finely chopped
1 cup cooked rice
2½ cups water
1 packet chicken noodle soup

1 tablespoon curry powder
4 cups finely shredded cabbage
1 x 440g (15oz) can* pineapple
pieces, drained
¼ cup chopped chives

Combine all ingredients, with the exception of the cabbage, pineapple and chives, in a 9 cup casserole. Stir thoroughly, cover and microwave on HIGH for 10 minutes. Add the cabbage and pineapple, combine thoroughly, then microwave on MEDIUM-HIGH for a further 8 minutes.   Serves 5-6.
*nearest eqivalent can size.

PHOTOGRAPH   PAGE 254

OFFICIAL OPENING OF THE NEW NATIONAL PARLIAMENT HOUSE BY QUEEN ELIZABETH II, HERE ACCOMPANIED BY THE AUSTRALIAN PRIME MINISTER, MR BOB HAWKE, CANBERRA AUSTRALIAN CAPITAL TERRITORY

TASTY HAMBURGERS (RECIPE PAGE 259)

FRUIT SALAD BASKET (NO RECIPE) TOP; PEACH AND RUM CHEESECAKE (RECIPE PAGE 266) BOTTOM

Spiced Lamb Cutlets

This recipe is excellent cooked outside on a barbecue. Pre-cook lamb cutlets in the microwave on HIGH for 4 minutes, then barbecue, brushing them with the delicious plum sauce as they continue cooking.

2 tablespoons tomato sauce
2 tablespoons honey or brown sugar
2 tablespoons soy sauce
2 tablespoons plum jam
1 tablespoon dry mustard

2 teaspoons Worcestershire sauce
8 lamb cutlets, trimmed
1 tablespoon toasted sesame seeds
wedges of fresh pineapple
sprigs of herbs, for garnish

Combine the tomato sauce, honey, soy sauce, jam, mustard and Worcestershire sauce in a bowl. Arrange the lamb cutlets in a large, shallow casserole and top with a tablespoon of the mixture. Microwave on HIGH for 5 minutes then turn each cutlet over, spoon on more sauce and cook for a further 3 minutes on HIGH. If cutlets are a little thick, allow an extra 30 seconds to 1 minute. Transfer to a serving plate. Cover and allow to stand for 2 minutes. Reheat sauce and spoon over cutlets, sprinkle with sesame seeds. Serve with pineapple wedges. Garnish with fresh herbs.

PHOTOGRAPH   THIS PAGE

Serves 4-6.

Sweet Lamb Curry

Serve with fluffy rice and sauteed mixed blanched nuts, papadams, and a plate of fresh fruits such as paw paw, sliced banana, apple wedges and pineapple.

500g (1lb) lean lamb, cubed
2 tablespoons seasoned flour
2 cloves garlic, crushed
1 onion, chopped
1 stick celery, sliced
2 tablespoons oil

1 tablespoon curry powder
2 tablespoons fruit chutney
1-1½ cups beef stock
1 teaspoon lemon juice
½ green apple, diced
¼ cup sultanas

Toss meat in the flour and set aside. Microwave the vegetables in the oil on HIGH for 3 minutes, add curry powder and microwave for a further 2 minutes on HIGH. Stir in the lamb and add the beef stock. Cover and microwave on HIGH for 5 minutes, then stir in the sultanas, lemon juice and apple. Microwave on MEDIUM-HIGH for 15 minutes, stir and microwave for a further 10 minutes.

PHOTOGRAPH   PAGE 269
Serves 4.

SPICED LAMB CUTLETS (RECIPE PAGE 264)

Chicken and Mushroom Casserole

An ideal recipe for an informal dinner, as it can be prepared ahead of time and reheated in the microwave.

60g(2oz) butter or margarine
2 tablespoons oil
seasoned flour
1.5kg (3lb) chicken pieces
4 sticks celery, sliced
2 large onions, sliced
125g (4oz) mushrooms, sliced

4 rashers bacon, roughly chopped
2 cloves garlic, crushed
3 tablespoons flour
2½ cups chicken stock
seasoning to taste
⅓ cup parsley sprigs

Melt the butter in the oil, using a large saucepan, and saute the lightly floured chicken pieces on both sides until golden brown. Remove from pan. Add celery, onions, mushrooms, bacon and garlic and cook for approximately 2 minutes. Add flour, stir for 1 minute, then add the stock and seasoning. Stir until sauce boils and thickens. Place chicken into an ovenproof casserole, pour the sauce over and bake, covered, at 180°C (350°F) for 40 minutes or until chicken is tender. Sprinkle with chopped parsley and serve.

Serves 4-6.

Glazed Chicken Wings

These delicious wings can be served hot or at room temperature. They are very versatile and can be served as a main course, entree or as an excellent picnic food.

2 tablespoons peanut oil
⅓ cup soy sauce
2 tablespoons honey
2 tablespoons dry sherry

1 clove garlic, crushed
2 teaspoons Hoi Sin sauce
½ teaspoon finely grated root ginger
20 chicken wings

Make the marinade by combining the first seven ingredients. Place chicken wings in a large baking dish and pour over the marinade. Marinate for 2 hours, turning occasionally. Cover and microwave on HIGH for 6 minutes. Turn over wings and move centre ones to outside of dish. Microwave a further 6 minutes on MEDIUM-HIGH. Stand for 5 minutes before serving.

Serves 6-8.

PHOTOGRAPH   PAGES 256-257

Tuna Asparagus Casserole

Serve as a quick snack on muffins, toast or with rice or noodles.

1 x 440g (15oz) can* cream
asparagus soup
1 x 425g (13oz) can* tuna, drained,
flaked
3 hard boiled eggs, quartered

1 x 280g (9oz) can* champignons,
drained
1 cup frozen peas
1 cup potato chips, lightly crushed

Combine all ingredients with the exception of the potato chips in a 5 cup casserole. Top with the chips. Cover and microwave on MEDIUM-HIGH for 5 minutes. Serves 4-5.
*nearest equivalent can size.

REFRESHING MINT TEA (RECIPE PAGE 271)

Spaghetti Marinara

1 tablespoon oil
1 onion, finely chopped.
1 green capsicum, finely chopped
4 cloves garlic, crushed
4 tomatoes, peeled, chopped
3 tablespoons tomato paste

1/3 cup dry white wine
seasoning to taste
1 tablespoon oregano
1 teaspoon sugar
500g (1lb) mixed seafood
Parmesan cheese

Place all ingredients, with the exception of the seafood and Parmesan cheese, in a 3 cup casserole dish. Cover and microwave on HIGH for 10 minutes, stirring occasionally. Add prepared seafood and microwave for a further 3-5 minutes. Serve seafood sauce spooned over hot spaghetti, with the Parmesan cheese served separately. Serves 6.

Jaffa Nut Cake

125g (4oz) butter or margarine
1/2 cup sugar
2 teaspoons grated orange rind
2 eggs, lightly beaten
1 1/3 cups self-raising flour sifted
1/3 cup orange juice, approximately

60g (2oz) coarsely grated dark
chocolate
60g (2oz) walnuts, finely chopped
orange flavoured icing
cherries and pecan nuts for decoration

Cream butter and sugar together with the grated rind until light and fluffy. Gradually beat in the eggs, then fold in the flour, juice, chocolate and nuts. Pour mixture into a large, greased ring dish and microwave on MEDIUM for 10 minutes. stand for 10 minutes to cool before turning out. Ice and decorate with cherries and pecan nuts. Serves 6.

PHOTOGRAPH   PAGE   259

Pineapple and Almond Upside Down Cake

180g (6oz) butter or margarine
1/2 cup brown sugar
450g (15oz) can* pineapple rings
glace cherries
whole blanched almonds
1/2 cup sugar

1/4 cup ground almonds
almond essence
2 eggs, beaten
1 1/4 plain flour
pinch salt
2 teaspoons baking powder

Place 60g (2oz) of the butter into a round container and melt in the microwave on HIGH for 1 minute. Add the brown sugar, mix well and spread evenly over base of container. Drain the pineapple, reserving 4 tablespoons of the juice. Place the rings in the prepared base and arrange the cherries and whole almonds decoratively in and around the pineapple rings. Cream the remaining butter and sugar together until light and fluffy, then add the ground almonds, almond essence and the beaten eggs. Sift the flour, salt and baking powder together and fold into the creamed mixture, together with the pineapple juice. Spread the mixture evenly over the pineapple rings and microwave on MEDIUM-HIGH for 8-10 minutes or until the mixture is well risen and cooked. Allow to stand 8 minutes then turn out onto cooking rack. Serves 6-8.
*nearest eqivalent can size.

Peach and Rum Cheesecake

2 cups sweet biscuit crumbs
125g (4oz) butter or margarine,
melted
750g (1 1/2lb) cream cheese
3 eggs, lightly beaten
2/3 cup caster sugar
1 tablespoon lemon juice
1 teaspoon grated lemon rind

2 x 425g (13oz) cans* peach halves,
drained, liquid reserved
The Rum Glaze
1/3 cup apricot jam, sieved
1/3 cup reserved peach juice
1 tablespoon brown rum
1 tablespoon hot water
2 teaspoons gelatine

Combine the melted butter with the biscuit crumbs and press into a 23cm (9") flan dish. Refrigerate until firm. Cut cream cheese into small portions and place in a large bowl and soften, uncovered in the microwave on MEDIUM-HIGH for 30 secs. Add sugar and beat until smooth. Add lemon juice, rind and beaten eggs. Select the firmest peach halves and set aside for garnish. Chop remaining fruit finely and add to cream cheese mixture. Pour into the chilled crumb base. Microwave on MEDIUM-HIGH for 12 minutes. Stand for 10 minutes before removing cake from the microwave. Cool thoroughly. Arrange reserved peach halves on top of cheese cake. Dissolve the gelatine in the water, stir into the combined remaining ingredients and microwave on HIGH for 1-2 minutes. Cool slightly, pour over the cheese cake and refrigerate until set. Serves 8-10.
*nearest eqivalent can size.

PHOTOGRAPH   PAGE   263

ABORIGINAL ELDER EATING NECTAR, DARWIN, NORTHERN TERRITORY

Brandy Peach Crumble

This dessert can easily be adapted with a choice of other fruits, either fresh or canned.

1 x 825g (24oz) can* sliced peaches
2 tablespoons brandy
2 bananas, peeled, sliced
60g (2oz) butter or margarine

1 cup self-raising flour
¼ cup brown sugar
1 teaspoon cinnamon
⅓ cup coconut

Drain the peaches and place in a 4 cup casserole, reserving ¼ cup of syrup. Pour the syrup over the peaches with the brandy and stir in the bananas. Prepare the crumble topping by rubbing the butter into the flour until it resembles breadcrumbs. Continue mixing and blend in the sugar, cinnamon and coconut. Sprinkle evenly over the fruit and microwave on HIGH for 7 minutes. Allow to stand 8 minutes before serving with whipped cream or custard.   Serves 6.

*nearest equivalent can size.

Marble Puddings

60g (2oz) butter or margarine
60g (2oz) brown sugar
1 egg
½ cup self-raising flour, sifted

1 tablespoon milk
3 teaspoons cocoa
1 tablespoon hot water
¼ cup vanilla essence

Grease 5 ramekins. Cream the butter and sugar together, beat in the egg and fold in the flour and milk, mixing well. Spoon 1 tablespoon of the mixture into each ramekin and add the combined cocoa, hot water and vanilla essence to the remaining mixture. Top up each ramekin and swirl the two mixtures together with a spoon. Place around the edge of the microwave carousel and microwave on MEDIUM for 4-6 minutes. Allow to stand 1-2 minutes prior to serving.   Serves 5.

DOYLES SEAFOOD RESTAURANT, WATSONS BAY, SYDNEY, NEW SOUTH WALES

SWEET LAMB CURRY (RECIPE PAGE 264)

Pecan Chocolate Mousse

125g (4oz) *cooking chocolate, chopped* ¼ *cup chopped pecan nuts*
4 *eggs, separated* 150ml (¼ *pint) cream*
⅓ *cup sugar* 30g (1oz) *cooking chocolate, grated*
1 *teaspoon vanilla*

Place chopped chocolate in the top of a double saucepan and stir over hot water until melted. Remove from heat. Place the egg yolks, sugar and vanilla into a food processor and process until pale in colour. Transfer to a bowl and stir in the melted chocolate and walnuts. Beat the egg whites until soft peaks form and fold through the chocolate mixture. Spoon into 4 individual glass bowls and refrigerate for several hours. Serve decorated with the grated chocolate and whipped cream. Serves 4.

Cherry Brandy Trifle

The Custard
1 egg
4 tablespoons flour
3 tablespoons sugar
½ teaspoon vanilla essence
2⅓ cups milk

The Trifle
1 Swiss roll
1 cup strawberries
2 small bananas
2 tablespoons cherry brandy
1 cup cream, whipped
glace cherries and angelica for decoration

Combine the egg, flour, sugar and essence in a bowl. Heat the milk in the microwave on HIGH for 4 minutes, pour into the egg mixture whisking continually and strain. Microwave on MEDIUM-LOW for 6 minutes, whisking 3 or 4 times throughout the cooking time. Allow to cool. Prepare the trifle by cutting the swiss roll into slices and lining a glass bowl. Scatter the fruit over the roll and sprinkle with cherry brandy. Pour over the custard and chill until firm. Decorate with whipped cream and glace cherries just prior to serving. Serves 6.

Rich Chocolate Cheesecake

A delightful Microwave dessert, easy to make.

250g (8oz) chocolate biscuits, crushed
125g (4oz) butter or margarine, melted
2 tablespoons milk
125g (4oz) dark chocolate, grated

750g (1½lb) cream cheese
⅔ cup caster sugar
3 eggs, lightly beaten
2 tablespoons brandy

Combine the biscuits with the melted butter and press around base and sides of a 23cm (9") round pie dish and refrigerate until firm. Place the milk and grated chocolate into a bowl and microwave on medium for 1 to 2 minutes, stirring twice until the chocolate has melted. Remove from oven and cool. Beat the cream cheese and sugar together in a bowl until smooth. Add the eggs, brandy and cooled chocolate mixture and stir until combined. Pour into the chilled biscuit base and Microwave on 'MEDIUM' for 7 minutes then 'MEDIUM LOW' for a further 7 minutes. Stand for 10 minutes then cool completely. Serve with whipped cream. Serves 8-10.

PHOTOGRAPH PAGE 184-185

White Wine Pears

Serve pears with scoops of vanilla ice cream and a little of the sauce spooned over the top.

1½ cups water
1½ cups white wine
5cm (2") cinnamon stick

½ cup sugar
½ teaspoon vanilla sugar
4 firm pears, peeled, cored, sliced

Place water, white wine, cinnamon stick, sugar and vanilla sugar into saucepan. Stir over a low heat until sugar dissolves, bring to the boil, then add the pears. Cover and simmer gently until pears are tender, approximately 5 minutes. Chill thoroughly. Serves 4-6.

Minted Orange Slices

A refreshing dessert, particularly suited to the summer months.

¾ cup brandy
½ cup water
½ cup sugar

⅓ cup dry ginger ale
1 tablespoon finely chopped mint
4 oranges, peeled, sliced.

Combine all the ingredients with the exception of the mint and oranges, in a medium casserole. Microwave on HIGH for 5 minutes, stirring once. Add the mint and allow to cool. Pour over the sliced oranges and serve in chilled glass bowls; garnished with a sprig of mint. Serves 4.

Choco Nut Cream Pie

Crumb Crust
220g (7oz) plain biscuits, crushed
60g (2oz) hazelnuts
90g (3oz) butter or margarine, melted
Filling
150g (5oz) cooking chocolate, roughly chopped

2 teaspoons gelatine
2 tablespoons boiling water
60g (2oz) hazelnuts, finely chopped
2 tablespoons brandy
1¼ cups cream
extra whipped cream for decoration
30g (1oz) cooking chocolate, grated

Make the crust by combining the biscuits, nuts and butter together and pressing the mixture into a 20cm (8") pie plate. Refrigerate until firm. Melt the roughly chopped chocolate in the top of a double saucepan. Allow to cool. Dissolve the gelatine in the boiling water. Combine the hazelnuts, chocolate, brandy, cream and gelatine. Pour into the crumb crust and refrigerate until set. Decorate with whipped cream and grated chocolate, prior to serving. Serves 6-8.

Tasty Baked Apples

This recipe is a most popular microwave dessert because it is just so quick and easy.

4 granny smith apples
½ cup of water
3 tablespoons butter or margarine
3 tablespoons brown sugar

1 tablespoon sultanas
1 tablespoon chopped walnuts
cinnamon

Wash and core apples and place into a 4 cup dish with ½ cup water. Soften butter in the microwave on HIGH for 20 seconds and beat in the sugar, sultanas, walnuts and cinnamon. Fill the apples with the fruit mixture, cover and microwave on HIGH for 4-6 minutes. Allow apples to stand for 3 minutes before serving. The cooking time may vary, depending on the size of the apples. Serves 4.

Refreshing Mint Tea

Chilled mint tea makes a delicious summer thirst quencher. Keep in a jug in the refrigerator. Serve over ice cubes and decorate with slices of lemon or strips of cucumber skin.

4 cups boiling water
2 tea bags
1 cup fresh mint leaves, washed, bruised

4 teaspoons sugar
4 thin slices lemon
4 sprigs fresh mint

Place water, tea bags, mint, sugar and lemon into a large teapot or heatproof jug and infuse for a minute. Strain into cups and serve with a sprig of fresh mint. Serves 4.

PHOTOGRAPH PAGE 266

Mulled Wine

3 cups red wine
2-3 drops Angostura bitters
3 cloves
small piece cinnamon stick

twist of lemon peel
3 teaspoons caster sugar
pinch allspice

Place all ingredients into a large jug or bowl. Microwave on HIGH for 4 minutes but do not allow to boil. Strain into heatproof glasses and serve warm. Serves 4.

Brandied Coffee

3 mugs hot coffee
3 teaspoons raw sugar
3 teaspoons brandy

3 tablespoons whipped cream
nutmeg

Stir sugar into each mug of coffee. Float the brandy on top and serve with a bowl of whipped cream, flavoured with grated nutmeg. Serves 3.

EXPO 88, BRISBANE QUEENSLAND

SUNRISE ON TROPICAL CARDWILL BEACH, QUEENSLAND

The Australian way of
NUTRITION AND HEALTH

A Chinese physician of the 11th Century, once said "Experts in the use of medicines are inferior to those who recommend proper diet." This physician obviously was an advocate of preventative medicine.

It is true that with the knowledge of nutrition available to us today, we can all take better control of our health. We do not have to resort to medication to put right the wrong we have done to our health through bad diet.

The temptations to eat incorrectly are many. With the vast variety of foods available to Australians, there is a tendency to over nutrition in our society, brought about by the incorrect choice of food. Many factors influence our choice of food, the one which is difficult to resist is the media, which continually promotes foods which should be eaten only occasionally at best. However, the choice is there and the best approach is to maintain a well balanced diet selected from the five food groups, then practice a policy of moderation in the amount of fatty foods, sweet foods and alcohol consumed

Common health problems which are related, at least in part, to a poor choice of food and drink are:

*obesity   *constipation
*heart disease   *some cancers
*high blood pressure   *gallstones
*diseases of the digestive system   *liver disease
*tooth decay   *diabetes

In an effort to improve the diet of Australians, a set of Dietary Guidelines has been developed. People from all backgrounds can follow these guidelines and still prepare food creatively and enjoy eating while maintaining health.

The Dietary Guidelines

1. Eat a variety of foods each day: select foods from the five food groups which are
1. Breads and Cereals
2. Fruits and Vegetables
3. Lean meat, fish, poultry, eggs, legumes
4. Milk, cheese, yoghurt
5. Butter, oil, margarine

Each of these groups provides a number of nutrients, so selecting from within each group, a full compliment of nutrients necessary for health will be obtained.

2. Maintain your weight within the accepted range : this means to maintain a healthy weight in relation to height. People who are overweight are more likely to develop conditions such as high blood pressure, heart disease, and gall bladder problems. Also, be careful of taking slimming to an extreme, which can also be detrimental to health.

3. Limit the fat in your diet: a high-fat diet is often associated with excess weight and a number of other health problems. It may contribute to high levels of cholesterol in the blood. The Australian Heart Foundation and other health authorities recommend that only about 30% of kilojoule intake should come from fat.

4. Avoid eating too much sugar: sugars of all types contribute kilojoules but no protein, dietary fibre, minerals or vitamins. They are considered empty energy foods, which means they contribute energy to the body but no nutrients. Complex carbohydrates contribute energy as well as other valuable nutrients.

5. Eat more wholemeal breads,wholegrain cereals, vegetables and fruit: breads, cereals, vegetables and legumes provide complex carbohydrates and dietary fibre. Fruit is also a source of fibre. These foods supply many necessary vitamins and minerals. The various types of fibre they contain are helpful in preventing constipation, and diseases of the colon.

6. Use less salt: salt contains sodium, and a high intake has been linked with high blood pressure and strokes.

Many processed foods contain high levels of sodium in the form of salt and other sodium compounds such as monosodium glutamate. Is is wise to limit the consumption of these foods and refrain from adding salt at the table.

7. Limit alcohol consumption : alcoholic drinks have no nutritional value, but they are high in kilojoules and may contribute to excess weight. Heavy drinkers may develop a range of health problems including liver disorders and some vitamin deficiencies.

8. Promote breast feeding : breast milk meets the infant's nutritional needs more exactly than formula. It also contains valuable antibodies to protect the infant against a number of diseases. Breast milk may help prevent allergies in the infant.

THE SIX ESSENTIAL NUTRIENTS

1. Proteins: are needed by the body to build all body tissues. They are essential for growth and to maintain and repair the cells of the body. Protein foods are meat, fish poultry, dairy products, pulses, wholegrain cereals and nuts.

2. Carbohydrates: supply the body with energy, and come in two forms, sugar and starches. Sugars are mainly in cane sugar, fruits, honey. Starches are contained in cereals and cereal products (such as breakfast cereal products, bread, porridge) and vegetables particularly legumes and root vegetables. It is important to have a high intake of the starches or complex carbohydrates as these provide other nutrients and dietary fibre. Foods containing a high proportion of refined cane sugar should be limited as they have a lot of energy but no other nutrients and no fibre eg. sweets, soft drinks.

3. Fats: in small amounts eg. butter, oil, fat on meat etc., are essential in the diet for they contain fat soluble vitamins such as vitamin A, D and E and some essential fatty acids. They supply twice the kilojoules as proteins or carbohydrates. Most Australians have too much fat in their diet, for health reasons it is advisable to restrict fat intake.

4. Vitamins: are essential for life and health, they are needed for various chemical reactions to occur in the body. Vitamins are found mainly in fresh fruits and vegetables, and it is important to have a daily supply of these foods. As some vitamins are destroyed during cooking include some raw fruit and vegetable in the daily diet.

5. Minerals: like vitamins, are important to help in complex chemical reactions, and are needed by the bones and blood. Dairy products, fruits and vegetables provide minerals.

6. Water: comprises about 70% of the human body. Water is continually leaving the body in air breathed out from the lungs, in sweat from the skin and other body functions. Although some foods have a natural water content, it is necessary to have six to eight glasses of water a day.

The Australian way of
VEGETABLES

The ancient world, about 250 B.C., had already accumulated a large variety of fresh vegetables which later were taken into Europe either through trade routes or by the Romans. With the fall of Rome and the era of the dark ages, the tribes of Europe were more concerned with warring with each other, than with the tillage of their soil. Over the centuries there was little vegetable cultivation, the main food being meat and cereals, mostly, cereals, which did not require the attention that vegetable patches demanded.

Emperor Charlemagne who united in one superstate all the Christian lands in Western Europe (768-814) was responsible for the re-establishment of vegetable growing in all his domains. He travelled around his vast empire issuing orders and instructing his stewards in the management of the estates down to a detailed list of what vegetables to plant. His empire survived only for one generation after his death and again the vegetable gardens became extinct through preoccupation with war and unrest. King Henry IV of France, in the 17th Century, led the way for their revival, encouraging vegetables to be grown and vineyards to be planted.

By this time the vegetables from the New World had made their appearance in Europe and England and they were to have a profound influence in the cuisines of many nations and the diets and well being of the people.

Artichoke:

Artichokes grew wild around the Mediterranean. In ancient times the Romans made use of them for a short while, but they soon became a forgotten vegetable. Cooks in Florence, in the 14th Century, began creating dishes using artichokes which became very popular. They have remained part of the Italian cuisine ever since. The French, learning from the Italians, elevated the artichoke to a sophisticated vegetable.

Asparagus:

Throughout its history the cultivated asparagus has been considered a luxury vegetable. The ancient Egyptians cultivated asparagus and considered it a worthy offering to the Gods. The Greeks and Romans prized the cultivated asparagus highly. The wild form originated on the steps of Eastern Europe and came via Asia Minor to the Mediterranean.

Broccoli:

Belongs to the cabbage family, originated in Asia Minor and around the Mediterranean. The Romans were extremely fond of broccoli; it remained in the area until Italy gave the broccoli to the modern world, together with the name which remained unchanged in other countries. By 1560 it was grown in France and appeared in England in 1720. Broccoli is one of the western vegetables adopted by the Chinese, and is used extensively in their cuisine.

Okra:

Okra originated in Ethiopia and spread into the Middle East. It was taken to North Africa by the Arabs and travelled south with traders to the Ivory Coast. From here it was taken to Brazil and the Carribean and the southern states of U.S.A. Negro cooks made it so popular that it prompted its introduction back into Europe.

Potato:

The conquest of Peru by the Spanish (1530) yielded much treasure, but none so lasting as the potato. This amazing vegetable was to conquer cuisines of the world, although at the beginning many were reluctant to accept it. The potato was brought back to Spain in 1553 and was well received as it was in Italy a little later. It was planted in Ireland where it soon became the major crop. England, France and Germany hesitated for many years before they too finally succumbed.

Tomato:

Originated in Peru and spread north to Mexico. The Spanish brought the seeds to Spain, and they were passed onto Italy almost immediately. It was the Italians who cultivated the tomato to the large, red variety we know today, and who were the first to use it in cooking. In England they, for a time, only used it in the making of Tomato Ketchup.

Onion:

It is difficult to trace the origin of the onion for its use goes back a long time. However its recorded history begins in Mesopotamia in 3,000 B.C. From there they spread west to Ancient Egypt, Greece and Rome, and east to China and India. The American continent also had its own indigenous variety of onions. They grew in abundance on the shore of Lake Michigan. Later a city which developed near the area took for its name the Indian word for "their odour", Chicago.

Spinach:

Compared to other vegetables, spinach is a recent arrival. It is believed to have originated in Persia and that the plant travelled westwards in 650 A.D. and eastwards to China about the same time. It arrived in Europe and England about the 12th Century.

Capsicum:

Originated in tropical America and includes many varieties. They became known to the world after voyages of Columbus and made great changes to many cuisines. The capsicum became a favourite in Italy, the Balkans and Middle East. Hungary coloured and flavoured her cooking with the paprika, and India 'hotted' her curries with the chili.

Green Beans:

Native of Mexico and Guatemala, were unknown until the Spanish Conquistadors entered Mexico. The plant had already penetrated into North America and was growing in the North East and the dry South West. It was well received in Europe and England and eventually replaced the broad bean which was the only bean growing in the Old World. It is now one of the most commonly used vegetables throughout the world.

The Australian way of
FRUITS

Fruits were early man's first food. Prehistoric man survived on fruit and nuts before he learnt to hunt, gather grains and cultivate vegetables. The species of fruits our planet offered in their natural state varied with climatic zones and continents.

With the development of civilization man learnt to tame the wild variety and to improve the quality of the fruit. He was also responsible for transporting the species from its indigenous location to other areas, thus increasing the food supply available.

How these foods found their way around the world is

a fascinating and exciting study. At first there was an interchange between Asia and Europe for there existed land routes which connected them. With the opening up of sea routes and the discovery of the Americas, there was a far greater interchange which benefited both the Old and the New World. By the time Australia was settled in 1788, the cycle of exchange was almost completed, and she was able to stock the new countries larder with the fruits of the thousands of years of exchange and development.

Strawberry:

Wild strawberries of many varieties have always grown on the European and American Continents. Repeated attempts to cross wild varieties to produce a larger, sturdier fruit failed, until by chance, plants from Virginia found themselves side by side with plants from Chile in the same strawberry patch in Brittany, France. This resulted in the beautiful fruit we enjoy today.

Strawberries are a rich source of Vitamin C.

Oranges:

A native of South China and known there from around 2,000 B.C.

It remained a Chinese secret for many centuries. India and Persia were the next to enjoy the orange from around the 1st or 2nd century A.D., but it was not until the 8th century that the European continent received the orange, brought with the Arab conquerors to Spain.

Columbus took orange seedlings back to the New World on his second voyage and planted them on a Caribbean Island in 1493. Some twenty years later, the orange was growing in Panama and Mexico, and a little later it made its first entrance into North America, being planted in Florida. The famous Californian oranges began with plantings in 1707.

Oranges are an excellent source of Vitamin C.

Mango:

Sometimes called "the apple of the tropics". It is native to Eastern India and adjacent tropical areas. The mango was slow to travel abroad, but it eventually did, firstly to Africa in the 10th Century. Brazil received the mango around 1700 and a little later it was planted in the West Indies. Florida plantings date from 1825 and about this time tropical Australia received them.

India produces about 80% of the total world output.

Mango is a good source of Vitamin A.

Plums:

It is not possible to identify a native location for the plum as it grew wild on all continents except Antarctica. The many varieties we now enjoy are the result of centuries of crossbreeding the wild varieties.

In ancient times it was the Damascus plum that was highly prized. Today, the Domestica with its many varieties is the most popular.

Plums contain some Vitamin A and C.

Apples:

Carbonized apples dated 6,500 B.C. have been found in Asia Minor although many theories place the origin of the wild apple much further north. The Ancient Egyptians, Etruscans and Greeks all cultivated apples. Apples feature prominently in ancient mythology and the folklore of many nations. It is considered the "king of fruits".

The varieties of apples that now exist in the world run into tens of thousands but it is the few popular varieties that are produced to satisfy the market. Of these, the Delicious is the most popular.

Apples are a good source of fibre and a fair source of Vitamins A & C.

Paw paw:

A native fruit of the Caribbean, also know as papaya. Columbus referred to the fruit as a tree melon called "the fruit of angels". It very quickly took flight from the area and was soon thriving in many tropical areas in the East and in the Orient.

Paw paw is a good source of Vitamin A and Vitamin C.

Grapes:

The wild grape flourished in the Caucasus and it was probably there that the first cultivation began. By 3,000 B.C. it was established in Mesopotamia and later travelled through to the Mediterranean.

Greek colonists planted vines in the Marseilles area of Southern France and Sicily, this being its first foothold in Western Europe. It penetrated further into Europe with the Romans.

There are approximately 8,000 varieties of grapes, natural and cultivated which are used to make wine, for table grapes and are also used for drying to make sultanas and raisins.

Grapes are a fair source of Vitamin C and calcium.

Apricot:

Chinese records show that apricots were cultivated in China around 2,000 B.C.. They travelled a long road through Persia to the Middle East and Mediterranean area about 100 B.C. Being a fragile fruit they did not progress far from there until the Moors planted them in Granada, Spain after the 8th Century. Their big step into Europe came with the return of the Crusaders, but did not arrive in England until 1562. About 1629 they were introduced into America, their first plantings being in Virginia, and much later, planted by the Mission Fathers in California.

Apricots are a fair source of Vitamins A and C.

Pineapple:

A native fruit of Central and South America. It was first encountered when Columbus and his crew landed on the Caribbean Island of Guadaloupe. It did not take long for Spanish and Portugese traders to take it to India and the East Indies, they were already well established there by the mid 1500's. Africa also received the pineapple around this time.

The Pacific Islands received the pineapple when Captain Cook planted it on some of the islands in 1777. Hawaii, which is the world's largest pineapple producer, first received the plant in 1790. Pineapple is a very good source of Vitamin C.

Banana:

The banana is a native plant of South East Asia and India. It was very slow in making its way around the world; Africa received the banana early in the Christian era, possibly brought by Indonesian invaders to Madagascar. But the big step for the banana was when it was introduced into the New World and planted on a Caribbean Island in 1516. Central and South America are now the major banana producing countries.

Bananas are a good source of carbohydrate and a fair source of Vitamin C.

HERBS

The Australian cook is now very conscious of the variety and use of fresh herbs. Parsley and mint which once dominated the kitchen now have many companions: fresh basil, chives, dill, sage and sorrel to name but a few.

The use of fresh herbs goes back to ancient times where they were used for culinary and medicinal purposes as well as making dyes, cosmetics, perfumes and essences. Many herbs grew naturally around the Mediterranean area, but cultivation of herbs was first begun by the Romans who added species from other areas to the indigenous variety. In the Middle Ages, monks planted formal herb gardens in their

monasteries, mainly for medicinal purposes, importing species from Eastern areas in the course of trade with the spice lords. In France the nobility planted herb gardens in their castle grounds and encouraged their cooks to create new and exciting dishes which later became the Haute Cuisine of France.

All cultures have their favourite herb which predominates in their cuisine. Dill predominates in Scandinavian and Russian cooking, basil in the Italian cuisine, rigoni or oregano in the Greek, and the French love their 'fines herbes' selection which include chervil, chives, parsley and tarragon.

Basil:

Basil originated in India. It has a spicy aroma which enhances salads, tomato dishes, poultry, omelettes and spaghetti dishes. Its name, from the Greek basilikon, means "kingly". It is held in reverance by the Greeks as it was growing over the Holy Cross when found by St. Helen, the mother of Emperor Constantine, who first allowed freedom of worship to the Christians.

Bay Leaf:

Used in soups, stews, sauces and casseroles, one leaf is enough to impart flavour. Its true name is Bay Laurel, and it originated in the Mediterranean area.
There were no gold medals for the first Olympians of Ancient Greece, the winning athletes were crowned with a wreath of laurel leaves. It was also considered a symbol of honour given to victors in battle and to outstanding men of letters.

Chervil:

Has a subtle flavour which is lost when cooked, so is best added to the dish in the last 5 to 10 minutes of cooking or finely chopped and sprinkled over the cooked dish. It is used in soups, many sauces, in egg dishes, cream cheese and salads. It also enhances poultry and fish.
Chervil is a native of South-western Russia. It is considered the "herb of joy" as its Greek name 'chairephyllon' testifies.

Chives:

Have a mild onion-garlic flavour and are used on egg and cheese dishes, salads, soups and over cooked vegetables. Chives are said to have originated in Siberia and some have theorised that they spread across the top of the world into Alaska then America before they appeared in Europe.

Coriander:

Is both a herb and a spice; the dried seeds from the plant being the spice. It originated in the Eastern Mediterranean area and was known and used in early ancient times in the Aegean, Egypt, Babylon and Assyria. Its aroma was praised by some and abhorred by others. It is used to flavour soups, salads, curries and stews, and used extensively in oriental dishes.

Dill:

Finely snipped dill leaves go with almost all foods, the pleasing flavour being especially good in lettuce salads and spinach dishes. Although dill originated in the warm Mediterranean area it is the cold countries of the north that make the most use of the herb. Dill is an essential flavouring in Scandinavian, Russian, Polish, Czechoslavakian and Hungarian cooking.

Fennel:

Is used widely in Italian cooking. Its mild aniseed flavour enhances fish and potato dishes, green tossed salads and tomato based dishes.
Fennel is indigenous to the Mediterranean area.

Mint:

There are many varieties but the Spearmint is the variety mostly used in the kitchen. This is the mint which gives flavour to mint sauce, mint jelly and used with green peas. Mint originated in the Mediterranean area where it was used widely for medicinal purposes in ancient times.

Marjoram:

The subtle aroma of this herb gives flavour to chicken, fish and egg dishes. Shakespeare referred to it as "the herb of grace". In Ancient Greece and Rome, bridal bouquets included sprigs of marjoram to ensure a happy marriage. The custom found its origin in mythology, which tells us that Aphrodite, the goddess of love first gave the plant its sweet perfume from her handling of it. Marjoram is indigenous to the Mediterranean area.

Oregano:

Resembles marjoram but is stronger and spicier in aroma. The two herbs are often confused. Oregano is the main flavouring in many Italian and Greek dishes. It is used in lamb and beef dishes, in tomato sauces and soups.

Parsley:

Originated around the Mediterranean. From ancient times to the present day, parsley has retained its reputation as the herb most frequently used.

Rosemary:

Is yet another herb which originated in the Mediterranean area. In ancient times it was highly regarded for its health properties, particularly for relieving nervous headaches. Students in Ancient Greece placed sprigs of rosemary in their hair while studying, for they believed it stimulated their memory. It came to be known as the "herb of remembrance". Rosemary has a fresh resinous flavour which suits lamb, veal, beef and pork dishes, as well as many vegetable dishes.

Sage:

Sage was first used as a medicinal plant and was often added to dishes such as sausages and stuffings, only to counteract the richness of the dish and aid in its digestion. It gradually gained favour as a culinary herb and is used in many meat and vegetable dishes. Sage is indigenous to the Mediterranean area.

Sorrel:

Has a sharp flavour which enhances soups and sauces. A few sorrel leaves torn into a tossed salad gives a pleasant tangy flavour. Sorrel originated in Southern France and is widely used in French cooking.

Savory:

This herb is also noted for its medicinal properties, and was included in foods to aid digestion . It is added to leguminous vegetables, pulses and lentils for flavour and to aid in their digestion. Savory is indigenous to the Mediterranean area.

Tarragon:

Has a tart flavour and is used to season sauces, soups, stews and salads. It is also good for chicken and fish dishes. A plant of the Mediterranean area although its place of origin is not clear. Some say it originated on the steppes of Asia. It is widely used in French cooking.

Thyme:

The pungent flavour of thyme adds zest to stews, casseroles, meat loaves, rissoles and stuffings. It is used in mixed herb blends. A native of the Mediterranean area, it was widely acclaimed for its medicinal qualities, particularly for the treatment of coughs and colic.

The Australian way of
CEREALS AND GRAIN

The word cereals comes from the latin 'ceres', the name of the goddess the Romans worshipped to protect their wheat crop.

Nature provided these small grains, and at first, they were carried by the wind, or by birds to grow further afield. They were sometimes carried by man in his wanderings. Maize, which is a heavy grain, depended only on man for its expansion. After their systematic cultivation began they travelled further through trade, until all peoples had one or several kinds of these valuable grains.

In areas where each grain thrived they became the staple food of that area. Thus the seven cereals came to be identified with certain areas. Wheat was the grain of Southern Europe and the Middle East, rye and oats of Northern Europe. Millet was important to Africa, rice to Asia and maize to the Americas. With the development of new strains of the various grains, cereals are able to grow in more varied climatic areas.

Maize:

The Spaniards reported back to Columbus, after exploring the interior of Cuba, that they came upon a grain which tested well when baked and made into flour. It was maize or corn as it is more commonly called.

This amazing grain was found in systematic cultivation in many parts of South, Central and North America. Its probable place of origin was Mexico, Honduras or Guatemala, and it had already spread north and south long before the voyages of discovery.

When maize came into Europe, about 1520, it was introduced into an already civilized and organized world, and within fifty or sixty years, it was being grown in Europe, Africa and Asia. In Africa it greatly improved the diet of the people who had little grain to nourish them. In Europe, large amounts of corn or maize was consumed more through the pork, eggs and poultry it produced than the grain itself.

Oats:

Oats were cultivated in Northern Europe about 1,000 B.C. It was first noticed as a weed in the wheat fields and was usually pulled out and fed to the horses. At times when the wheat crop failed, the farmers took to eating the oats, and so its recognition as a food began. The Germanic Tribes sowed oats for their horses as well as themselves. As the horse gained importance as a means of transport, its cultivation increased.

In the Celtic lands, oats were always appreciated and used mainly as a food. The Scots love their oatmeal porridge and the Welsh love their oatcakes. Oats progressed from an animal fodder to a health food, for today it is in great demand for high fibre and low cholesterol diets.

Rice:

Much research and investigation has gone into establishing the place of origin of the rice plant. All evidence now points to Thailand or thereabouts, as grains found at an archeological site date back to 3,500 B.C. China and India had rice under cultivation some 800 years later. Japan received the grain about 100 B.C. It was considered so important that during feudal times, a man's wealth was estimated on how much rice he produced. Rice completed its eastern march as all of South East Asia accepted it as their staple food.

The western march took longer. It was taken to Persia and passed on to the Arabs in the Middle East. The Arabs took rice further west into Spain in the 8th Century. By the 11th Century, Italy was cultivating rice in the north. The rest of Europe may have sampled rice but cultivation there is difficult, if not impossible.

The New World was to receive rice in the rapid exchange of foods which took place after its discovery. It is used extensively in Mexican and South American Cooking.

Wheat:

When early man decided to plant wheat and wait around to harvest it, nomadism was abandoned, fixed settlements began, and civilization was born.

This occurred around 1,000 B.C. in Mesopotamia, there is also evidence that the cultivation of wheat and urban settlement was happening about the same time in some areas of Europe.

Wheat is an amazing plant, and will grow almost anywhere. In its wild state it spread over a vast territory, both west and east of its place of origin which was Asia Minor. Altitude is no problem to wheat, it grows from below sea level as in Jericho which is 825 feet below, to over 10,000 feet as in Columbia. As for latitude, wheat flourishes from Siberia to the equator. The ideal territory for growing wheat is between 30 and 60 degrees of latitude in areas where annual rainfall is from 12 to 35 inches. The Prairies of the United States and the pampas of Argentina, both within these ranges, are considered the greatest grasslands in the world.

Rye:

Many believe that rye originated in the same area as wheat, for it was always found growing as a weed in a wheat field. The further north wheat was planted, the more rye was present, till ultimately, to quote a historian "the farmers were reduced to harvesting the weeds rather than the wheat."

One theory places rye as originating in North Eastern Europe, which seems more realistic as that is the climate where it grows best. Rye became the staple cereal of Northern Europe. It is used to make their famous black breads such as pumpernickel, and other lighter rye breads which contain wheat or barley.

Millet:

Millet was probably the first crop to be cultivated in Neolithic times. It is thought to have originated in Africa or Asia. Its small seeds were carried by the wind and birds, and thus the plant spread naturally over a vast area.

The role of millet seems to be to give grain to peoples who otherwise would have none, for it can grow in poor soil in semi-arid areas. In the absence of moisture, millet goes into a dormant state, and with the return of moisture, it begins to grow rapidly. The people of the Sahara plant it. Wherever a rare heavy rainfall fills hollows with water, it grows and ripens, ready for harvest in 45 days. It is therefore well suited for nomadic tribes in arid areas. It is used to boil into a porridge or gruel, or to grind to a flour to make flat breads. It is still the staple food of half a billion people in parts of Africa, Asia and China. It has a higher protein content than rice and maize, but not as high as wheat, and it will grow in areas where wheat will not grow. In the western world it is grown for stockfeed.

PULSES

Dried beans, peas and lentils are referred to as pulses. The word pulse is from the latin word 'puls' which means 'a moss or paste'. A paste or thick porridge eaten in ancient times was made with some kind of bean, pea or lentil and the three collectively became known as pulses, or as a pulse, singularly. They belong to the leguminous species of plants and so are referred to as legumes, but not correctly so of lentils.

Pulses together with grains were the staple food of early mans diet, dating back to prehistoric times. At that time they were eaten in a simple form out of necessity, but gradually they were combined with herbs, spices and flavoursome vegetables, and tasty and interesting dishes evolved. They have always been associated with poor mans food, for they are cheap

to produce and a much cheaper source of protein than animal protein. Today they are recognised for their nutritional value and are gaining popularity in western diets. Their protein content is not complete as they do not contain all the essential amino acids. But this is overcome by combining them with proteins from nuts, grains and cereals. They are rich in valuable minerals and vitamins and do not contain fat as other protein foods do. There are also strong indications that pulses reduce the level of cholesterol in the blood.

It may be quicker to grill a steak than to make a bean dish, but with a little planning, their preparation and serving is less of a hassle than co-ordinating a meat dish with vegetable accompaniments.

Soaking of beans may be done in two ways:

> **Long Soak:** Wash beans well in a colander under running water. Place in a large bowl with three times their volume of water and leave to soak for six hours in a cool place or overnight in the refrigerator. Soaking water may be used for cooking, but some find the flavour too strong. It may be drained and replaced if preferred.

> **Quick Soak:** Place washed beans and water in a saucepan, bring quickly to the boil and boil for two minutes. Remove from heat, cover and stand for 40-60 minutes. Water may be replaced if preferred.

When cooking it is best to add salt and tomato or tomato paste after beans begin to tenderise, as salt and the acid content of tomatoes slows down the tenderising process.

Adzuki Beans:

Tiny reddish brown beans with a strong sweet slightly nutty flavour. They are ideal to serve with rich meat dishes, in meat loaves and in vegetarian burgers. In the Asian cuisine they are mashed, flavoured with sugar and used in cakes, buns and jellies. Pre-soak, then cook for 30-45 minutes.

Black Beans:

Small almost round black beans feature in African, West Indian and Chinese cooking. Use in soups and Chinese style sauces. Pre-soak and boil gently for 1-1¼ hours.

Black-Eyed Beans:

Small, creamy white beans with a black spot. They are easier to digest than most pulses. They combine well with spinach, in tomato based soups and stews. Pre-soak then boil gently for 1-1½ hours.

Borlotti Beans:

Long in shape with speckled pink colour. They are moist and sweet when cooked and are ideal for bean salads as well as adding to soups and stews. Pre-soak and cook gently for 1 hour.

Broad Beans:

Large, flat beans, greenish brown colour. Skins may sometimes be a little tough and may be removed after pre-soaking if preferred. Makes a tasty bean puree, used in stews and bean salads. Requires longer cooking than other beans. Pre-soak and boil gently for 2 hours.

Butter Beans:

Large white beans with a buttery flavour. They go well with pork and also make delightful bean salads. Popular in stews, soups and casseroles. Pre-soak and boil gently for 1-1½ hours.

Chick Peas:

Round and rough textured. Made into a puree, used in stews with vegetables or lamb. Also tasty when flavoured with curry. Used to make hommus. Pre-soak then boil gently for 1½-2 hours.

Haricot Beans:

Small, oval beans, white in colour. Sometimes called Boston beans for they are used to make Boston baked beans. They also feature in the French Cassoulet. Use in soups and stews. Pre-soak and boil gently for 1½ hours.

Lentils:

Red, green and brown lentils are the most popular in Australia although there are many more varieties. Brown and green lentils do not disintegrate in cooking and may be served as an accompaniment with butter and herbs, also used in soups and stews, or mashed to make lentil patties. Red lentils disintegrate in cooking and are usually served as a puree. The have little flavour of their own so need spicing. Lentils require no soaking.

Lima Beans:

Flat, kidney shaped beans, white in colour. There are two types: large limas and baby limas. They have a sweet, nutty flavour and are excellent for bean salads. Also good served hot. Pre-soak and cook gently for 1-1½ hours until tender.

Pinto Beans:

Beige coloured beans speckled with brown. They make attractive salads and side dishes. They are used to make the popular chili beans, spiced with red chili. Used also in mince meat dishes, soups and stews. Puree and refry and use for taco filling. Pre-soak and boil gently for 1-1½ hours.

Red Kidney Beans:

Kidney shaped, dark red beans. Served in soups and salads. Traditional use is with minced or cubed meat to make chili con carne. Pre-soak then boil for 1-1¼ hours. They need to be boiled first for 10 minutes to destroy a slightly toxic enzyme which is present in the bean.

Soya Bean:

Small, very hard, beige coloured bean. They are the toughest of the pulses, and need long soaking and cooking. They also have no taste and so need plenty of added flavouring. They are preferred, particularly by vegetarians, for they have complete protein and can be used as a meat substitute. Pre-soak, overnight if possible, then boil for 3-4 hours.

Split Peas:

Both yellow and green split peas are available. Popular use is hearty pea soup flavoured with bacon or ham bones. Split pea puree dotted with butter is a delicious accompaniment for a main course. They do not require soaking. Boil gently without stirring for 1-1½ hours.

The Australian way of

PASTA

The story that Marco Polo introduced pasta to Italy, having brought the idea from China is told and retold. The possibility that the Romans were eating pasta centuries before is very evident.

The evidence comes with a type of pasta made in Greek villages today, which has its origin in antiquity. It consists of pasta dough made with flour, eggs and milk, sieved to form little balls which are dried in the sun. It is then used in soups and stews. It is called Trahana. Trahana is very similar to a Hungarian pasta which consists of small pellets of pasta dough, dried in the sun. It is boiled and served with stews and casseroles. It is called "Trahonya". The Hungarians claim their pasta dates back to the Roman times when

they were part of the empire. It is well documented that many Greek cooks were taken to Rome, after Greece was conquered, to cook for the nobility and officials, and that they refined and enriched the cuisine at that time. Is it possible that Trahana and Trahonya are connected?

Whatever its origin, pasta is now enjoyed in many countries. There is a great interest in pasta in Australia, many shops supplying fresh pasta daily. The commercial variety is extensive and there are frozen packs of the filled pasta variety available. The following are amongst the more popular varieties of pasta.

Spaghetti:

Long thin strands of pasta. It comes in varying degrees of thinness. It is usually boiled and served with tomato or meat sauces and sprinkled with grated cheese.

Vermicelli:

A very fine pasta strand formed in a coil or nest. It is used in soups.

Tagliatelle:

A flat ribbon pasta 6mm (1/4") wide. Served with a variety of sauces including cream based sauces, rich meat sauces, chicken or fish toppings.

Tagliarine:

Similar to tagliatelli, but smaller in width.

Macaroni:

Tubular pasta of varying widths. May be in long strands or cut in short pieces. The long variety is cooked and served with sauces. The short variety is used to make macaroni cheese, pasta salads or used in soups.

Shell Pasta:

The correct name is conchiglie rigata'. It is shaped like sea shells. Boil until tender, toss with butter and serve to accompany braised meats. Use also in pasta salads.

Fusilli:

Spiral or corkscrew pasta shapes. Use as for shell pasta.

Fettucine:

A flat ribbon pasta, made in long strands. It may be flavoured with spinach which makes it green or it may be plain. Served with a variety of sauces. Fettucine Marinara is a popular dish; a seafood sauce with tomato base served over boiled fettucine.

Lasagne:

Very wide, flat pasta sheets. Use to layer in a dish alternating with meat sauce, tomato sauce and bechamel sauce. Top with grated cheese and bake in the oven. Vegetarian versions can also be made using spinach or lentil and vegetable mixture in place of meat sauce.

Torellini:

Small, stuffed pasta dumplings. A variety of ingredients may be used in the stuffing, such as chopped chicken, pork, ricotta cheese. Top with a cream or tomato sauce.

Ravioli:

Square shaped pasta dumplings stuffed with spinach, ricotta cheese and herbs or meat mixture, and served with a gravy or sauce.

Cannelloni:

Large hollow, cylindrical pasta shapes. They are filled with a meat stuffing, topped with a sauce and baked.

Pastine:

Tiny pasta shapes, used to add to meat or chicken broth to give substance to the soup. Shapes vary from stars, circles, rice shapes to alphabet shapes.

The Australian way of
FISH, SHELLFISH AND CRUSTACEA

A wealth of food abounds in the sea, and from early times sustained all cultures who were fortunate enough to live by the seaside. They had no problem with supplying the diet with the valuable protein that man needs.

Early man firstly made use of shellfish and molluscs which were easy to gather. He then used clubs and spears to catch fish basking in shallow waters. Small fish were also trapped by damming the streams with stakes and laced branches. Later he learnt to 'bail o line' and make nets to catch fish.

As time progressed and there was a larger population to feed, he realised the need to venture safely on the sea. First came the dugout canoe and the reed raft. During the Neolithic era, oars were developed which enabled the fishermen to fish further offshore.

The commercial manufacture of ice played a major part in expanding the fishing industry. In the 1860's, 1870's, steam trawlers were developed which could travel fast and carry stocks of ice in their holds. Fish were packed in ice at the point of catch and were able to remain chilled during its transport back to city fish markets. This provided fish to inland people for the first time.

Today the fishing is a vast and highly technical industry. Vessels have all manner of equipment for the catching of fish in deep waters, and for refrigeration and freezing at the point of catch. Thus many vessels fish thousands of miles from their home base.

Pilchard:

These small fish are best used whole to grill, fry or bake.

Leatherjacket:

As the name implies it has a tough skin which must be removed before pan frying or grilling.

Snapper:

Its delicate flavour makes it suitable to steam, bake, fry or grill.

Trevally:

Its subtle flavour makes it suitable to bake or fry.

Redfish:

Grill whole without scaling, then remove scales and skin when cooked. Fillets may be fried.

Flathead:

At its best when fillets are coated with flour and fried. Whole fish may be baked.

Silver Bream:

One of the most popular fish. It is a fine textured, white flesh fish with a delicate flavour. Fry, steam or grill.

Mullet:

This fish has a rather strong flavour and is oily. It is best grilled or barbecued.

John Dory:

Soft, moist flesh with a mild flavour. May be cooked whole or filleted to fry or grill.

Sea Bream:

Its fine white texture and delicate flavour make it a fine table fish. Pan fry or grill.

Ling Fillets:

Medium textured fish with a mild flavour. Bake, grill or casserole.

Gemfish Fillets:

A firm fleshed fish with few bones. Suitable for all cooking methods.

Kingfish:

This fish has a pink, soft flesh, is very tasty and is cut into cutlets to casserole and fry.

Latchet:

Has a slightly dry, firm texture. Cook whole to retain moisture. Fry, bake or poach.

Mirror Dory:

A white fish with fine texture and mild flavour. Fillets may be fried or grilled.

Ocean Perch:

It is slightly oily and has a pleasant taste. Suitable for all cooking methods.

Garfish:

This fish has a most delightful, sweet taste and is best fried or grilled. It also has many fine bones, so take care.

Jewfish or Butterfish:

A firm textured fish suitable for casseroles and grills.

Calamari Squid:

May be cut into rings to fry or whole hoods may be stuffed and baked.

Elheridge Squid:

Small and very tender. Lightly fry and serve with garlic, oil and lemon juice dressing.

Mud Crab:

Drown in cold water or place in freezer to kill. Boil lightly and serve with lemon dressing.

Blue Swimmer Crab:

The finest of all crabs. Boil or grill and serve with a lemon dressing.

Lobster:

Treat as for mud crab.

Octopus:

Cut into pieces, marinate in oil and lemon juice, and grill, barbecue or saute.

Oysters:

There are many ways of serving oysters, the best is 'au natural'.

Balmain Bugs:

Mild, sweet flesh. Uncooked bugs may be barbecued or grilled.

Scallops:

Must be cooked gently to prevent toughening. May be poached, pan fried, grilled or baked.

Mussels:

Overcooking toughens the mussels. Cook in shell by steaming or poaching.

Spanner Crab:

Sold already cooked. Open and remove flesh and serve with a dressing.

King Prawns:

Sold cooked and uncooked. Uncooked prawns may be grilled, barbecued, boiled or fried.

Cuttlefish:

Must be cooked for 2 or 3 minutes only. Grill, fry or barbecue.

The Australian way of
WINES

If one person is to be given credit for beginning the Australian wine industry, it should be Governor Arthur Phillip. He ordered the planting of the first vines in Australia (brought from the Cape and Rio de Janeiro) at Farm Cove and further west along the Parramatta River. His two attempts failed, but the inspiration and interest remained even after his departure in 1792.

Private settlers soon began planting vines; the "Sydney Gazette" dated March 5, 1803, published an article on how to plant a vineyard. The authorities encouraged their efforts to establish wine to minimize the excessive use of hard spirits; namely rum. The Australian wine industry slowly got underway and many people, with their pioneering spirit and determination, contributed to the infant industry. It has grown steadily over 200 years and today Australia is acknowledged as a wine producing country of standing. There is an increasing demand for Australian wines at home and abroad.

Wine Production Areas

South Australia is the premier wine producing state in Australia with New South Wales and Victoria also having a substantial industry. The other states have wine growing on a smaller scale, but still manage to produce some outstanding wines.

South Australia

The Barossa Valley is the largest quality wine growing area in Australia. The names and traditions of most of the wine making in the region were brought to Australia by the German Lutherans who settled in the area. Their wines are mostly made in the German tradition. Some of the famous wineries in the area are Chateau Rosevale, Chateau Yalders, Hardy's Siegersdorf.

The area around Adelaide is surrounded by vineyards. There are three old and well-established wineries in this area, Reynella, planted in 1838, Hardy's and Seaview. The Coonawarra Estate which is close to the Victorian border, is a narrow strip of red coloured land which has the reputation of being Australia's coolest vineyard, produces a well balanced red wine.

Victoria

The two main wine-growing districts are Tabilk and Great Western. The Great Western estate is famous for its sparkling wines. Mildura, Robinvale and Swan Hill are other well know areas.

New South Wales

The best known district is the Hunter Valley, the oldest and warmest wine producing area. Established names such as Penfold, McWilliam, Lindemans, Drayton, Tulloch and Tyrell all have wineries in this area. The Murrumbidgee Irrigation area is also an old and well established wine area, some vineyards even began before irrigation came into the area.

Serving Wines with Food

Drinking wine with meals is a delight to be enjoyed. A background knowledge of how to choose the best wines, what to serve with what foods, when to serve etc. to the pleasure of serving to people who appreciate good wine. So much importance has been placed on the 'correct' wines to serve with certain foods, that many people feel inadequate in making the choice and a little self conscious and hesitant. Always remember that the correct wine to serve is the wine you like. You may have to experiment a little, try different wines to get to know them and how they compliment certain foods. Keep a personal record of the new wines you taste and note your reactions to that wine, it will help you to be able to choose wines with confidence.

Guide to Wine with Food

For those who need assistance and assurance in the choice of wines with meals, the following is a basic guide to the styles of wine which will best compliment the various foods being served.

Aperitif Wines

Those which are normally served before the meal to stimulate the appetite.

Sherry

Fino, Dry, Amontillado, Olorosso or sweet — of varying degrees of flavour and sweetness for individual tastes. Served straight or with ice.

Vermouth

Dry, Bianco or Sweet — fortified wines with aromatic herbs and spices. Served straight, with ice or with soda, spa etc.
Chilled Champagne, Rosé, White or Sparkling wines are also ideal aperitifs in warmer weather or on particular occasions.

Table Wines

Those which are normally served throughout the meal.

White Wines

Hock, Chablis, Riesling, White Burgundy and Moselle — wine styles served at commencement, with early courses or throughout the meal.
Spatlese, Auslese, Sauternes have sufficient sweetness to accompany desserts and fruit.

Red Wines

Claret and Burgundy styles — usually served to compliment the main course of the meal.

Rosé Wines

In varying degrees of dryness, served for part of, or throughout the meal.

Sparkling Wines

Brut (Dry); Demi sec (medium sweet); Sec (sweet) — served throughout the meal or with the dessert course.

Dessert Wines (fortified)

Marsala, Madeira, Muscat, Port, Tokay, Frontignac and Sweet Sherry are served with dessert, cheese, sweetmeats and coffee.
Brandy may also be served as the finale of a special occasion.

Wine and Food Selection:

Serve light wines before heavy wines; dry wines before sweet wines. This is the general rule but you may choose to depart from the format and serve one good wine throughout the meal.

The following, more detailed selection of wines with particular foods may be of further assistance.

Soups

A small glass of wine is usually sufficient to accompany the liquid content of soup:-

Consomme:	Dry or medium dry Sherry
Cream Soup:	Light dry white wine
Cold Soup:	Light dry white wine
Vegetable Soup:	Dry white wine
Meaty Soup:	Dry white, rose or light red wine.

Seafood

Unless the accompanying sauces or seasonings are of a stronger flavour, all seafoods taste best with light wines.

Fish:	Light dry or medium dry white wine.
Shellfish:	Medium dry or dry white wine.

Poultry

Method of cooking and accompanying sauce or seasonings will determine the wine choice.

Chicken:	Light dry or medium dry white wine
Duck:	Dry, full bodied white or rosé wine
Turkey:	Full bodied white, rosé or light red wine
Game Birds:	Rosé, light or fruity red wine

Meats

Veal:	Dry or full bodied white or rosé wine
Lamb:	Full bodied white, rosé or light red wine
Beef:	Light or full bodied red wine

Barbecue Foods

Depending on the occasion, the choice of wine is vast. . .quality cask or flagon wines being the most popular.

Suggested choice: medium dry white or dry redwine. . .light or full-bodied to suit.

Salads, Cold Platters

Care must be taken when choosing wines with foods having dressings containing, lemon, vinegar etc. as the acid taste will affect the wine flavour.

Salads:	Dry or medium dry white wine
Cold Platters:	Dry white, rosé or light red wine

Oriental and Eastern Dishes

The varying flavours of most Oriental and Eastern foods will determine the choice of accompanying wines – serve well chilled.

Bland dishes:	Light dry white wine
Sweet-sour dishes:	Fruity or ginger flavoured white wine
Spicy dishes:	Dry or medium dry white wine
Curry dishes:	Full-bodied, fruity white wine

Casseroles, Rice and Pasta Dishes

Choice of wine will depend upon the basic fish, poultry or meat ingredient and the accompanying sauce and seasonings.

Light, bland dishes:	Dry or medium dry white wine
Spicy, piquante dishes:	Full bodied white or red wine

Sauces

The accompanying sauce to fish, poultry or meat is often the determining factor choosing the wine.

White, cream sauce:	Dry or medium dry, fruity white wine
Tomato sauce:	Dry white, rosé or light red wine
Brown sauce:	Full bodied white, rose or dry red wine
Piquant sauce:	Dry or full bodied white, or red wine.

Desserts

The sweeter taste of most desserts harmonise well with the sweeter, spatlese and fruity wines of both the table and fortified styles.

Custard cream dishes:	Fruity, sweet white wine, Marsala
Fruit dishes:	Semi sweet or sparkling wine
Chocolate dishes:	Sweet Sherry, Marsala
Hot Puddings:	Fruity white wine, Port, Muscat
Flambe dishes:	Sweet or semi sweet sparkling wine

Cheese and Coffee

When served as a platter at the completion of a meal the degree of "piquancy" of the cheese will determine the choice of wine.

Mild Cheese:	Dry white or red wine, dry sherry, Port
Tasty Cheese:	Rich, fruity red wine, Port
Specialty Cheeses:	Port, sparkling wine

Sweetmeats, Nuts

Fortified wines, brandy or brandy liqueurs or sparkling wine would be the perfect finale.

The Australian way of Cooking Pictorial
TO THE AMERICAN AND CANADIAN READER

The Australian Way of Cooking applies to your way of cooking also, for although our beginnings as nations happened at different periods in time and on different continents, there are many similarities. Similarities in our colonization by the British; in the people who came from other countries to find a new home; in the vastness of our countries; the varied climatic zones we occupy and therefore the foods we both produce.

The Australian cuisine began with the traditions of the Anglo-Celtic heritage, the heritage of the first settlers in Australia. The same traditions began the North American cuisine with the Pilgrim Fathers in New England and the first settlement in Virginia.

The settlement of North America differs from Australia in that people of many different nations arrived in large numbers very early in its beginning, creating pockets of various ethnic cuisines in well defined areas. Over a time this melded into a whole, giving the North American cuisine that special multi-cultural flavour and yet new creativity with which it is identified. Australia arrived at the same point through a different route. The cuisine remained Anglo-Celtic for more than 150 years, but it was not until the great influx of post war migration that it turned into the exciting and varied cuisine it is today.

This book was written with the North American reader in mind, for in its pages you will find old recipes that have been lost to you through the technological advancement of food production. You may find that favourite recipe that grandma used to make, just as we have. You will also find new ideas using the wonderful array of fresh food produce common to our respective countries, and new combinations of flavour and taste sensations will be discovered and enjoyed by all.

Some cooking terms and names of ingredients used in the book will differ from American and Canadian terminology. The following list gives the equivalent or near equivalent; it is set out with the Australian term or name first, followed by the American/Canadian term.

AUSTRALIAN — AMERICAN/CANADIAN

Ingredients

Australian	American/Canadian
Baking Powder	Double acting baking powder
Bicarbonate of soda	Baking soda
Butter	Salted butter
Unsalted Butter	Sweet butter
Caster Sugar	Superfine sugar
Copha	White vegetable shortening
Cornflour	Cornstarch
Cornmeal flour	Cornmeal
Cream	Heavy cream
Cream thickened	Whipping cream
Desiccated coconut	Shredded coconut
Essence	Extract
Flour	All pure flour
Flour self raising	Self rising flour
Flour wholemeal	Whole wheat flour
Gelatine	Unflavoured gelatin
Glacé cherries	Candied cherries
Glacé fruit	Candied fruit
Greaseproof paper	Wax paper
Icing sugar	Confectioners sugar
Jelly crystals	Flavoured gelatin
Macaroons	Ratafia cookies
Stock cubes	Bouillon cubes
Sultanas	Golden raisins (seedless)
Sweet biscuit crumbs	Graham cracker crumbs
Tomato sauce	Tomato catsup
Vanilla essence	Vanilla extract

Utensils

Australian	American/Canadian
Absorbent paper	Paper towel
Cake cooler	Cooling rack
Cake tin	Cake pan
Baking tray	Baking sheet
Flan tin	Tart pan
Frying pan	Skillet
Kitchen paper	Paper towel
Lamington tin	Slab pan
Melon baller	Melon scoop
Oven slide	Cookie or baking sheet
Patty cups	Paper cupcake pans
Pie plate or dish	Pie pan
Recess cake pan	Sponge flan tin
Ring tin	Tube pan
Sandwich tin	Layer pan
Swiss roll tin	Jelly pan
Tea Towel	Dish towel/glass cloth

Cooking Terms

Australian	American/Canadian
Biscuits	Cookies
Chopped (onion)	Minced (onion)
Grill/Griller	Broil/Broiler
Pan fry	Pan broil
Pastry	Pie crust
Scones	Biscuits
Shell (to)	Shuck (to)
Sieve	Strain
Stone/seed	Pit
Whisk	Whip/beat

Fruits and Vegetables

Australian	American/Canadian
Capsicum	Sweet or bell pepper
Celery stick	Celery rib
Choko	Chayote
Cooking apple	Sour apple
Egg plant	Aubergine
Paw paw	Papaya
Rockmelon	Cantelope melon
Shallots	Scallions or welsh onions
Silverbeet	Swiss chard
Snow peas	Sugar peas, mange-tout
Spring onions	Scallions or green onions

Meat and Poultry

Australian	American/Canadian
Bacon rashers	Canadian bacon, slice
Boiling chicken	Stewing chicken
Chuck steak	Round or stewing steak
Corned silverside	Corned brisket or tip roast
Cutlet	Chop
Fillet of beef	Beef tenderloin
Gravy beef	Stewing beef
Lamb cutlet	Lamb rib chop
Minced meat	Ground meat (beef or lamb)
Pork fat	Fat back
Pork neck	Pork blade
Rump steak	Sirloin
Scotch fillet	Boneless rib steak
Shin (of meat)	Shank
Skirt steak	Flank steak
Veal cutlet	Veal rib chop
Veal knuckle	Veal shank

Fish (acceptable alternative)

Australian	American/Canadian
Bream	Sole (Porgy)
Jewfish	Halibut
John Dory	Porgy, soup (John Dory)
King prawns	Jumbo shrimps
Ling fillets	Sword fish fillets
Mussels	Clams (Mussel)
Prawns	Shrimps
Red fish fillets	Red snapper
Snapper	Sea bass
Trevally	Blue fish or cod

MEASURES, WEIGHTS & CONVERSIONS

Metric measurements are now used in Australia, but there are still many amongst us who relate better to the Imperial measures, that is the use of ounces and pounds. The tables on these pages will assist those who may still be confused.

Ingredients such as meats, fish, poultry and vegetables only are given in weights. However, a little more or less of grams or ounces will not effect the success of the recipe.

Only in structured recipes such as cakes, pastry, biscuits, breads and the like need accurate measurements. Australian standard 250 ml cup, 20 ml tablespoon and 5 ml teaspoon have been used to test the recipes. The recipes will work just as well with the U.S. or Canadian 8 oz cup or the U.K. 300 ml cup. Graded cup measures have been used in preference to tablespoon measures so that proportions will remain the same. Where tablespoon measures have been given, the smaller U.S. or U.K. tablespoon measure will not affect the recipe's success as these are not crucial measures. However, if accuracy is necessary for structured recipes, use 1 U.S. tablespoon (14.8 mls) plus 1 teaspoon (5 mls) for every Australian tablespoon (20 mls).

Recipes have been tested using 55 g (1¾ oz) eggs and all spoon and cup measures are level.

English and American Measures

ENGLISH

All measurements similar to Australian with two exceptions; the English cup measures 10 fluid ounces (300 ml), whereas the Australian cup measure is 8 fluid ounces (250 ml). The English tablespoon measures 14.8 ml against the Australian tablespoon of 20 ml.

AMERICAN

The American reputed pint is 16 fluid ounces, a quart 32 fluid ounces, a gallon 128 fluid ounces. The Imperial measurement is 20 fluid ounces to the pint, 40 fluid ounces a quart and 160 fluid ounces one gallon. The American tablespoon is equal to 14.8 ml, the teaspoon is 5 ml. The cup measure is 8 fluid ounces (250 ml) the same as Australia.

Cup Measurements

One cup is equal to the following weights.

	METRIC	IMPERIAL
Breadcrumbs, packet	125 g	4 oz
Breadcrumbs, soft	60 g	2 oz
Cheese, grated	125 g	4 oz
Coconut, desiccated	75 g	2½ oz
Flour	125 g	4 oz
Fruit, dried (mixed, sultanas etc)	125 g	4 oz
Honey, treacle, golden syrup	315 g	10 oz
Nuts, chopped	125 g	4 oz
Rice, cooked	155 g	5 oz
Rice, uncooked	185 g	6 oz
Shortening (butter, margarine)	250 g	8 oz
Sugar, brown	155 g	5 oz
Sugar, granulated or caster sugar	250 g	8 oz
Sugar, sifted icing	155 g	5 oz

Oven Temperatures

The centigrade temperatures given here are not exact; they have been rounded off and give a guide only. Follow the manufacturer's temperature guide, relating it to oven description given in the recipe. Remember gas ovens are hottest at the top, electric ovens at the bottom and convection-fan forced ovens are usually even throughout. We have also included Regulo numbers for gas cookers which may assist.

	C	F	REGULO
Very Slow	120	250	1
Slow	150	300	2
Moderately slow	160	325	3
Moderate	180	350	4
Moderately hot	190/200	370/400	5/6
Hot	210/220	410/440	6/7
Very hot	230	450	8
Super hot	250/290	475/550	9/10

Cake Dish Sizes

(Measurements relate to diameter.)

METRIC	IMPERIAL
15 cm	6 in
18 cm	7 in
20 cm	8 in
23 cm	9 in

Loaf Dish Sizes

METRIC	IMPERIAL
23 x 12 cm	9 x 5 in
25 x 8 cm	10 x 3 in
28 x 18 cm	11 x 7 in

Liquid Measures

METRIC ml millilitres	IMPERIAL fl oz	CUP AND SPOON fluid ounce
5ml	1/6fl oz	1 teaspoon
20ml	⅔fl oz	1 tablespoon
30ml	1fl oz	1 tablespoon plus 2 teasp
60ml	2fl oz	¼cup
85ml	2½fl oz	1.3cup
100ml	3fl oz	
125ml	4fl oz	½cup
150ml	5fl oz	(¼pint) 1 gill
180ml	6fl oz	¾cup
250ml	8fl oz	1cup
300ml	10fl oz	(½pint)
360ml	12fl oz	1½cups
420ml	14fl oz	1¾cups
500ml	16fl oz	2cups
600ml	20fl oz	(1pint) 2½ cups
1litre	35fl oz	(1¾pints) 4 cups

Standard teaspoon measures in Australia, New Zealand, U.S.A, Canada and U.K. are 5 ml in capacity or $\frac{1}{6}$ of a fluid ounce.

Dry Measures

All the measures are level, so when you have filled a cup or spoon, level it off with edge of a knife. The following scale is the "cook's" equivalent, it is not an exact conversion of metric to Imperial measurement.

METRIC	IMPERIAL	METRIC	IMPERIAL
15 g	½ oz	315 g	10 oz
20 g	⅔ oz	345 g	11 oz
30 g	1 oz	375 g	12 oz (¾lb)
60 g	2 oz	410 g	13 oz
90 g	3 oz	440 g	14 oz
125 g	4 oz (¼ lb)	470 g	15 oz
155 g	5 oz	500 g (0.5 kg)	16 oz (1lb)
185 g	6 oz	750 g (0.75 kg)	24 oz (1½lb)
220 g	7 oz	1000 g (1 kg)	32 oz (2lb)
250 g	8 oz (½lb)	1.5 kg	3 lb
280 g	9 oz	2 kg	4 lb

g = grams   oz = ounces
kg = kilograms   lb = pounds

Length

In this book we have used both metric and Imperial measurements. The measures have been rounded off to the easiest-to-use and most acceptable figures.

METRIC	IMPERIAL
mm = millimetres	in = inches
cm = centimetres	ft = feet
5 mm 0.5cm	1.4 in
10 mm 1.0cm	½ in
20 mm 2.0cm	¾ in
25 mm 2.5cm	1 in
5 cm	2 in
8 cm	3 in
10 cm	4 in
12 cm	5 in
15 cm	6 in
18 cm	7 in
20 cm	8 in
23 cm	9 in
25 cm	10 in
28 cm	11 in
30 cm	12 in (1 ft)

The Australian way of Cooking Pictorial

GENERAL INDEX

This book is a revision of
the Australian Heritage Cookbook.

The Australian way of Cooking Pictorial

PICTORIAL CREDITS
& ACKNOWLEDGEMENTS

1   Australian Picture Library
    Page 2-3, 4-5. 12-13, 14-15, 19 , 26, 27, 32, 33, 34, 36,
    40-41, 42-43, 45, 47, 51, 55, 63, 66, 68-69, 71, 73, 75, 79,
    80-81, 80, 87, 90-91, 98, 99, 105, 111, 114, 115, 116,
    118-119,.120-121, 123, 125, 130, 132, 134-135, 136, 137,
    139,.147, 149. 155, 157, 158-159, 162, 167, 170-171,
    196-197, 199, 200, 202, 210-211, 219, 222-223, 225, 226,
    227, 228, 232. 233. 235. 240, 241, 242-243, 245, 251, 252,
    255, 258, 261, 270-271, 272-273, 274, 276, 278, 280, 282,
    284,286, 288, 290, 292, 298, 302
2   David Ball, Front Cover, Page 8-9
3   D & J Heaton, Page 23, 60-61, 169-197
4   D. Rolf, Page 126
5   Fisher — Zefa, Page 280
6   Gary Lewis, Page 89, 94-95, 123, 232, 245, 252, 258
7   G. Ede, Page 226
8   Imagery Gallery, Pge 111
9   J. Carnemolla, Page 66, 74, 99, 136, 155, 170-171, 235, 261

10 John P. Baker, Page 29,39, 132, 232
11 M. Lees, Page 32
12 N. Kelly, Page, 270, 271
13 Owen Hughes, Page 10-11, 272-273, 292
14 R. Armstrong, Page 16-17
15 R. Garvey, Page 116
16 Richard Eastwood, Page 241
17 R. Dorman, Page 24-25
18 F. Preuzel, Page 202, 219
Additional photography provided by: Bread Institute of
Australia.

ACKNOWLEDGEMENTS
Special Thanks
The publishers wish to thank their friends and family and the
many other persons for making this book so successful. In
particular, thank you Annie and Kay.